Resurrection and Early Christianity

MW00850049

"This is a ground-breaking study of the literary antecedents for the resurrection stories in the Gospels, with wide-ranging implications for Christian history and theology. Never again can the resurrection stories be read and interpreted apart from their ancient literary context." —*Dennis Smith, Phillips Theological Seminary, USA*

"Early Christianity emerged in a world of intense interaction among the devotees of different cults and religions. Narratives, images, ritual practices, and ideas continually crossed the boundaries of religious groups. With the interdependence of ancient religions as his starting point, Richard Miller shows the close relation of the early narratives of Jesus' resurrection with pre-existing pagan and Jewish narratives of divine translation. This study makes a significant contribution to the study of Early Christianity and the religious trends of the Roman Empire." —*Angelos Chaniotis, Professor of Ancient History, Institute for Advanced Study, Princeton, NJ, USA*

"Richard Miller's reading of ancient Greco-Roman narratives concerning the disappearance of heroes and demi-gods successfully challenges the traditional reconstructions of the formation of resurrection accounts in the Gospels. Miller moves with theoretical sophistication through an impressive array of ancient texts and shows how early Christian stories about Jesus were developed in the context of literary imitation and emulation that characterized the Mediterranean world in antiquity." —*Giovanni Bazzana, Harvard Divinity School, USA*

This book offers an original interpretation of the origin and early reception of the most fundamental claim of Christianity: Jesus' resurrection. Richard Miller contends that the earliest Christians would not have considered the New Testament accounts of Jesus' resurrection to be literal or historical, but instead would have recognized this narrative as an instance of the trope of divine translation, common within the Hellenistic and Roman mythic traditions. Given this framework, Miller argues, early Christians would have understood the resurrection story as fictitious rather than historical in nature. By drawing connections between the Gospels and ancient Greek and Roman literature, Miller makes the case that the narratives of the resurrection and ascension of Christ applied extensive and unmistakable structural and symbolic language common to Mediterranean "translation fables," stock story patterns derived particularly from the archetypal myths of Heracles and Romulus. In the course of his argument, the author applies a critical lens to the referential and mimetic nature of the Gospel stories, and suggests that adapting the "translation fable" trope to accounts of Jesus' resurrection functioned to exalt him to the level of the heroes, demigods, and emperors of the Hellenistic and Roman world. Miller's contentions have significant implications for New Testament scholarship and will provoke discussion among scholars of early Christianity and classical studies.

Richard C. Miller is an adjunct professor in the Department of Religious Studies at Chapman University, USA.

Routledge Studies in Religion

For a full list of titles in this series, please visit www.routledge.com

Resurrection and Reception in Early Christianity

Richard C. Miller

Routledge
Taylor & Francis Group

NEW YORK AND LONDON

First published 2015
by Routledge
711 Third Avenue, New York, NY 10017
2 Park Square, Milton Park, Abingdon, Oxfordshire OX14 4RN

First issued in paperback 2017

*Routledge is an imprint of the Taylor & Francis Group,
an informa business*

© 2015 Taylor & Francis

The right of Richard C. Miller to be identified as author of this work has
been asserted by him/her in accordance with sections 77 and 78 of the
Copyright, Designs and Patents Act 1988.

All rights reserved. No part of this book may be reprinted or reproduced or
utilized in any form or by any electronic, mechanical, or other means, now
known or hereafter invented, including photocopying and recording, or in
any information storage or retrieval system, without permission in writing
from the publishers.

Trademark Notice: Product or corporate names may be trademarks or
registered trademarks, and are used only for identification and explanation
without intent to infringe.

Library of Congress Cataloging-in-Publication Data
Miller, Richard C. (Adjunct Professor)
Resurrection and reception in early Christianity / by Richard C. Miller. —
   1 [edition].
      pages cm. — (Routledge studies in religion ; 44)
   Includes index.
   1. Jesus Christ—Resurrection—History of doctrines—Early church, ca.
30–600. I. Title.
   BT482.M54 2015
   232'.509015—dc23
   2014033662

ISBN 13: 978-1-138-04827-0 (pbk)
ISBN 13: 978-1-138-82270-2 (hbk)

Typeset in Sabon
by Apex CoVantage, LLC

I dedicate this book to my three marvelous sons,
Riley, Owen, and Sebastian.
May you ever be
three true brothers and three fine gentlemen.

Contents

Acknowledgments

As I first embarked on this project in 2003, more than one well-intended scholar advised me to select a topic of particular enjoyment to me, for, by the end of the project, I would certainly grow weary of my subject matter. This, no doubt, has been the common experience of many a Ph.D. candidate. For me, however, the topic of this book has continued to be a tremendous source of invigoration. Indeed, with each fresh reading of an early Christian passage on the resurrection of Jesus or discovery of an ancient Greek or Latin tale of divine translation, a call within me awakens, my heart gallops with delight.

Now with over twelve years of absorbed, focused study into the topic, I see quite plainly that this book exists as a privileged collaboration, the aggregate contribution of good company. Among them, I must first express unmitigated gratitude to my dear wife, Sandra Lynn Miller, for her abiding encouragement during the composition. Several of my teachers in the academy especially merit mention at this time. I wish to thank Veronika E. Grimm of the Department of Classics at Yale University who first immersed my ripe mind in the legends of Romulus over a decade ago. I must also thank my thesis advisor at Princeton Theological Seminary under whom I served as Research Assistant, James H. Charlesworth, whose kindness and mentorship matured my depth of interest in such academic pursuits. I am grateful as well for the tremendous, undiluted wisdom of my advisor at the Yale University Divinity School, John J. Collins, who cultivated my interest in Hellenistic and Roman studies so many years ago. I am indebted also to James M. Robinson for his wise tuition, emboldening me to pursue diligently and with great care such topics of ultimate consequence. I am forever obliged to those who read and reread the earliest drafts of the manuscript, namely, my dissertation committee: Tim Whitmarsh of Cambridge University, Ellen D. Finkelpearl of Scripps College, Karl Galinsky of the University of Texas at Austin, and Dennis R. MacDonald of the School of Religion at the Claremont Graduate University. I could not have selected a superior quartet of qualified experts in classical and early Christian studies. Alongside them, I must also thank Dale B. Martin of the Department of Religious Studies at Yale University, for his friendship and gracious critical feedback with the final revision, as well as the unsolicited kind contribution of the late Prof. François Bovon of Harvard University, who mailed me several of his notes on the topic before his passing. I regard this as my highest honor, namely, to see this book counted worthy of the charm and sophistication of the Routledge yearly list. In this, I must express my humble thanks to the Routledge editorial board and to Margo Irvin and Nancy Chen, editors of the Routledge Studies in Religion series.

1 Justin's Confession

ὅτι τὰ ὅμοια τοῖς Ἕλλησι λέγοντες μόνοι μισούμεθα

Although we say the same things as the Greeks, we alone are hated!

[Justin, *1 Apol.* 24.1]

Ca. 150 C.E., in response to a most grievous and escalating persecution of Christians under Roman Emperor Antoninus Pius, the earliest surviving written apology (i.e., sustained rhetorical defense) of Christianity confessed:

τῷ δὲ καὶ τὸν λόγον, ὅ ἐστι πρῶτον γέννημα τοῦ θεοῦ, ἄνευ ἐπιμιξίας
φάσκειν ἡμᾶς γεγεννῆσθαι, Ἰησοῦν Χριστὸν τὸν διδάσκαλον ἡμῶν, καὶ
τοῦτον σταυρωθέντα καὶ ἀποθανόντα καὶ ἀναστάντα ἀνεληλυθέναι
εἰς τὸν οὐρανόν, οὐ παρὰ τοὺς παρ᾽ ὑμῖν λεγομένους υἱοὺς τῷ
Διΐ καινόν τι φέρομεν. πόσους γὰρ υἱοὺς φάσκουσι τοῦ Διὸς οἱ
παρ᾽ ὑμῖν τιμώμενοι συγγραφεῖς, ἐπίστασφε· Ἑρμῆν μέν, λόγον τὸν
ἑρμηνευτικὸν καὶ πάντων διδάσκαλον, Ἀσκληπιὸν δέ, καὶ θεραπευτὴν
γενόμενον, κεραυνωθέντα ἀνεληλυθέναι εἰς οὐρανόν, Διόνυσον δὲ
διασπαραχθέντα, Ἡρακλέα δὲ φυγῇ πόνων ἑαυτὸν πυρὶ δόντα, τοὺς
ἐκ Λήδας δὲ Διοσκούρους, καὶ τὸν Δανάης Περσέα, καὶ τὸν ἐξ
ἀνθρώπων δὲ ἐφ᾽ ἵππου Πηγάσου Βελλεροφόντην. τί γὰρ λέγομεν
τὴν Ἀριάδνην καὶ τοὺς ὁμοίως αὐτῇ κατηστερίσθαι λεγομένους;
καὶ τί γὰρ τοὺς ἀποθνήσκοντας παρ᾽ ὑμῖν αὐτοκράτορας, οὓς ἀεὶ
ἀπαθανατίζεσθαι ἀξιοῦντες καὶ ὀμνύντα τινὰ προάγετε ἑωρακέναι ἐκ
τῆς πυρᾶς ἀνερχόμενον εἰς τὸν οὐρανὸν τὸν κατακαέντα Καίσαρα;

(Justin, *1 Apol.* 21)

When we affirm that the Logos, God's first-born, begotten without a sexual union, namely, our teacher Jesus Christ, was crucified, died, rose, and ascended to heaven, we are conveying nothing new with respect to those whom you call the sons of Zeus: Hermes, the interpreting word and teacher of all; Asclepius, who, though he was a great healer, was struck by a thunderbolt and so ascended to heaven; and Dionysus too, after he had been torn limb from limb; and Heracles, once he had committed himself to the flames to escape his toils; and the sons of Leda, and the Dioscuri; and Perseus, son of Danae; and Bellerophon, who, though sprung from mortals, rose to heaven on the horse Pegasus. For what shall I say of Ariadne, and those like her who have been declared to be set among the stars? And what about the emperors who die among you, whom you deem worthy to be forever immortalized and for whom you bring forward someone who swears to have seen Caesar, once having been consumed by fire, ascend into heaven from the funeral pyre.[1]

Justin Martyr's *1 Apology* presented the framing contours of the Gospel narrative as having resided within a mythic mode of hero fabulation. Considering the plea's broader context, one may best summarize the larger argument as follows: "We, O Romans, have produced myths and fables with our Jesus as you have done with your own heroes and emperors; so why are you killing us?" Central to the earliest great apology of the Christian tradition, this grand concession casts a profound light on the nature of early Christian narrative production.[2]

This synopsis of the text, however, begs further complication and clarification and, as such, shall serve as the heuristic stone pathway for embarking upon the present study. The critic may pause to consider: Could the apology indeed have admitted that the earliest Christians had composed Jesus' divine birth, dramatically tragic death, resurrection, and ascension within the earliest Christian Gospel tradition as fictive embellishments following the stock structural conventions of Greek and Roman mythology, specifically the narrative traditions of the fabled antique Mediterranean demigod? Would not such an admission have utterly crippled earliest Christian kerygma, at least as historians have typically imagined the so-called orthodox movement's claim in the first two centuries of the Common Era? The text becomes all the more disturbing when considering that the argument did not even qualify as an "admission" per se but merely arose as a statement in passing, as though commonly acknowledged both within and without Christian society. Indeed, the implied author even included himself, as well as all Christians, as complicit in this mythopoeic enterprise: οὐ παρὰ τοὺς παρ' ὑμῖν λεγομένους τῷ υἱοὺς Διί καινόν τι φέρομεν.[3] Did this earliest defense of Christianity deliver a candid assessment when stating that there was "nothing unique" or *sui generis* about these dominant framing contours of the Jesus narrative?

The apology's at times overt rejection of antecedent iconic figures of classical antiquity, however, yet further complicates the matter. In *1 Apology 5*, for instance, the apology asserted that the classical pantheon was, in truth, a cast of demons. Notice that the apology did not argue this point; the denigration did not arise out of a reasoned progression of thought. The text simply asserted that the gods were to be understood as wicked and impious. Only out of ignorance did the classical world regard such demons as deities.[4] So, despite the confession that the early Christians "say the same things as the Greeks" (*1 Apol.* 24.1), the Greek analogues, according to the defense, arose by the inspiration of "evil demons" through the "myth-making of the poets" (*1 Apol.* 23.3). By thus discrediting the prior Greek literary renditions of the sons of Zeus as deceptions, the apology distinguished the analogous Christian narratives, regarding Jesus alone as being "true," though again providing no further evidence or reasoned argumentation.

Marshaling an all the more radical ambivalence than those sentiments previously articulated by the Epicurean Lucretius in his *De rerum natura*, the apology's claim appears to be unstable, pendulating between two paradoxical propositions.[5] On the one hand, the stock themes of the tales of the Greek demigods equal those applied to his Christian demigod, thus indicating conventional adaptation. While on the other hand, all such prior Greek stories were mere deceptions arising out of the corrupt influence of demons upon the classical poets; the Gospel narrative alone warrants credulity. If one mistakenly holds the early Christian apologetic tradition to the generally accepted standards of reasoned argumentation, in this aporetic moment, the apology's thesis collapses, undercutting itself. The Derrida within may find amusement in watching Justin's text deconstruct with such alacrity. This observed lack of coherence, however, instead emerged from the apology's fluid, non-systemic rhetorical style. As Robert Price has observed, "It is to the history of Christian rhetoric rather than of Christian doctrine that Justin and the other Greek Apologists belong."[6] As with his Christian movement, Justin's position was in motion, that is, echoing a shift upon a developmental trajectory of early Christian rhetoric in contestation with the cultural structures of classical civilization. This refraction in the works of Justin of a chronological strategic development becomes the more visible when one notes the several intermediate, hybridic (*tertium quid*) positions and tactics throughout *1–2 Apology*. The works, for instance, as did the Johannine school, sought to appropriate the Greek philosophical conception of universal reason (λόγος) as metaphysically establishing the underlying wisdom and machinations of the cosmos, thus having seen this principle as fully embodied by and culminating in the Christ. Socrates not only knew this divine reason, but by extension, according to the apology, knew Christ himself (*2 Apol.* 10.8). *1 Apology*, moreover, boldly asserted that all who lived according to universal reason (λόγος) prior to Christ were in fact Christians, listing such examples as Socrates and Heraclitus among the Greeks (*1 Apol.* 46.3–4), Gaius Musonius Rufus, the Roman Stoic philosopher (*2 Apol.* 8.1–3), and Abraham, Ananias, Azarias, Misael, Elijah, and many others from among the "barbarians" (*1 Apol.* 46.3–4). As previously understood in Greek philosophical tradition, this supreme reason existed as universally accessible to all peoples throughout time. The apology merely made explicit that which the prologue to John's Gospel had already implied (Jn 1.1–14). Contrary to Adolf von Harnack's conception, Justin did not attempt to Hellenize the alleged original Judeo-Christian "kernel" of Christianity (*"umlagerte noch den Kern"*).[7] Setting aside the matter of the historical Jesus, one may observe that the New Testament documents previously displayed the inchoate, thoroughly Hellenistic disposition of early Christian proclamation. Justin's works were not "Hellenizing," but providing rhetorical exposition of the already well-established Hellenistic hybridity of earliest Christian kerygma. Indeed, the present book succeeds inasmuch as the analysis demonstrates the apology's claim that the Gospel renditions of Jesus presented "nothing new" with respect to the stock themes of the classical "demigod" tradition of Mediterranean culture. Such a claim, according to this study, was not a Hellenizing or Romanizing innovation in *1 Apology*, but merely a moment of explicit concession regarding that which had already been broadly recognized.

With the mimesis of such iconic figures admitted, rather, the apology's rhetorical innovation came in the endeavor to denigrate such classical archetypes, thus participating in a more pronounced phase of contestation in the second century.[8] The text continued:

> Ἵνα δὲ ἤδη καὶ τοῦτο φανερὸν ὑμῖν γένηται, ὅτι ὁπόσα λέγομεν μαθόντες παρὰ τοῦ χριστοῦ καὶ τῶν προελθόντων αὐτοῦ προφητῶν μόνα ἀληθῆ ἐστι καὶ πρεσβύτερα πάντων τῶν γεγενημένων συγγραφέων, καὶ οὐχὶ διὰ τὸ ταὐτὰ λέγειν αὐτοῖς παραδεχθῆναι ἀξιοῦμεν, ἀλλ᾽ ὅτι τὸ ἀληθὲς λέγομεν.
>
> (Justin, *1 Apol.* 23.1)

> In order that this also may become plain to you, only the things which we say and which we learned from Christ and the prophets who came before him are true, and they are older than all those who were [the classical] writers. It is not merely because we say the same things as they do that we ask to be accepted by you, but because we say what is true.

Interestingly, the apology did not propose any argument in support of this claim that the two groups of stories were distinguishable by the alleged veracity of the Christian narratives and falsity of the analogous classical Mediterranean narratives; this statement again provided merely an assertion, attempting to assign archaic precedence to Judeo-Christian tradition. The obvious step, were this an attempt at a historical argument, would have been to propose eyewitness testimony attesting to the historicity of such early Christian tales, an argument that may have perhaps appeared compelling considering Justin's proximity to the region and time period.

As was indicated in the reading of *1 Apology* 21, however, the apology confessed that the two groups were identical in kind (οὐ . . . καινόν τι φέρομεν), the very point that prompts the investigation at hand. The apology simply proposed what the logician may deem a genetic fallacy, namely, that demons inspired the classical writers to produce lies or fictions that proleptically mimicked the Christian Gospel narratives, thus seeking to preempt and undermine their veracity and legitimacy by apparent generic association. Δαίμονες, according to Justin's works, had inspired the classical literary authors to produce classical culture's principal figures.

The repositioning reflects an underlying shift in the proposed modality of the Gospel narratives, moving along the continuum from fictive mythography toward historical fact. Such a shift corresponds with rising second-century demands being placed upon the Gospels. Whereas, at first, such stories succeeded inasmuch as they were capable of appropriating, riffing on, and engaging the conventions and themes of the classical literary tradition, by the middle of the second century, early Christians had their sights on a higher prize: a comprehensive cultural revolution of the Hellenistic Roman world.[9] This claim to a new order required a foundation of distinct superiority, which placed new, unprecedented weight upon the etiological myths of the movement, that is, the Gospels. The founder must be better than, truer than, more virtuous than, of a more archaic tradition than, and more prophetically legitimated than the established classical cultural forms. No longer was it enough that Jesus should join the classical array of demigods as an exciting Near Eastern installment or instance; he must obtain a *sui generis* stature, while condemning all prior Mediterranean iconic figures. The new pressure placed upon the Gospel narratives in the second and third centuries called for creative reinterpretation and rhetorical prowess readdressing those points about the founding narrative(s) that seemed most strained or problematic to the shift. This fundamental purpose served as the implicit metanarrative functioning throughout both of Justin's apologies and driving the particular passage here under consideration, namely, *1 Apology* 21.

1.1 EVIL DEMONS

1 Apology 21 has set forth with clarity, with geographic, chronological, and social proximity to the Gospel compositions, an early Christian admission of the generic basis of Jesus' resurrection narrative within the broader translation topos.[10] Besides the apology's candid disclosure, several other subsequent early Christian works within the "orthodox" patristic trajectory broadly acknowledged and confirmed this receptive awareness (e.g., Tertullian, *Apol.* 21.20–23; *Nat.* 1.10.29–33; *Marc.* 4.7.3; Minucius Felix, *Oct.* 21.9–10; Origen, *Cels.* 2.55–56; 3.22–31; and Theophilus, *Autol.* 1.13; 2.27). Justin's works *et alii* only distinguished the story by alleging that demons had proleptically imitated the sacred Christian narrative, somehow anticipating and thus weakening its distinctive importance. Since Justin's apologies provided no support for this claim, one better classifies this as rhetoric, better studied as such through the lens of social anthropology, rather than as reasoned apologetic. In his broadly referenced article appearing in a 1978 *Principat* volume of *Aufstieg und Niedergang der römischen Welt*, Jonathan Z. Smith concluded similarly:

> [Such a use of Δαίμονες] is confined to Christian texts and represents a unique attempt to overcome similarity rather than the perception of

dissimilarity which was to the fore in all other instances [in surveyed classical literature]. It is the apologetic argument that the rituals and myths of other religions which resemble the Christian do so as a result of post facto or proleptic demonic plagiarism (μιμησάμενοι οἱ πονηροὶ δαίμονες, "the evil demons, in imitation of this," in Justin Apology 62, 66, Cf. 23, 25, and 54).[11]

Justin's works applied the Mediterranean term δαίμων, it seems evident, as little more than a subconscious trope in disdain for the dominant icons of Mediterranean culture, reflecting a second-century phase in the early Christian orientation toward and contestation with Greco-Roman civilization. The writings do not seem to necessitate any supporting evidence for his use of δαίμονες in these various instances, except perhaps inasmuch as the term provided an alternative explanation for the Mediterranean analogues to his own sacred religious myths and rites, analogues that had vitally served the initial rise of Christianity, rendering its forms and significations, though in variation, intelligible to the cultural Mediterranean mind through the use of conventional semiosis. These analogues were, however, by the mid-second century, beginning to undermine the religion's rising interests to effect a full-scale cultural revolution. Awareness of this diachronic transition thus serves to delimit one's inferences from the various literary moments to be investigated within the present study.

Peering through the lens of socio-cultural anthropology, Smith perceived that the demonic in such instances functioned in a locative sense to designate or relegate that which one should regard as existing beyond the civilized, that is, the acceptable mapped boundaries of civilization.[12] By relegating the central icons and narratives of Greco-Roman myth, ritual, and culture to the uncivilized margins, Justin's works tacitly placed their own (self-designated) subaltern community at the center. Such a bold assertion effectively defined Christian society as the "contestant other," the mimetic, liminal opponent to classical civilization, legitimate bearer of its true legacy. The intended rhetorical performance of this language, as such, sought to transfer anthropological alterity from subject to object.

In this regard, postcolonial theory seems particularly promising as applied to explain the rhetorical, strategic disposition of Justin's apologies. Contrary to this proposal, however, the counter-cultural disposition of the early Christian movement(s) appealed to nearly all segments of Roman society, not merely to the disenfranchised of Rome's far-flung empire. Other permutations of early Christianity arising beyond the occupied outer provinces of the Roman Empire, while few, were quite different in nature. Manichaeism, for instance, originating in Sassanid Persia, contained little if any of the mythic attributes of the Mediterranean forms of Christianity, specifically those with analogues to be found within the conventions of Greek and Roman mythology. Manichaeism instead applied the philosophic features of earliest Christianity in syncretism with Zoroastrian, Buddhist, and Indic traditions, thus configured toward, appropriating, and contesting a non-Roman, Oriental context.[13] Just as Homi Bhabha has described the "menace of mimicry," one may describe the mimetic policies and strategies of the Mediterranean forms of nascent Christian literature as being, at their heart, culturally and politically subversive. This strategy, then, as seen here in the works of Justin, underwent another iteration, building back upon itself and thus becoming further reinscribed. The works claimed that the Greeks and Romans, through the inspiration and agency of demons, had perpetrated the mimicry. The archaic, pure tradition of the Christians was in fact the genuine theology of classical antique order. All other analogues were either impostors, counterfeits, or ignorantly misperceived manifestations of the divine, spermatic λόγος.

As this study in part explores, the early Christian writers endeavored to eclipse Greco-Roman mythology with early Christian mythology. Just as the English poet William Blake (1757–1827) once observed, "The foundation of empire is art and science. Remove them or degrade them, and the empire is no more. Empire follows art and not *vice versa*." The distinctions made by the early Christian writers compared to those made previously by the Romans, as they appropriated, imitated, and subsequently sought to eclipse Hellenistic mythology through a program of rhetoric and denigration. In classical antiquity, mimesis not only had become the sincerest form of flattery; mimesis was the most potent device of rivalry.[14] Note, for instance, Philip Hardie's assessment of Virgil's epic:

> The audacity of embarking on a comprehensive imitation of Homer was compounded by the prevalent ancient view that Homer was not only the earliest poet writing in the grandest genre, but that he was a universal poet, the source of all later literature and wisdom, of almost god-like stature, and one who saw into the deepest mysteries of the universe. It is a mark of the success of the *Aeneid's* ambition that later centuries saw Virgil himself as a universal and almost divine poet. This act of literary aggrandizement also makes the *Aeneid* a peculiarly apt complement to the ideology of the new *princeps* Augustus, buttressed as it is by a claim to the universal power of Rome; Virgil's poetic triumph, as vividly described at the beginning of the third *Georgic*, makes of him the fitting poet for the *triumphator* Augustus; the literary imperialist rides by the side of the military imperialist.[15]

Though the *Aeneid* admittedly stood as perhaps the most barefaced instance of literary *rivalitas*, composed imitation was never innocent, and the Oedipal hostility found in Justin became all the more rapacious in Tatian's apology, *Oratio ad Graecos,* a generation later. By the time of Tertullian, ca. 200 C.E., such a program of degradation had become fully engorged. Tertullian's *De Spectaculis,* for instance, delivered an unmitigated, ruthless denunciation of the best and most illustrious cultural attainments of the classical world.[16]

Justin's Christianity had come to a place wherein the movement could propagate its most severe rhetorical claims toward a cultural apposition, opposition, and revolution against the established socio-cultural institutions and structures of classical antiquity. Thus varying on Price, one may also conclude that it is to the history of Christian social and ideological rhetoric rather than of compelling argumentation that Justin and the other early Christian apologists belong.[17] Accordingly, Justin's works provided no historical argument supporting the resurrection; one may properly adduce such conspicuous absences in concluding that early Christians held no such position. Indeed, scanning the multitude of documents, one finds that the early Christians apparently never did make such a claim or attempt such an argument, unlike modern Christian apologists, because that was not their perspective nor was this the story's conventional function.[18]

1.2 ZEUS'S OTHER SONS

The fundamental question then resurfaces: To what extent were the framing contours of the Gospel narratives "nothing new" with respect to the established mythic conventions of the Mediterranean demigod, as Justin's work conceded (*1 Apol.* 21)? The supposed gravity of this confession, it would appear, extended well beyond the language of mere comparison, contrary to the summary of many. *1 Apology* juxtaposed the Christian deity's son, not merely as a proposed analogue to the sons of Zeus. The Hellenistic Roman world, according to *interpretatio graeca et romana*, commonly identified the Judeo-Christian deity as indeed being Father Zeus (Jupiter), the supreme god of the classical pantheon, thus interpreting Jesus as agnate to the array of other demigods born of the god's dalliances with mortal women.[19] The apology's assertion thus brings to the fore two matters quite central to the study of Christian origins: 1. the cultural and socio-religious phenomena inherent to Hellenistic Judaism in the urban Greek East, and 2. the relational dynamic that the rise of early Christianity had to Hellenistic Judaism. Proper delineation of these matters proves essential to discerning questions of syncretism between early Jewish theologies, early Christian theologies, and the standing Hellenic and Roman theologies of the urban Levant.

Hellenistic Judaism and the Urban Greek East

During Roman governance of the Levant, the majority of Jews of the Hellenistic Diaspora resided in the central hubs of Hellenistic culture. Each major Hellenistic πόλις contained a sizable Jewish quarter, making up a major portion of the city's total resident population. This continually awkward religious segregation existed not so much on matters of Hellenism—Indeed, both Jews and non-Jews of these Eastern Levantine cities committed variously to Hellenism—, but operated along the maintenance of lines of social and religious identity. The cultural aggravation of this semi-assimilated status perpetually reinforced the alterity of the Jews in antique urban society. Hellenism, moreover, did not exist as a mere phenomenon of influence in the East, contrary to the descriptions of many; from the time of Alexander's conquests onward, Hellenism constituted a movement, a belief, a way of life that had captivated and come to distinguish the best and highest of cultural expression in the eastern Mediterranean.[20] All Hellenists aspired to Hellenize, that is, to exhibit a fashionable measure of Greek cultural *savoir-faire* and refinement through mastery and interplay with recognized Hellenic cultural capital, *le capital culturel*, to follow the parlance of French sociologist Pierre Bourdieu. In cultural expression in the Hellenistic Orient, this process of syncretism typically meant the appropriation of Hellenic forms under significant indigenous names or, conversely, the appropriation of indigenous forms under significant Hellenic names. In the complex negotiation of Jewish identity in the urban Greek East, Jewish modes of Hellenism typically implied the former and not the latter. For, fundamental to being Jewish came the signification of distinctly Jewish symbolisms to the exclusion or demotion of non-Jewish symbolisms. Thus, Philo of Alexandria's *De vita Mosis*, for instance, portrayed Moses as the perfect philosopher whose consummate stature eclipsed that of Socrates, Plato, and Aristotle. While such Hellenizing Jewish works wholly operated in reference to the Greek literary *oeuvre*, with little exception this referential quality came implied; these works typically made explicit only a secondary, surface intertexuality with Jewish sacred texts (customarily the Septuagint).

In this manner, due to Hellenism and Romanism, early Jewish sacred tradition came variously to mimic Greek and Roman forms as a matter of sophisticated acculturation. As an indissoluble religion, however, as John J. Collins has well analyzed, such Jewish assimilation, no matter how extensive, always came accompanied with some measure of social and cultural antagonism.[21] For Hellenistic Jews, the mechanics of a maintained tension between assimilation and dissimilation kept to the fore the ongoing negotiation and reinscription of Jewish identity in urban Greek society. Indeed, the very essence of Hellenistic Jewish identity obtained in this restlessness between a cosmopolitan Hellenism and cultural-religious separatism as the persecuted religious other. Obversely, non-Jewish Hellenistic society, from the opposite side of this culturally fraught delineation, struggled as well to classify and to cohabit with Jewish populations, the struggle itself becoming inherent to Jewish definement.[22]

One particularly precarious example of this dynamic came with the syncretic identification of the Jewish god with Zeus-Jupiter, supreme father of all. Considering such Hellenistic Jewish theologies, George H. van Kooten's recent edited volume documents substantial ancient indications that both Hellenistic Jews and non-Jews equated the two deities, analogous to the syncretism of Ammon-Zeus in Ptolemaic Egypt.[23] With regard to Hellenizing protocols in the Near East, specifically the policy of religious assimilation by Alexander and the subsequent Seleucid and Ptolemaic dynasties, Martin Hengel has observed, "As the '*interpretatio graeca*' of foreign gods shows, they had long been ready to accept alien forms of the divine into their pantheon, the new masters gave the old Semitic gods Greek names."[24]

In ancient civilization, the practice of identifying the deity of a neighboring culture with one's own deity helped to mitigate a sense of difference and foster understanding and familiarity between historically disparate peoples. During their sweeping Hellenistic campaigns, the Seleucids and Ptolemies deployed such a policy as a strategy to give coherence and unification to their extensive empires. Maintaining the success of Alexander's conquests in the East largely relied upon the infusion of Hellenic culture and the subsumption of Eastern cultural structures to cultivate a sense of unity and a common, fundamental order under an ambiance of Hellenism. Myth and religion were, of course, of central importance to the endeavor to assimilate the East. In tandem with *interpretatio graeca*, and hardly separable, came the renovation of the Eastern city into ἡ πόλις ἡ ἑλληνική. The Greeks, beginning with Alexander the Great, brought their advanced architectural expertise, masonry skills, and lavish resources to bear on the massive enterprise of upgrading select cities in the East. In nearly every case, these sweeping upgrades were not only welcomed, but sought by the non-Greek indigenous peoples. This typically entailed the building of colonnades (for *stoae* and *porticos*), markets, gymnasia, as well as revamping the local temples and sacred spaces in keeping with *interpretatio graeca*.[25] The Jerusalem temple cult underwent quite a complex history with regard to this policy, both internal to Judaism and from Hellenistic and Roman governance. Reading against the grain of early Jewish sacred history, one sees that both the temple on Mt. Gerizim (dedicated to Ζεὺς Ξένιος) and the temple on Mt. Moriah (dedicated to Ζεὺς Ὀλύμπιος), under powerful Jewish and Samaritan support, converted to syncretic worship of Yahweh-Zeus, with only the latter having been met with considerable resistance.[26]

The Romans succeeded the Seleucids and Ptolemies and largely adopted these same strategies in their own campaign to Romanize the outlying provinces and frontiers of the empire, thus the parallel phrase *interpretatio romana*, a phrase coined by Tacitus (*Germania* 43.4).[27] Cicero comments:

> Age et his vocabulis esse deos facimus quibus a nobis nominantur? At primum, quot hominum linguae, tot nomina deorum. Non enim, ut tu Velleius, quocumque veneris, sic idem in Italia Volcanus, idem in Africa, idem in Hispania.
>
> (*de Natura Deorum* 1.83–84)

> Come now. Do we assert that the gods actually go by the same names that they are called by us? Yet, the names of the gods are as many as the human languages spoken. For it is not an issue with the gods, but with us. You are Velleius wherever you go, but Vulcan is not Vulcan in Italy and in Africa and in Spain.

One observes that the rendition of the foreign deity need not be altered in order for her or him to be regarded as a member of the Roman pantheon, though called by a non-Roman name.[28] Clifford Ando has problematized the policy, discussing the inevitable incongruities among competing divine renditions in lore, literature, and iconography.[29] The Romans, for instance, sought to assimilate the best of Greek religion and mythology, subsuming these under Roman renditions and nomenclature. Yet, along with this process of *interpretatio romana* often came the propaganda of Roman superiority, the Romans in effect saying to the Greeks, "Our renditions surpass yours." However further radicalized, one finds this central dynamic at play in the works of Justin and the other early Christian apologists.

For the Jews and Romans, Jerusalem became the nucleus of these conflicted forces. Foiled only by the matter of his own death in 40 C.E., the emperor Caligula almost had succeeded in his attempt to convert the Jerusalem temple, nearly having installed a "colossal statue" of Jupiter in the temple's innermost sanctum.[30] Not quite a century later, however, after a period which included the razing of Jerusalem during the First Jewish War under the Flavian Dynasty (66–72 C.E.), the Emperor Hadrian rebuilt the city, renaming it Aelia Capitolina and dedicating the Jerusalem temple to the worship of Jupiter Capitolinus. This dramatic move provoked various reactions among the Jews, most notably the sizable, failed conservative resistance movement in Judea led by Bar Kokhba.[31] Both the Emperor Hadrian and the Emperor Antoninus Pius, to whom *1 Apology* was metonymically addressed, moreover, revamped the Samaritan temple on Mt. Gerizim for syncretic worship of Jupiter (dedicated to Jupiter Perigrinus).[32]

Seleucid, Ptolemaic, and Roman vexation in their perpetually troubled attempts to assimilate Judea under their own governance fomented anti-Jewish stereotypes throughout the Greek-speaking world. By visible evidence, this animosity spawned countermeasures from the philhellenic end of the Jewish spectrum, that is, elaborate Jewish apologetic efforts appealing to Hellenistic and Roman cultural sensibilities and values.[33] With few notable exceptions, the Romans found the more liberal Hellenistic and Romanistic Judaisms of the urban Diaspora to be far less problematic and provocative vis-à-vis Roman rule than their more separatist counterparts in Judea. In truth, the study of Diaspora Hellenizing Jews, as an urban Mediterranean religious segment, suitably resides under the larger field of classical studies. Their writings, while distinct, exist as garden-variety manifestations of classical urban cultural production, even despite the often contemptuous, near-ethnic distinction variously present in Roman sentiment.

Judaistic Hellenism and the Levantine Christian Movements

One need not have been born and raised, as Justin, in Neapolis, the urban Hellenistic center of Samaria at the foot of Mt. Gerizim, to have become rather familiar with these foremost issues of syncretism altogether straining and polarizing the religious complexion of Jewish and Samaritan theism. In the crucible of these forces (namely, through the Jewish Wars, growing stereotypical orientalist myths of Jewish Palestine, Roman discouragement and bans on circumcision, *et cetera*), the earliest Christian movements were forged. The sheer *dynamis* of Greek, Roman, Jewish, and Persian cultures compressed into a singularity had given rise to a new cultural dialectic, a "Christian" synthesis that partially resolved several of the deepest, most long-standing tensions of classical antiquity, all the while igniting new ones.

For emerging early Christian communities in the Greek East, Hellenistic Judaism had served as the jumping-off point. As a fundamental metanarrative or theme running throughout the letters of Paul, the Gospels, and Acts of the Apostles, one observes in these communities the systematic abrogation of nearly every isolationist, separatist practice of early Judaism. Of particular importance to the present study, one notes that the other works of a more reserved Jewish character known from earliest Christian writing (e.g., Matthew's λόγια tradition or "Q," Hebrews, James, and the *Didache*) give no trace of the Hellenistic, theopoetic themes outlined in *1 Apology* 21 (i.e., divine birth, translation, and ascension). Such themes of Hellenistic *exaltatio* in Paul, the Gospels, and Acts of the Apostles survive as the celebrated textual products of these early Christian movements of the urban Greek East. Drawing in waves of Hellenist converts from both Jewish and non-Jewish backgrounds, these early Christian urban communities defied the conventional lines of both early Jewish tradition and Hellenistic tradition. How was it that Paul, for all of his Judaic training, appeared at the core more to resemble an itinerate Stoic philosopher than any known rabbi of the Roman Levant? That is to say, the *forms* of these urban early Christian constructions were, more often than not, at their core lifted from the structures of classical antique culture, often with a mere outward Judaistic decor.[34]

The first steps of early Christianity in the urban Greek Levant were to exit the Jewish quarter, flipping Hellenistic Judaism on its head, thus giving way for a new social modality. For these burgeoning house assemblies in the principal cities of classical antiquity, which seems the more accurate description: Judaism was being Hellenized, or Hellenism was being Judaized?[35] Innovative displays of appropriation and adaption from both worlds coalesced into an unprecedented movement that swept the urban Mediterranean Roman world, forming the originary communities that produced and signified the resurrection narratives of the New Testament. Indeed, the Gospels and Acts of the Apostles belie any effort at contextualizing their language or composition in Jewish Palestine. Knowledge of the literary context inscribed *within* the documents themselves presents not the markings or signs of a mundane, local familiarity with Galilee, Samaria, or Judea, but general, wayfaring descriptions more typical of festival pilgrims of the Jewish Diaspora, returning Roman troops, and disposed emigrants romanticizing the setting of a distant homeland.[36] First composed, signified, and sacralized in the Hellenistic urban world of Roman Syria, Anatolia, Macedonia, and Greece, these works typically reflected and played on crudely stereotypical myths of Jewish Palestine.[37] The inculpatory themes of the Gospels and Acts with respect to Judaism in Palestine referenced collective critical attitudes in the Hellenistic Roman East, growing vexation over reports of an ongoing, seemingly needless struggle with perceived insolent, pertinacious religious mentalities in the region. Such vexation threatened to upset the already tenuous urban cohabitation between non-Jews and Jews in cities throughout the Hellenistic world. Within these unbearably strained urban contexts, the Gospels found their remarkable early traction and purposefulness.

1.3 PROPER INFERENCE

The above sketch underscores the ongoing dramatic strain upon and, perhaps more important, *within* ancient Abrahamic religion to synthesize with the broader cultural theologies of the Hellenistic kingdoms and the Roman Empire. Appreciation of these prevailing Hellenizing and Romanizing forces, both those within and those without the early Jewish social landscape, elevates the ultimate cultic and theological implications of this inclination to synthesize the two theologies. Through improved awareness of the recurring centrality of this conflict, one better contextualizes and comprehends the divine Christian υἱὸς θεοῦ.[38] One thus accurately adduces such instances of the syncretic language in early Christian theology as indicating a Christian adaptation of antique Greco-Roman forms. Could any fresh, third-party observer not immediately perceive the pattern: a Judeo-Christian version of Zeus-Jupiter, with his own storied demigod son born of a mortal woman? Such syncretic, adaptive traits applied as much to the demigod tradition as to the early Christian endeavored subsumption of the Platonic θεός, thus appropriating (or expropriating) the classical philosophical tradition. Justin's argument stood on the prevalent acceptability of this most basic premise: On the one hand, the apology described a continuity between these classical generic forms, while, on the other hand, the apology denigrated all prior instances as false, illegitimate, and even demonic, with the immorality of Zeus, in this instance, often being cited.

1 Apology has, in this passage, specified the broad semiotic connotation for the title υἱὸς θεοῦ applied in the Gospel tradition. Thus, while in significant agreement with the analysis set forth by Michael Peppard, the present book broadens the association from an exclusively Roman imperial use (*divi filius*) to include the larger "demigod" tradition of the classical world, that is, as prompted by Justin's explicit appraisal.[39] *1 Apology* 21 sets out a brief paradigm, moreover, revealing a correct understanding that the deification of the Roman emperor, following antecedent traditions found in the Hellenistic kingdoms, derived from the classical tradition of the demigod.

Topic of Inquiry

Plainly stated, this book explores the ancient conventionality and significance of the "resurrection" and "ascension" narratives of Jesus in the New Testament. The investigation, more specifically, seeks to discern any semiotic-linguistic relationship between what Plutarch described as a Mediterranean "translation fable" tradition in classical antiquity (*Vita Romuli* 27.3–28.6) and the postmortem accounts of the New Testament Gospels and Acts of the Apostles.[40] To this end, the study conducts close philological readings of all four Gospels, providing a methodologically robust analysis of the likely earliest socio-cultural performance of the Gospel resurrection narratives in light of a thorough cultural and literary understanding of the "translation fable" convention as found in broader Mediterranean hero fabulation and the Roman apotheosis traditions of the period. As such, the analysis includes substantial cultural and linguistic exploration of many relevant primary texts taken from both literary domains, that is, both classical and early Christian works, and catalogues numerous remaining pertinent passages. Indeed, the book should serve, among other purposes, as a useful, extensive published compendium of such tales under the stated rubric, contributing to both fields of study, aiding the accuracy of inference taken from any given instance of the cultural convention to be encountered in antique Mediterranean literature.

In 1942, Harvard classicist Arthur Stanley Pease published "Some Aspects of Invisibility" (*HSCP* 53 [1942]: 1–36) in which he concisely surveyed several stories of invisibility scattered throughout the Greek and Latin writings of antiquity. As often has been the case with the scholars of classical studies, Pease treaded all-too-lightly when his survey finally reached its curious destination, Jesus' empty tomb, after sampling an assortment of translation fables. When finally addressing most directly this question of whether the resurrection and postmortem appearance and ascension narratives of the New Testament must fall under his outlined rubric, Pease adroitly eluded, writing:

> Whether Jesus was considered divine because of the possession of miraculous powers—including the faculty of invisibility—, or was believed to possess such powers because he was considered divine is hardly a question which can be decided by such studies as present. Or, as Pfister puts the problem for classical antiquity, does legend develop from cult or cult from legend? From the same Biblical data the Fundamentalist and the Modernist and the Sceptic will answer these questions in quite different ways.

This discretion suggests that he had an answer, but did not wish to propound his answer upon the religious neurosis of some readers and thus attract undesired reprisal. He walked to the (arbitrary) discursive bounds of his discipline and did all but cross its well-monitored threshold into the τέμενος of Western sacred history. Classicists have long been (self)trained not expressly to disrupt the sacred tenets of the Christian West and thus have leveled veiled criticisms, albeit at times most thinly, within the relative privacy of their privileged society. Now, seventy years later, the present transdisciplined book endeavors to fulfill the task introduced by Pease, at a time when, one may hope, the academy is better prepared to brave and to engage its implications.

The answer to this question, however, at least as the matter yet domiciles with New Testament academics, remains to be known. Sadly, with only minor shifts, Burton Mack's criticism a generation ago may still characterize the discourse:

> All scholars seem to agree . . . on the importance of the resurrection. Three terms are frequently used, each encoded by custom within the discourse of the discipline, to refer euphemistically to the resurrection of Jesus from the dead: Easter, appearance, and spirit. The casual reader may not notice how often recourse is made to these terms in the language of New Testament scholarship, thinking perhaps that their occurrence is to be attributed to the idiosyncrasy of an occasional confessional writer. After reading seriously into the field and at length, however, the repetition of these terms creates a crescendo that becomes quite shrill. These coded signs, usually capitalized, do not enlighten because they mark the point beyond which reasoned argument must cease. They serve as ciphers to hold the space for the unimaginable miracle that must have happened prior to any and all interpretation. They have become an all too convenient rhetorical device for evoking the myth of Christian origins without having to explain it.[41]

The academy still all too often applies the definite article to demarcate a *sui generis*, enigmatic moment imagined and collectively supposited as the singular impetus for the birth of Christianity: the Resurrection, the Empty Tomb, the Event, the Mystery. The guild rather quietly has designated and relinquished this unique partitioned space, a discursive lacuna wherein ultimate critical declarations are often considered taboo. Instead, a vague politesse has grown fashionable, one content to consign the question of the historicity of Jesus' narrated resurrection to a blinkered bin of agnosticism. The present study finds this sacralized obstruction wholly unsatisfactory and intellectually vacant. The early Christians themselves did not designate any such claim as the sacred, originary impulse of the movement, let alone promulgate a corresponding historical case. Proceeding from this myth of origins, moreover, would not one reasonably expect to find a throng of early Christian martyrs expressly having died for such a claim? Contrary to this, however, one finds little if any evidence of the kind in the chronicles of early Christian history.

What then should the undaunted scholar make of such tales of the raised Jesus? How would such stories have registered within the cultural-linguistic framework of Hellenistic and Roman antiquity? This precisely constitutes the present item of inquiry. While the term "comparative analysis" may suggest a decoupled, loose juxtaposition of two, until now, disparate traditions, the study endeavors to identify a detailed, shared conventional system between the Gospel resurrection narratives and the extant translation narratives of Hellenistic and Roman literature. If established, such a finding would then expose the directing, interpretive signals of early Christian accounts, thus elucidating the earliest readings of such texts. This discussion would then expand to include the various genres and respective relevant expressions within the broader, early Christian literary domain.

Although preliminary research has provided ample evidence toward these prospects, the nature and extent of such findings require a more formidable, methodologically sophisticated inquiry. A sketch of the data and initial observations suggest a developmental, contiguous trajectory, or set of trajectories, beginning with, so to speak, the subsumption of "resurrection" language under the broader "translation" topos. As has been shown, for the Hellenistic and Roman cultures, the tradition functioned in an honorific capacity; the convention had become a protocol for honoring numerous heroes, kings, and philosophers, those whose bodies were not recovered at death. In Roman propaganda, the translation of Romulus, perhaps originating in Ennius, served as the quintessential, archetypal account for a pronounced "apotheosis" tradition in the funerary consecration of the *principes Romani*. The Romulean legend thus deserves special attention when considering the emerging (counter-)cultural station of the *rex regum* in Roman cultural history. To what extent did the Romulean translation narratives provide a mimetic backdrop for the Gospel narratives? The monograph seeks to posit the most satisfying thesis for explaining the extensive structural semiotic similarities. How, for instance, might Hellenistic and Roman archetypal mimesis account for such literary-cultural patterns? Did other substantial examples of this exist within the earliest literary depictions of Jesus and/or elsewhere within Greek and Roman cultures and literatures? Does such mimesis imply *aemulatio* or *rivalitas* when endeavoring to know the socio-cultural disposition and orientation of a given literary piece? If determined that the textualized Romulus indeed figured prominently within early Christian resurrection narrative construction, what mimetic, rhetorical performance might this have likely achieved within the cultural milieu of a Romano-Greek East, that is, in the primitive centuries of the rise of Christianity?

As a proper result of this analysis, the book also tacitly delivers a rather forceful critique of standing theories regarding the likely antecedents of the early Christian "resurrection" accounts. These tend to fall into two large pools: early Jewish resurrection tradition or the denial of any antecedent, thus positing a *sui generis* status, a perspective typically arising out of faith-based discourse. This study sets forth a more satisfying thesis, a model that more comprehensively explains the available data, namely, that such narratives fundamentally relied upon and adapted the broadly applied cultural-linguistic conventions and structures of antique Mediterranean society.

Some Definitions and Framing Considerations

While the title of this work may *prima facie* appear quite straightforward, some key definitions should lend additional clarity to the ensuing subject matter.

As for the operative expression "translation fable," for instance, Plutarch applied the descriptor μυθολογέω in his explanation of the "translation" motif (to be taken up in Chapter 2), a term Perrin translated as "fable writing." The study thus applies the term "fable" with the broader application as understood by—this must be emphasized—its Latin etymological term *"fabula,"* that is, not in the narrow sense of talking animals and anecdotes as, for instance, given in the apologues of Aesop, that is, the *Aesopia* of Phaedrus and Babrius. "Fable" or *"fabula,"* within the bounds of this book, refers to culturally owned and cherished, even sacralized narratives, ranging from the playful and whimsical to the dramatic and dire. Like the more narrow use of the term, however, "fable" often undertakes a didactic subtext, at times latent or even enigmatic and may thus require socially governed interpretation. The term's use here denotes a quite adjacent semantic scope as that meant by mythologists when applying the term "myth." Alan Dundes defines "myth" as "a sacred narrative explaining how the world and man came to be in their present form."[42] The present study, however, presumes to alter the definition to indicate that a myth is a sacred narrative or account that has served or serves to frame the present for a person, group, society, nation, or all of humanity. Such a definition would thereby include eschatological myths, apocalyptic myths, cosmic myths, and etiological myths. "Fable" adds to this description of "myth" the qualification of self-consciousness, that is, the "fable" exists as a myth to be understood as such. If one chooses to suspend disbelief, that person does so more consciously in the case of the "fable." The "fable" also comes to include didactic tales, that is, stories constructed only for the sake of making some point, such as Plato's Myth of Er (*Rep.* 10.614–10.621) or Jesus' Parable of the Sower (Mk 4.1–20). The study only proposes this particular definition of "fable" for use within the confines of the present book and, as such, does not necessarily suggest or promote a wider application or acceptance. The analysis, moreover, endeavors to elucidate the cultural-literary genus and nature of the translation fable as variously instanced. Indeed, the translation fable resided under the larger Latin rubric *fabula,* a conclusion yet to be established in Chapter 2 with the Gallery of various instances.

"Myth," as herein applied, may also refer to a mental sketch or image commonly operative in human conception.[43] Myth-making (μυθοποίησις), in this sense, denotes the all-too-human mental enterprise of producing operative sketches, often grossly reductionistic, distorted models referencing persons, concepts, places, notions, experiences, accounts, or any other topic of mental encapsulation. Myths prove helpful and necessary to human cognition inasmuch as they are manageable in size and detail for the sake of expediting human thought. Some myths may be true in the sense of being fit for a particular purpose, not unlike a sketched pocket map that proves reliable for the purpose of indicating how one might walk to a nearby bakery. Other myths may be true in the sense of being functional or wise, that is, they lead to desirable or virtuous outcomes. Shared myths may become valued for their social function within a community and are often applied in identity formation. All human understandings of persons, even historical persons, are myths.[44] The nature and limits of the human mind impose such a state. Stereotypical or reductionistic mental constructions aid in the expedition of cognitive processes, even (indeed perhaps especially) when one considers those of most intimate acquaintance, such as a parent, a significant other, or even the self. Such conceptions serve as crude, hurried working mental images. When governments, communities, societies, groups, or individuals seek to project and administer such myths (working caricatures or images), one calls the product of this activity "propaganda." Culturally or socially owned, iconic figures, as a rule, become untethered to their original persons (whether historical, legendary, or fictive) as such figures obtain new roles in emerging social performance. Indeed, in some instances, consideration of the "original" person becomes all but irrelevant (e.g., Davy Crocket, Saint Patrick, or Joan of Arcadia). Such figures become paragons or emblems, that is, metonymic symbols often embodying particular ideologies, movements, values, or social constructions.

Along the way, the present examination prompts the satisfying address of various formidable framing questions. To what degree and in which instances was early Christian mythopoiesis meant either as an accretion to Mediterranean mythology or as an alternative, competing system, that is, an abstracted, emulative alternative thinly dressed in early Jewish garb? To what extent are its core literary conventions taken from the larger literary-cultural domain of the Greek East? Jason König and other prominent classicists appear prepared to include earliest Christian literature within the broader Greek literary domain of the Roman world.[45] The proposed study contributes to this negotiation by further demonstrating what may come to appear as all too obvious in later generations of scholarship, namely that, despite the at times overt counter-cultural orientation, early Christian literature fundamentally and pervasively relied upon and varied upon the standing cultural-literary conventions of the Hellenistic Orient. Particularly pressing with respect to the earliest literary works, how might such writings have been made intelligible, from a structuralist and semiotic perspective, within the metropolises of the Romano-Greek Levant without extensive, substantive reliance upon the rich conventional literary forms operative in the region, a region altogether enchanted with Greek linguism?

The study thus must explore matters of literary composition, παιδεία, and the implied valence(s) of early Christian works. Were the Gospels regarded as *klein Literatur, hoch Literatur,* or both? Who were their implied authors/narrators and implied readers? Were these works understood as Jewish, Roman, cosmopolitan, or something else? What then may be known or assumed about their frame(s) of reference, that is, about their applied semiotic grammar? How might the earliest readings have registered or been meant to register in cities such as Antioch on the Orontes, the third-largest metropolitan center of the Roman world and cradle of earliest Christianity in the late first and early second centuries?

The investigation directly elucidates what many early Christian scholars identify as the most sacred narrative of early Christian kerygma. The analysis thus contributes significantly to early Christian studies by achieving a higher resolution of comprehension of the earliest performance of resurrection narratives within evident societies. Concerning classical studies, the monograph contributes to a much-needed negotiation between two artificially bifurcated fields of cultural-literary study, thus subsuming earliest Christian literature under the broader domain of classical Mediterranean study.

NOTES

1. Unless otherwise stated, all translations within the monograph are those of the author.
2. This same summary of the argument in *1 Apology* appears in my essay in the *Journal of Biblical Literature.* Richard C. Miller, "Mark's Empty Tomb and Other Translation Fables in Classical Antiquity," *JBL* 129, no. 4 (2010): 775.
3. Here Justin aligned himself with the Socratic tradition in an appeal to gain sympathy. The infamous charges brought against Socrates by Meletus, namely, that Socrates had fabricated "new gods" (Plato, *Euthyphr* 3b), later served to legitimate and delineate space for a philosophic disposition toward classical society. Socrates tells Euthyphro, Ἄτοπα, ὦ θαυμάσιε, ὡς οὕτω γ᾽ ἀκοῦσαι. φησὶ γάρ με ποιητὴν εἶναι θεῶν, καὶ ὡς καινούς ποιοῦντα θεούς, τοὺς δ᾽ ἀρχαίους οὐ νομίζοντα, ἐργάψατο τούτων αὐτῶν ἕνεκα, ὡς φησιν. Cf. Diogenes Laertius 2.40. Justin, however, here did not deny that the earliest Christians had introduced a "new god," but stated that this introduction had fit under a long-standing tradition including various other demigods or "sons of Zeus," namely, as part of an established honorific protocol inherent to classical custom. In this regard, the embellished Jesus narrative proposed nothing new or novel.
4. If one follows the compelling arguments of Pervo and Tyson in dating Luke-Acts to the early second century, then the rhetorical exordium of the "Mars Hill" speech in Acts 17 stood adjacent to and nearly contemporaneous with Justin's criticism of the Greeks worshipping their pantheon in a state of ignorance. Richard I. Pervo, *Dating Acts between the Evangelists and the Apologists* (Santa Rosa, CA: Polebridge Press, 2006) and Joseph B. Tyson, *Marcion and Luke-Acts, a Defining Struggle* (Columbia: University of South Carolina Press, 2006).
5. Regarding the critical ambivalence of Lucretius regarding the classical poets, see Monica Gale, *Myth and Poetry in Lucretius* (Cambridge: Cambridge University Press, 1994).

6. Robert M. Price, "Are There 'Holy Pagans' in Justin Martyr," *StPatr* 31 (1997): 171.

7. Adolf von Harnack, *Die Grundlegung,* book 2 of *Lehrbuch der Dogmengeschichte* (5th ed., reprint of the 4th ed. of 1909; Tübingen: Mohr, 1931), 343. Harnack's entire second book (here, in Band 1) contained his pervasively influential thesis that the Apologists were culpable for the Hellenization of the original movement's message. Such a thesis no doubt arose out of Harnack's Protestant German disposition vis-à-vis Catholicism. The corrupting "paganism" of the Catholic Church, an influence according to Harnack that took hold in the second century, had obscured the purity of the original gospel and, as such, has rendered Catholic Christianity perverse.

8. By the early third century, Tertullian continued to struggle with the same difficulty, namely attempting to disentangle and subsequently denigrate these same archetypal heroes of the classical age, distinguishing them as a "mythic class": *Sedenim in isto mythico genere, quod poetae ferunt, quam incerti agitis circa conscientiae pudorem et pudoris defensionem!* (*De Nationes* 7.8); cf. Tertullian, *Apologia* 12–13.

9. The shift also followed a long-standing disdain for the mythopoeic traditions of classical antiquity, a disdain that arose out of the Hellenic philosophical traditions. Cf. Tertullian, *de Spectaculis* 29: *Si scaenicae doctrinae delectant, satis nobis litterarum est, satis versuum est, satis sententiarum, satis etiam canticorum, satis vocum, nec fabulae, sed veritates, nec strophae, sed simplicitates.* "If erudition of theater delight you, we have sufficiency of literature, of poems, of aphorisms, sufficiency of songs and voices, not fables, but truths; not artifice but simplicity."

10. N.B., this study deliberately brackets the term "orthodox" in describing a socio-political religious movement that came to prominence in the Late Antique period of Christian history, in general alignment with Bauer's seminal thesis understanding the politics, complexity, and untidy diversity of early Christian philosophy, myth, and ideology. Walter Bauer, *Rechtgläubigkeit und Ketzerei im ältesten Christentum* (Tübingen: Mohr, 1934). The term here becomes perhaps useful to the extent that "orthodoxy" has tended to accrue a stereotypical profile, a profile wherein the alleged historicity of Jesus' resurrection has often been its most fundamental premise. The present study thus boldly challenges this unsupported, though pervasive misunderstanding.

11. Jonathan Z. Smith, "Toward Interpreting Demonic Powers in Hellenistic and Roman Antiquity," *ANRW* II.16.1 (1978): 428.

12. Ibid., 429–30.

13. Cf. Iain Gardner and Samuel N. C. Lieu, *Manichaean Texts from the Roman Empire* (Cambridge: Cambridge University Press, 2004). This fundamental observation (namely, that the permutations of early Christianities formed vis-à-vis the respective cultures that each sought to counteract or to contest) not only applies in contexts where the Romans had subjugated prior great empires (Greece, North Africa, Egypt, and Syrian-Palestine). Earliest Christianity variously developed as counter-cultural composites, hybridities appropriating and countering various Mediterranean and Oriental cultural-semiotic forms and patterns. The elements most familiar to a given region within which Christianity arose thus became dominant. Those elements that were most foreign tended to fall off or were substantially reinterpreted. Early Christianity in Roman Egypt likewise manifests this principle. See Gregory J. Riley, *One Jesus, Many Christs: How Jesus Inspired not One True Christianity, but Many* (Chicago: University of Chicago Press, 1997).

14. Cf. Ellen Finkelpearl, "Pagan Traditions of Intertextuality in the Roman World," in *Mimesis and Intertextuality in Antiquity and Christianity* (SAC;

Harrisburg, PA: Trinity International Press, 2001), 78–90. See also Homi Bhabha's related notion of mimicry as a menacing mode of resistance to domination, a matter taken up in Chapter 3 below, "Critical Method and the Gospels." Homi K. Bhabha, *The Location of Culture* (New York: Routledge, 1994), 121–31.

15. Philip Hardie, *Virgil* (Greece & Rome New Surveys in the Classics No. 28; Oxford, 1998), 57.

16. See especially *Spect.* 30, the final chapter. Later, once it became apparent that Roman culture would not abolish all prior mythography and fable, early Christian writers instead demoted these as inferior, base modes of theologizing (e.g., Augustine, *Civ.* 6.7).

17. Robert M. Price, "Are There 'Holy Pagans' in Justin Martyr." Price concludes his essay writing: "It is to the history of Christian rhetoric rather than of Christian doctrine that Justin and the other Greek apologists belong."

18. The only noteworthy seeming exception to this observation presents itself in Paul's correspondence with the church at Corinth (1 Cor 15), a matter to be taken up in Chapter 4.

19. Regarding Zeus as the "father of men and gods," see Walter Burkert, *Greek Religion* (Cambridge, MA: Harvard University Press, 1985), 129.

20. Despite Edward Saïd's valuable correctives over the politically freighted, stereotypical use of the term "Orient" in modern thought, the present study often applies the term as connoting ancient perceptions, namely, to signify a common ancient Occidental romanticization and mythologization of the East. Regrettably, many scholars since Saïd's publication have come to avoid the term altogether. This seems particularly unwarranted, since Saïd himself readily applied the terms "Western" and "Eastern" in his own writings. A substantive awareness, moreover, of these ancient connotations proves vital to comprehending the lively cultural, inferential associations of ancient classical society. Romanticization, generalization, and stereotype inherently constitute much of human thought. He rightfully called the academy to cease the careless, uncritical use of the term, particularly that which promotes social, political, or economic injustice. Saïd's own tendency to generalize and make broad characterizations has drawn valid criticisms to his work. Major elements of his argument deconstruct once one turns the methodology in upon itself (e.g., past criticisms of *Orientalism* leveled by George P. Landow of Brown University). Notwithstanding these problems, the present book notes Saïd's considerable contribution to the discourse. Edward W. Saïd, *Orientalism* (London: Routledge and Kegan Paul, 1978).

21. John J. Collins, *Between Athens and Jerusalem: Jewish Identity in the Hellenistic Diaspora* (Grand Rapids: Eerdmans, 2000). Cf. John M. G. Barclay, *Jews in the Mediterranean Diaspora from Alexander to Trajan (323 BCE— 117 CE)* (Edinburgh: Clark, 1996).

22. One finds a panoply of evidence of this unsettled awkward dynamic in Menahem Stern, ed., *Greek and Latin Authors on Jews and Judaism* (3 vols.; Jerusalem: Israel Academy of Sciences and Humanities, 1974–1984).

23. Perhaps most famously expressed in Aristobulus and Ps.-Aristeas. See George H. van Kooten, ed., *The Revelation of the Name YHWH to Moses: Perspectives from Judaism, the Pagan Greco-Roman World, and Early Christianity* (Themes in Biblical Narrative 9. Leiden: Brill, 2006).

24. Martin Hengel, *Judaism and Hellenism* (2 vols.; trans. John Bowden; Eugene, OR: Wipf and Stock Publishers, 1974), 261. Cf. Marice Sartre, *The Middle East under Rome* (trans. Catherine Porter and Elizabeth Rawlings; Cambridge, MA: Belknap Press of Harvard University Press, 2005), 299–318.

25. Seth Schwartz explains the process of Hellenization as the creation of "hybrid" cultural expressions, expressions that both preserved the city's original

ethno-cultural traditions, while celebrating Greek innovation and high culture. Seth Schwartz, "The Hellenization of Jerusalem and Shechem" in *Jews
in a Greco-Roman World* (ed. Martin Goodman; Oxford: Clarendon Press,
1998), 37–45. For a further elaboration of Hellenization in Syria and the Near
East, see Marice Sartre, *The Middle East under Rome*, 274–296. Palmyra and
the cities of Ptolemaic and Roman Egypt provide excellent studies of such
hybridity in the Levant.

26. Cf. *2 Macc* 6:1–12. *1–2 Maccabees* applied denigrative labels to these pro-
Hellenization movements of Seleucid Palestine, endeavoring to marginalize
both Samaritan religion and the Jewish masses who succeeded in Hellenizing
Jerusalem. *1 Maccabees* applied the term ἄνδρες παράνομοι throughout the
history as a designation for those Jews who favored Antiochus's reforms in
Jerusalem (*1 Macc* 1.11, 1.34, 2.44, 7.5, 9.22, 9.69, 10,61, 11.21–25, 14.14;
the NRSV translates the term as "renegades"). Note the implied size, capacity, and power of the pro-Hellenization Jewish faction in Jerusalem; they were
able to revamp the city, including major building projects, through their own
labor and resources. Modern treatments often mischaracterize the Hellenizing reforms that provoked the Maccabean Revolt as not internal to Judaism,
but as wholly superimposed by the Seleucids, thus indulging in the biased
propaganda of these tendentious histories. The strength of the Jewish Hellenizing party grew so formidable that they were able to hold and defend
Jerusalem from the attacks and advances of Mattathias and his resistance
movement (*1 Macc* 1.29–40). Though Mattathias was said to have defeated
the Hellenists (*1 Macc* 2.42–48), they continually rematerialized in ever more
substantial numbers according to the narrative. *1 Maccabees* would have the
reader suppose that the resistance movement under Mattathias, Judas Maccabeus, *et alii* enjoyed divine providence and heroic dominance during the
decades in question, but a critical reading, one running against the subtextual
grain, readily reveals that neither side by any means dominated the conflict for
long, as *1 Macc* 9.23 exemplifies: "After the death of Judas, the 'lawless men'
reemerged in all parts of Israel; all of the wrongdoers reappeared."

27. Cassius Dio, for example, provides an excellent detailed description of Hadrian's expansive, Romanizing building campaigns. The outlying provinces of
Asia and Africa, with the notable exception of second-century Jewish matters,
welcomed the overhaul of their respective cities and indeed petitioned Hadrian
to include their cities in his building and renovation projects. For a careful
historical analysis of this, see Mary T. Boatwright, *Hadrian and the Cities of
the Roman Empire* (Princeton, NJ: Princeton University Press, 2000).

28. Cf. Origen's quotation of Celsus in Origen, *Contra Celsus* 1.24; 5.41; Cf.
Augustine's quotation of Varro in Augustine, *De Civitate Dei* 4.2; 4.9. For
further discussion and primary references see Hengel, *Judaism and Hellenism*,
261–67.

29. Clifford Ando, "*Interpretatio Romana*," *CP* 100 (2005): 41–51.

30. Cf. Philo, *Legat.* 29–46; Josephus, *Ant.* 18.257–309; *B.J.* 2.184–203.

31. Dio Cassius, *Historicus* 69.12.1; Eusebius, *Historia ecclesiastica* 4.6–7; Pausanias, *Graeciae Descriptio* 1.5.5.

32. Eusebius, *Theoph;* cf. Origen, *Cels.* 2.13.

33. The works of Josephus and the works of Philo provide two of the most famous
extant examples of this apologetic character. Collins likewise observes this
theme as common to Hellenistic Jewish writings. John J. Collins, *Between
Athens and Jerusalem*, 14–16, 261–72.

34. The present monograph, in an effort to capture the verbal directive nature
of the movement as *in process*, coins the term "Judaistic," a word parallel in
function to the better-known term "Hellenistic" and more or less linguistically

equivalent to the term "Judaizing," that is, endeavoring the process of rendering something more "Jewish."

35. As set forth in Chapter 3, much confusion over these types of questions has arisen from the traditionally privileged role assigned to the earliest Christian authors, as opposed to the cultural *langue* and implied readers who signified these documents. With the Pauline letters, for instance, many have sought early Jewish antecedents, ever interested to explore the person of Paul in order to uncover the ideological and conventional underpinnings of the text. The movement, however, that Paul helped to ignite in urban Greece, Macedonia, and Anatolia comprised mostly non-Jewish Hellenists. The movement was they, not Paul alone. This authorial orientation to Hellenistic urban Christianity in the Roman provinces and the texts that they most sacralized appears in the otherwise magisterial work of Wayne Meeks, to give but one of countless examples from prior generations. Wayne A. Meeks, *The First Urban Christians: The Social World of the Apostle Paul* (New Haven: Yale University Press, 1983), 32–50.

36. The invective and specific character of regional references (typically north of Judea) present in the Synoptic Sayings Source (Q) provide the visible exception to this observation, a matter taken up again in Chapter 3.

37. For this reason, efforts by well-intended scholars, perhaps most notably those in the published work of E.P. Sanders, at reconciling portrayals of Judaism in Paul and the Gospels and Acts with an historically accurate understanding of Judaism(s) in Palestine often seem contrived and overly strained. These documents were not internal to Palestinian Judaism, but quite external, and referenced the categories, orientation, and currents of these Hellenistic northern cultural contexts during a period of severe Roman encroachment and upheaval in the region.

38. Often the Gospel traditions rendered one or both nouns as anarthrous (e.g., Mk 1.1 and 15.39). Irrespective of the presence of an article, however, the phrase did not presuppose a monotheistic or doctrinal valence for the term, contrary to later, ecclesiastical readings, but applied established Mediterranean language typical of demigods. One should understand the presence of the article, as with common grammar, as demonstrative in function: the (previously identified or understood) son of the (previously identified or understood) deity. Here, proper linguistic principles untangle a needlessly complicated syntax. Where the Greek article is absent, the noun simply becomes indefinite: a son of a deity. The Gospels did not require of or impose upon their ancient reader a monotheistic or Christological starting place, but presumed a general Hellenistic cultural-linguistic paradigm.

39. Michael Peppard, *The Son of God in the Roman World: Divine Sonship in Its Social and Political Context* (Oxford: Oxford University Press, 2011).

40. My 2010 article appearing in the *Journal of Biblical Literature* "Mark's Empty Tomb and Other Translation Fables in Classical Antiquity" (*JBL* 129, no. 4 [2010]: 759–76) has provided the premise for this present book now broadening the analysis beyond Mark's narrative to encompass all four canonical Gospels and Acts.

41. Burton L. Mack, *Mark and Christian Origins: A Myth of Innocence* (Philadelphia: Fortress Press, 1988), 7.

42. Alan Dundes, editor's introduction to *Sacred Narrative: Readings in the Theory of Myth* (Berkeley: University of California Press, 1984), 1.

43. The term "myth" serves several semantic uses in the English language. For a consideration of other valid denotations for the term, see Lauri Honko, "The Problem Defining Myth," in *Sacred Narrative: Readings in the Theory of Myth* (ed. Alan Dundes; Berkeley: University of California Press, 1984),

41–52; Laurence Coupe, *Myth* (The New Critical Idiom; New York: Routledge, 1997), 1–12.

44. This statement is but a subset of the larger assertion, one held by the writer of this thesis, that all human conceptions are essentially and inexorably myths. Blumenberg provides a full philosophical treatise on this single point, arguing against the notion that humankind can progress toward a "myth-free" society. We simply trade some myths for others, according to Blumenberg, and thus never escape our myth-making mental processes. Inference rightly gains legitimacy, however, through fidelity to experience and the scientific method. Hans Blumenberg, *Work on Myth* (trans. Robert M. Wallace; Cambridge, MA: MIT Press, 1985). With respect to a metacritical characterization of academic work itself as myth, see Bruce Lincoln, *Theorizing Myth: Narrative, Ideology, and Scholarship* (Chicago: University of Chicago Press, 1999).

45. Jason König, *Greek Literature in the Roman Empire* (Classical World Series; London: Bristol Classical Press, 2009), 24–25, 63–64.

BIBLIOGRAPHY

Ando, Clifford. "*Interpretatio Romana.*" *Classical Philology* 100 (2005): 41–51.

Bauer, Walter. *Rechtgläubigkeit und Ketzerei im ältesten Christentum*. Tübingen: Mohr, 1934.

———. *Orthodoxy and Heresy in Earliest Christianity*. Translated by a team from the Philadelphia Seminar of Christian Origins. Edited by Robert A. Kraft and Gerhard Krodel. Mifflintown, PA: Sigler Press, 1971.

Bhabha, Homi K. *The Location of Culture*. New York: Routledge, 1994.

Birley, Anthony R. *Hadrian, the Restless Emperor*. London: Routledge, 1997.

Blumenberg, Hans. *Work on Myth*. Translated by Robert M. Wallace. Cambridge, MA: MIT Press, 1985.

Boatwright, Mary T. *Hadrian and the Cities of the Roman Empire*. Princeton, NJ: Princeton University Press, 2000.

Burkert, Walter. "*Caesar und Romulus-Quirinus*" *Historia* 11 (1962): 356–76.

Collins, John J. *Between Athens and Jerusalem: Jewish Identity in the Hellenistic Diaspora*. Grand Rapids: Eerdmans, 2000.

Coupe, Laurence. *Myth*. The New Critical Idiom. New York: Routledge, 1997.

———, ed. *Sacred Narrative: Readings in the Theory of Myth*. Berkeley: University of California Press, 1983.

Finkelpearl, Ellen. "Pagan Traditions of Intertextuality in the Roman World." Pages 78–90 in *Mimesis and Intertextuality in Antiquity and Christianity*. Edited by Dennis R. McDonald. Studies in Antiquity and Christianity. Harrisburg, PA: Trinity International Press, 2001.

Gale, Monica. *Myth and Poetry in Lucretius*. Cambridge: Cambridge University Press, 1994.

Gardner, Iain and Samuel N.C. Lieu. *Manichaean Texts from the Roman Empire*. Cambridge: Cambridge University Press, 2004.

Goldstein, Jonathan A. *1 Maccabees*. AB 41. Garden City, NY: Doubleday, 1976.

Hardie, Philip. *Virgil*. Greece & Rome New Surveys in the Classics 28. Oxford: Oxford University Press, 1998.

Harnack, Adolf von. *Lehrbuch der Dogmengeschichte*. 3 vols. 5th ed., reprint of the 4th ed. of 1909. Tübingen: Mohr, 1931.

Hengel, Martin. *Judaism and Hellenism*. 2 vols. Translated by John Bowden. Eugene, OR: Wipf and Stock Publishers, 1974.

Honko, Lauri. "The Problem Defining Myth." Pages 41–52 in *Sacred Narrative: Readings in the Theory of Myth*. Edited by Alan Dundes. Berkeley: University of California Press, 1984.

König, Jason. *Greek Literature in the Roman Empire*. Classical World Series. London: Bristol Classical Press, 2009.

Kooten, George H. van, ed. *The Revelation of the Name YHWH to Moses: Perspectives from Judaism, the Pagan Greco-Roman World, and Early Christianity*. Themes in Biblical Narrative 9. Leiden: Brill, 2006.

Lincoln, Bruce. *Theorizing Myth: Narrative, Ideology, and Scholarship*. Chicago: University of Chicago Press, 1999.

Mack, Burton L. *Mark and Christian Origins: A Myth of Innocence*. Philadelphia: Fortress Press, 1988.

Meeks, Wayne A. *The First Urban Christians: The Social World of the Apostle Paul*. New Haven: Yale University Press, 1983.

Miller, Richard C. "Mark's Empty Tomb and Other Translation Fables in Classical Antiquity." *Journal of Biblical Literature* 129, no. 4 (2010): 759–76.

Parvis, Sara and Paul Foster, eds. *Justin Martyr and His Worlds*. Minneapolis: Fortress Press, 2007.

Peppard, Michael. *The Son of God in the Roman World: Divine Sonship in Its Social and Political Context*. Oxford: Oxford University Press, 2011.

Pervo, Richard I. *Dating Acts between the Evangelists and the Apologists*. Santa Rosa, CA: Polebridge Press, 2006.

Price, Robert M. "Are There 'Holy Pagans' in Justin Martyr." *Studia patristica* 31 (1997): 167–71.

Riley, Gregory J. *One Jesus, Many Christs: How Jesus Inspired not One True Christianity, but Many*. Chicago: University of Chicago Press, 1997.

Saïd, Edward W. *Orientalism*. London: Routledge and Kegan Paul, 1978.

Sartre, Marice. *The Middle East under Rome*. Translated by Catherine Porter and Elizabeth Rawlings. Cambridge, MA: Belknap Press of Harvard University Press, 2005.

Schwartz, Seth. "The Hellenization of Jerusalem and Shechem." Pages 37–45 in *Jews in a Greco-Roman World*. Edited by Martin Goodman. Oxford: Clarendon Press, 1998.

Smith, Jonathan Z. "Toward Interpreting Demonic Powers in Hellenistic and Roman Antiquity." *Aufstieg und Niedergang der römischen Welt: Geschichte und Kultur Roms im Spiegel der neueren Forschung* II.16.1 (1978): 425–39.

Tyson, Joseph B. *Marcion and Luke-Acts, a Defining Struggle*. Columbia: University of South Carolina Press, 2006.

2 Translation Fables in Hellenistic and Roman Antiquity

καὶ ὅλως πολλὰ τοιαῦτα μυθολογοῦσι, παρὰ τὸ εἰκὸς ἐκθειάζοντες τὰ θνητὰ τῆς φύσεως ἅμα τοῖς θείοις.

To sum up, they produce many such myths, those who irrationally deify the mortal elements of nature together with the divine.

[Plutarch, *Rom.* 28.6]

An analogical examination here rationally begins with a cross-sectional sampling of the panoply of instances of the translation fable, with the fundamental purpose of deriving a generic class or structural type, along with variant patterns and subthemes, underlying the cultural and literary tradition. The survey, moreover, seeks to expose the modality of the narrative theme, whether presented as fictive or as historically plausible, as well as the generic implicit function of the convention. The study also endeavors to determine the semiotic signals requisite to and directing the recognition of this ancient trope, with an eye toward specific diachronic, archetypal, and intertextual dependence. Once having established these tropological-critical patterns of classification, the study then, in Chapter 3, turns attention to relevant matters of critical method and the New Testament Gospels. In Chapter 4, the book undertakes the analogical, linguistic assessment of the resurrection narratives within New Testament Gospels. The chapter concludes with a speculative first look at the implications that this study may reasonably indicate going forward, both for religious faith and for humanistic study. First, however, a cultural-literary investigation of the origins of the translation fable should prove enlightening.

2.1 THE HELLENIC ROOTS OF TRANSLATION

Plumbing the recesses of Hellenic archaism with the grand spirit of Frazer's *Golden Bough,* the scrupulous anthropologist of ancient lore discovers the roots of the translation fable, however peculiar, to occasion little surprise. Attending to Homer and Hesiod, the sacred canon of this Greek polytheistic paradigm, one witnesses the sprouts of the idea of the honorific afterlife emerging from the Greek Dark Ages, a conception fundamentally dependent upon the essential immortality of the human soul.

Homer's personal eschatology consisted of postmortem souls translated to Elysium, the Abode of Hades (the Fields of Asphodel), or Tartarus, mythical lands at world's end to the west beyond the bounding currents of Oceanus. In his rite of νέκυια, having sacrificed his sheep at the River Acheron's shore, just as the goddess Circe had instructed, Odysseus converses with the ghost of his deceased mother as she comes forth from gloomy Erebus at the Abode of Hades. At once, Anticlea describes the common state of the dead as shades:

ἀλλ αὕτη δίκη ἐστὶ βροτῶν, ὅτε τίς κε θάνῃσιν·
οὐ γὰρ ἔτι σάρκας τε καὶ ὀστέα ἶνες ἔχουσιν,
ἀλλὰ τὰ μέν τε πυρὸς κρατερὸν μένος αἰθομένοιο
δαμνᾷ, ἐπεί κε πρῶτα λίπῃ λεύκ ὀστέα θυμός,
ψυχὴ δ᾽ ἠύτ᾽ ὄνειρος ἀποπταμένη πεπότηται.
(*Od.* 11.218–23)

This is the way of mortals, when someone dies.
The tendons no longer hold the flesh and bones together,
but the stronger force of the blazing fire overcomes them,
once life first has left the white bones,
and the soul, like a dream, after having fluttered about, flies away.

In early Greek poetry, as Jan Bremmer aptly describes, the souls of the dead (τὰ εἴδωλα) abide in the underworld and "are witless shades who lack precisely those qualities that makes up an individual."[1] The heroic dead only awaken to full consciousness at the taste of sacrificial blood, in this case offered on the blade of Odysseus. Quite distinct from this characterization, however, divine Proteus indicated a more lively and blessed afterlife for King Menelaus (*Od.* 4.560–79), wherein he was to join yellow-haired Rhadamanthys in Elysium, land of refreshment and repose, unlike the slumberous dim of Asphodel.

Hesiod's classic familial pantheon, or *Theogony* (ca. 700 B.C.E.), detailed the requisite notion of the gods residing within an anthropomorphic family tree, with several (Ζεύς predominantly) having dalliances with mortal women. This masterwork established an elaborate order of graduated hierarchy in classical Greek civilization, ranging from the lowest échelon (mortal criminals, captives, and slaves) to the highest (the supreme king of Hellenic polytheology, immortal Ζεύς, πατὴρ ἀνδρῶν τε θεῶν τε [542]). In *Works and Days*, Hesiod depicted the Heroic Age, a fourth, just prior age in his five epochs, a romanticized dispensation when demigods and heroes walked among the common people. The poet versified their distinguished fate:

ἔνθ᾽ ἦ τοι τοὺς μὲν θανάτου τέλος ἀμφεκάλυψεν,
τοῖς δὲ δίχ᾽ ἀνθρώπων βίοτον καὶ ἤθε᾽ ὀπάσσας
Ζεὺς Κρονίδης κατένασσε πατὴρ ἐς πείρατα γαίης,

καὶ τοὶ μὲν ναίουσιν ἀκηδέα θυμὸν ἔχοντες
ἐν μακάρων νήσοισι παρ᾽ Ὠκεανὸν βαθυδίνην·
ὄλβιοι ἥρωες, τοῖσιν μελιηδέα καρπὸν
τρὶς ἔτεος θάλλοντα φέρει ζείδωρος ἄρουρα.

(166–73)

There the finality of death engulfed some of them,
but others, after granting them life and habitation afar off from
    people,
Father Zeus, son of Cronus, settled them at the ends of the earth,
and these dwell having minds free from sorrow
on the Isles of the Blessed alongside Oceanus, the encircling perimeter,
happy heroes for whom the life-giving land grows honey-sweet fruit,
yielding thrice yearly.

Elysium and the Isles of the Blessed functioned to grant a happy afterlife to a distinguished few in early Greek eschatology.[2] Despite appearances, unlike the gods, these do not enjoy tactile, palpable bodies in their postmortem state capable of interaction with the mundane world of objects.[3] Pindar, moreover, likewise established in his eschatology an immaterial, postmortem utopia for the classical heroes, a place where Zeus's son Rhadamanthys ruled over the μάκαρες at world's edge.[4]

This tradition of an immaterial afterlife in the underworld extended from the archaic period through to the Roman imperial writings and late antiquity. As when Odysseus sought to embrace his beloved mother, Anticlea (*Od.* 11.204–9), so did Virgil's Aeneas in vain strive to clasp his ghostly father, Anchises, mortal mate to Aphrodite (*A.* 6.700–2). "Thrice did he endeavor to place his arms about his neck; thrice vainly clasped did the phantom flee his hands, as light winds and like a winged dream."[5] The emergent translation fable of Hellenistic and Roman antiquity compares and contrasts with the decorative epilogisms of the great heroes of old who were granted a blessed afterlife in the underworld.[6] With the increase of geographic knowledge, Elysium gradually came to be understood as a subterranean region of the underworld, inhabited by non-physical heroes. Unlike Homer's Odysseus who voyaged to the boundaries of the earth to find the Abode of Hades, Virgil's epic hero needed only to find the right cave at Cumae (*spelunca alta;* 6.237–64), in order to descend into the birdless, cavernous depths of the earth in search of the spirit of his deceased father in Elysium. By the late Republican times of Virgil and Statius, however, the underworld had become a noticeably more lively and conscious existence, on its way to become Dante's bustling Renaissance epic portrayal of the subterranean afterlife, furnished in the *Divina Commedia*.

Instead of the submundane existence of the shades, following his defeat of the Chimera, Bellerophon sought, in his hubris, heavenly Olympus to join the supermundane existence of the gods by riding heavenward upon the winged

Pegasus. Zeus thwarted his ambition by sending a tiny gadfly causing him to plummet from his horse down to earth, meeting a wretched end. Famed Pegasus, however, the god kept as his pack horse, bearer of his divine bolts.[7] This myth contrasts with that of Ganymede, most beautiful of all mortals (κάλλιστος γένετο θνητῶν ἀνθρώπων), whom the gods consequently caught up to heaven to be cup-bearer of royal Zeus (Homer, *Il.* 20.231–6).[8] The pantheon, in like manner, granted Tantalus to become cup-bearer to Poseidon and to partake of the immortalizing ambrosia in Olympus. In classical antiquity, divine immortality came only to those most worthy, however. Pindar relates that Tantalus transgressed the hospitality of the gods in a most grievous manner by stealing away some of the honey-sweet fruit and feeding it to his drinking companions back in Anatolia (*O.* 1). For this, the gods damned Tantalus to cruel Tartarus, the lowest region of Hades (Homer, *Od.* 11.582–92). This story compares with that of the Thessalian king Ixion, whom Zeus had invited to sup with the gods. In his treachery, his ξεναπατία, he seduced Hera, thus provoking the wrath of Ζεὺς ξείνιος (Pindar, *P* 2; cf., Tityus).[9]

The anthropomorphic gods, moreover, of Greek and Roman antiquity enjoyed wholly perfect hyper-physical bodies, unlike the wispy hypophysical existence of the ghosts of Pluto's underworld. In his article "Mortels et immortels: Le corps divin," Jean-Pierre Vernant has provided the definitive treatment on the matter. With incisive critical percipience, the anthropologist lays out this mortal | immortal structural binary:

> Poser le problèm du corps des dieux ce n'est donc pas se demander comment les Grecs ont pu affubler leurs divinités d'un corps humain mais rechercher comment fonctionne ce systèm symbolique, comment le code corporel permet de penser le relation de l'homme et du dieu sous la double figure du même et de l'autre, du proche et du lointain, du contact et de la séparation, en marquant, entre les pôles de l'humain et du divin, ce qui les associe par un jeu de similitudes, de rapprochements, de chevauchements et ce qui les dissocie par effets de contraste, d'opposition, d'incompatibilité, d'exclusion réciproque.[10]

> To pose the problem of the body of the gods is thus not to ask how the Greeks could have equipped their gods with human bodies, but to seek how this symbolic system functions, how the corporeal code permits one to think of the relations between man and god under the binary figures of same and other, of near and far, of contact and separation, marking between the poles of human and divine that which associates an interplay of similarities, parallels, and overlap and that which dissociates them by effects of contrast, opposition, incompatibility, and mutual exclusion.

The bodies of the gods were more physical, more perfect than those of mere transient mortals. They possessed super-human traits, that is, bodies without the limitations of the quotidian human condition. They remained durable, imperishable, immortal, powerful, perfect, beautiful, robust, immune to disease and debilitation, and were physically able to travel through the air, to transform (undergo metamorphoses or adopt an incognito form), to appear and to vanish, to teleport, even to multilocate. Also, unlike the shades, the immortals were fully capable of interacting with the physical world in all human respects to the extent of fighting in battles, eating mundane foods, and even having intimacy and offspring with mortals.

This distinction between mortal and immortal bodies proves crucial both to comprehending ancient Mediterranean translation tales and to establishing the semiotic limits of inference for Hellenistic readers of the earliest Christian resurrection narratives, a matter entirely central to the present book to be taken up in Chapter 4. The popularized fascination with stories of metastasis manifested in whole works of Hellenistic poetry, such as the second-century Nicander of Colophon's epic *Heteroeumena* and the mythographon *Omithogonia* by Boeus. These works, in turn, inspired the homonymous *Metamorphoses* of Ovid, Apuleius, and Antoninus Liberalis in Roman antiquity, not to mention the mythographic thematic play of such writers as Lucian of Syria. The strongest conventional signals of the translation fable operate under a subtext of distinction, namely, in demonstrating one or more of the signature divine features of the translated *corpus*. Most typically this meant a "vanished body," though the class of fabulous tales drew upon a host of various signals within the available semiotic repertoire.

Prior to the translation fable and as a corollary to the Hellenic cult of the dead, early Greek funerary and honorific custom ritualized the missing body of great figures through the carving of κολοσσοί (also referred to as ἀγάλματα, εἴδωλα, and εἰκόνες), typically small statued effigies resembling the absent σῶμα of the hero.[11] Jean-Pierre Vernant, applying the structuralist methods of Claude Lévi-Strauss and the Prague school of linguistics, lucidly exposed the binary opposition inherent in this practice, namely, the immortal presence and permanence of the statue and the mortal absence and transience of the vanished body.[12] Deborah Steiner comments the practice:

> The impetus for making a substitute for a missing person and performing his or her symbolic (re)interment may have two sources: first, the belief that the *psuchē* of the dead cannot find its rest in Hades until the body has received appropriate burial (as Patroklos explains in *Iliad* 23.70–74); and second, the need to appease an unquiet soul, angry at the circumstances of its death and its deprivation of the customary honors and rites it could properly expect (the sentiment to which Orestes and Electra appeal when they attempt to rouse the ghost of Agamemnon in Aeschylus's *Choephori*).[13]

The *Letters of Themistocles* (5.15) and Plutarch's *Lectures on Homer* (fr. 126 in schol. Eur. *Alc.* 1128; *Mor.* 560e-f) reported that such a bronze statue of the fifth-century Spartan general Pausanias had been placed in the sanctuary of Athena of the Brazen House (on the Acropolis) in order to exorcise his restless φάσμα from the temple. Herodotus, in the same era, wrote of the honorific deaths of the Argive heroes Cleobis and Biton, sons of Cydippe, priestess of Hera. The legend stated that Cydippe had petitioned Hera that the goddess might bless her sons with highest honors, after which both sons fell asleep in the temple, never to awaken. At Delphi, the Argives placed two sculpted statues (εἰκόνες) of the athlete-heroes in honor of their surpassing excellence (. . . ὡς ἀριστῶν γενομένων; 1.31). While their bodies had not gone missing per se, this story very much fell in line with both later thematic patterns of the heroic athlete and the tradition of the venerated statue or double of the exalted hero.[14] The translated poet Aristeas, according to Herodotus, returned in physical form two hundred and forty years after his death, bidding that the people erect an honorary statue of himself to be placed next to the altar of Apollo. Then, he vanished. According to the fable, the people did as the raised Aristeas had commanded; thus Herodotus etiologized the venerated image (τό ἄγαλμα) through passing on this epichoric folktale (4.15). The archaic tradition of the κολοσσοί persisted as a Frazerian survival into Roman imperial culture, often combining with the popularized translation fable. The roots of postmortem romanticization and mythic embellishment of persons of renown during the Roman Principate extended deeply into the Hellenism of Roman republican culture. Penelope J. E. Davies describes such encomiastic renditions of the exalted dead:

> Inevitably, as a Roman anticipated his own demise he hoped to be remembered at his best, for beneficent works and good character. Yet admirable deeds could also offer a path to immortality through remembrance, since they transformed the deceased into an exemplum for the living. An excerpt from Polybius's description of Roman customs lends insight into the process. The passage records a practice of creating wax masks of the dead and placing them in wooden cupboards in the atrium, the most conspicuous part of a Roman house. At family funerals, he explains, living substitutes wore the masks in procession, dressed according to the rank of the deceased, riding in chariots and bearing appropriate insignia of office; they would then sit in ivory chairs upon the Rostra. "There could not be a more impressive sight of the images of these men who aspire to fame and virtue," he interjects. "For who could remain unmoved at the sight of the images of these men who have won renown for their virtues, all gathered together as if they were living and breathing? What spectacle could be more glorious than this?" A speaker delivers an oration over the body and "proceeds to relate the successes and accomplishments of the others whose images are displayed, beginning with the oldest. By this constant renewal of the good report of heroic men, the fame of those who have performed any noble deed is made immortal, and the renown of those who have served their country

well becomes a matter of common knowledge and a heritage for generations to come. But the most important consequence is that young men
are inspired to stand firm through extremes of suffering for the common
good in the hope of attaining the glory that attends upon the great."
In the role of exemplum, then, lay perpetuation in the respectful and
emulative minds of the living. For the living, in turn, the achievements
of ancestors, recounted or represented in public places and as part of
public ceremonies, offered prominent families recurrent validation, and
a pedigree of civic "heroes," as Harriet Flower notes, offered critical
support to a man seeking office. In effect, exalted histories maintained
the fabric of republican society.[15]

Like that of Aristeas, the stories of Alcmene, Aspalis, and Britomartis
presented later in this chapter provide vivid examples of such survival. Typically such statuary, when translation had been implied, resided within the
most prominent τέμενοι, often placed in association with a major deity of
the pantheon, with the translation fable providing the effigy's *raison d'être*
for pilgrims of these sacred precincts.

Just as the tradition of the κολοσσοί served as a corollary to the cult of
the dead in early Greek culture, so also did the translation fable serve as a
corollary to the related cult of heroes in Hellenistic culture(s), a domain of
honorary protocols.

2.2 STRUCTURE AND SIGNIFICATION

This survey most fundamentally aims to derive, through comparative examination of the linguistic *parole* of the convention, the underlying semiotic
grammar or *langue* governing its various expressions in Mediterranean
antiquity. What precisely were the signature traits of the convention, and
what meaning did such biographical endings impress upon their ancient
readers? While the convention displayed a seemingly endless multifarity of
manifestations with several linguistic permutations (signifiers) in subthemes
and cultural-literary adaptations, the basic import (signified) of the "translation fable" trope manifested a durable consistency over a thousand-year
period in the ancient Hellenized world of cultural instantiation. This stability, as such, reflects the customary and ritualized use of the convention
within a common semiotic grammar of Hellenistic language in antiquity.

The apparent widespread awareness of the translation fable, as with all
matters of linguistic grammar, deposes the author as the locus of primary
signification. Barthes, however, relocated the operation to a decentered multiplicity of readers. Barthes, for instance, wrote:

> Once the Author is removed, the claim to decipher a text becomes quite
> futile. To give a text an Author is to impose a limit on that text, to

furnish it with a final signified, to close the writing. Such a conception suits criticism very well, the latter then allotting itself the important task of discovering the Author (or its hypostases: society, history, psyché, liberty) beneath the work: when the Author has been found, the text is 'explained'—victory to the critic. Hence, there is no surprise in the fact that, historically, the reign of the Author has also been that of the Critic, nor again in the fact that criticism (be it new) is today undermined along with the Author. In the multiplicity of writing, everything is to be *disentangled*, nothing *deciphered*; the structure can be followed, 'run' (like the thread of a stocking) at every point and at every level, but there is nothing beneath: the space of writing is to be ranged over, not pierced; writing ceaselessly posits meaning ceaselessly to evaporate it, carrying out a systematic exemption of meaning. In precisely this way literature (it would be better from now on to say *writing*), by refusing to assign a 'secret,' an ultimate meaning, to the text (and to the world as text), liberates what may be called an anti-theological activity, an activity that is truly revolutionary since to refuse to fix meaning is, in the end, to refuse God and his hypostases—reason, science, law.[16]

The 1967 French essay, however, in a milieu of fresh liberal awakening, appears to have overreached. Fundamental linguistic operations rely upon a shared *langue*, despite variance, nuance, and complexity. Without this linguistic contract to which all willing participants agree, signifier and signified would constitute no reliable index (sign). Ironically, Barthes's paragraph itself, both in French and in the act and proposal of an English translation, wholly relied upon the common consent of language as a social institution. If Barthes's author has died, then indeed so has his reader. The semiotic lexicon exists as a shared linguistic resource. Connotation and denotation function first as shared operations of language, not as private ruminations of subjective whim or social interest. Neither a municipal judge nor any on-coming cross-traffic would allow one to indulge in a private "reading" of a traffic signal. Whatever sentiments one may harbor about any given relation of signifier and signified, whatever subjective evaluation one may place upon them, the grammar of connotation and denotation remains unyielding, except of course by those societal processes of common consent. The matter of linguistic denotation requires a conditioned membership within a given linguistic society, that is, sufficient semiotic socialization. The defiance of a reader and that reader's suspicion of an author become functions of the extent to which the reader adopts a critical disposition to a text's implied narrator and, as such, that reader's conscious disassociation with the text's implied narratee. The critic, in this way, stands outside and, as such, exposes the myths of the text, discerning and resisting its spell, that is, its metanarrative. All the while, the common linguistic significance of the text remains untouched, both by subjectivity and by criticism. One may thus distinguish what a text "says" as a singular, public signified, and what a text "means" as a social or private relation toward what a text "says."

Although exceedingly varied in representation, the *denotata* and *connotata* of the translation fable structure, as an artifact of antique culture, remained quite static throughout the millennium under investigation. The traditional, ritualized custom, as seen through the lens of structural anthropology, à la Claude Lévi-Strauss, accounts for this relative linguistic stability. Considering this rich multifarity of forms, might one speak of a generic type with respect to the translation fable without specifying some set criteria by which a given narrative must qualify? Following Cambridge philosopher Ludwig Wittgenstein, genre theorists have come to understand such questions of definition as falsely conceived. Wittgenstein instead proposed that the human identification of genre, class, type, or kind operates not under static definition, but under familial resemblance. In demonstrating this, he applied his illustrious analogy of the "game":[17]

Betrachte z.B. einmal die Vorgänge, die wir "Spiele" nennen. Ich meine Brettspiele, Kartenspiele, Ballspiele, Kampfspiele, u.s.w. . Was ist allen diesen gemeinsam?—Sag nicht: "Es *muß* ihnen etwas gemeinsam sein, sonst hießen sie ncht 'Spiele'"—sondern *schau,* ob ihnen allen etwas gemeinsam ist.—Denn, wenn du sie anschaust, wirst du zwar nicht etwas sehen, was allen gemeinsam wäre, aber du wirst Ähnlichkeiten, Verwandtschaften, sehen, und zwar eine ganze Reihe. . . . Ich kann diese Ähnlichkeiten nicht besser charakterisieren, als durch das Wort "Familienähnlichkeiten"; denn so übergreifen und kreuzen sich die verschiedenen Ähnlichkeiten, die zwischen den Gliedern einer Familie bestehen: Wuchs, Gesichtszüge, Augenfarbe, Gang Temperament, et. etc. .—Und ich werde sagen: die 'Spiele' bilden eine Familie.

Consider, for example, the proceedings that we call "games." I mean board-games, card-games, ball-games, Olympic games, and so on. What is common to them all?—Don't say: "There must be something common, or they would not be called 'games'"—but look and see whether there is anything common to all. For if you look at them you will not see something that is common to all, but similarities, relationships, and a whole series of them at that. . . . I can think of no better expression to characterize these similarities than 'family resemblance'; for the various resemblances between members of a family: build, features, color of eyes, gait, temperament, etc. etc. overlap and crisscross in the same way. And I shall say: 'games' form a family.[18]

The "operating system" of human cognition, as forged within the deep natural history of the species, parses the phenomenal world through the dynamic of genetic identification and taxonomy, not the stasis of definition. The cultural rubrics of creative work, without exception, live in heterogeneous, genetic flux, not statistical confinement.

The gallery of translation fables, therefore, not surprisingly, possesses no common, explicit thread, characteristic, or requisite set of features. Rather, one observes a cluster of various recurring formal traits or signals. The cluster of semiotic signals of the structure, as delineated in the broad cross-section of examples provided in this chapter, functioned as subthemes of the class (List 2.1):

List 2.1: Translation Subthemes

1. Heinous or ignoble injustice rectified by translation
2. Metamorphosis
3. Vanished / missing body
4. Eponymous etiology
5. Catasterism
6. Post-translation speech
7. Ascension
8. Postmortem translation
9. Translation associated with Zeus's thunderbolt
10. Post-translation appearance
11. Translation associated with a river
12. Translation associated with a mountain
13. Odious or dubious alternate account
14. Taken up by the winds or clouds
15. Feigned translation

The metastasis or transference of the σῶμα signaled the graduation or acceptance of the individual into the divine rank. Unlike the veneration of remains seen in the Hellenistic cult of heroes, immortalization required the utter absence of those remains. The most direct linguistic signs of the convention, therefore, became identical with the onset or exhibition of super-human somatic abilities within the narrative, such as disappearance, appearance, levitation, and metamorphosis.

As a matter of linguistic structural protocol, ancient Hellenistic works appear to have been quite conscious and deliberate in their application of the translation fable. After cataloguing a number of well-known translation fables, in his discussion of the Romulean disappearance story, Plutarch afforded a particularly candid exposition of the convention, concluding that ὅλως πολλὰ τοιαῦτα μυθολογοῦσι, παρὰ τὸ εἰκὸς ἐκθειάζοντες τὰ θνητὰ τῆς φύσεως ἅμα τοῖς θείοις ("they tell many such fables, those who unreasonably deify the mortal elements of nature along with those that are divine"; *Rom.* 28.6). Setting aside Plutarch's critical philosophic posture, one first may note the Middle Platonist's clear awareness of the convention as a distinct cultural-literary protocol, despite the whimsical variety in his examples. Justin likewise reveals a rich awareness of the conventionality of the translation tale in his discussions of similar examples (*Dial.* 69.1–3; *1 Apol.* 21).

As the Gallery in this chapter suggests, the translation fable became quite ubiquitous. Significantly, by the time of the Roman Principate, nearly every major glorified figure of Hellenistic and Roman culture obtained the myth of translation in some text or another, that is, *exaltatio memoriae*, particularly those whose remains could not be accounted for. In this sense, the embellishment served as a biographic protocol assigning a given figure the principal Hellenic honor of κλέος ἄφθιτον.

Minor figures achieved minor or epichoric fame as heroes, particularly those whose tombs could serve as sacred sites for veneration. Hellenistic and Roman antiquity was replete with lionized figures: athletes, generals, warriors, benefactors, and other individuals of renown, just as Pausanias, Apollodorus, and Strabo have abundantly displayed, romanticized individuals who, in the cultural mind, attained super-human stature. Publishing his 1920 lectures at University of St. Andrews, Oxford Vice-Chancellor Lewis Farnell provided what became the definitive English work of the twentieth century on the Greek cult of heroes. In the volume, Farnell seamlessly located the translated figures of the classical Greek tradition within the broader honorific patterns of the cult of heroes (e.g., Heracles, the Dioscuri, Asclepius, and other classical epic heroes).[19] Then, two decades later, Harvard classicist Arthur Pease analyzed the translation fable within a different rubric, namely, as a subclass of narratives of individuals in classical antiquity said to have disappeared or to have become invisible. As with Farnell, Pease described his larger category as most fundamentally honorific in function. Pease concluded his essay:

> For the accurate interpretation of any one instance of invisibility it should also be constantly born in mind that those whose vanishing has become a matter of tradition may, in many instances, have been themselves quite innocent of any such intention, the traditions having arisen from subsequent narration, first at the instance of admiring and well-meaning friends, and later through dissemination by a public delight in the dramatic, and unexpected, and the marvelous, and not overcritical in its application of logical or scientific criteria of truth. Hence, as with other forms of the miraculous, the superficial ascription of more than human powers is no sufficient evidence against an underlying historicity. For example, no one doubts the historic character of Alexander the Great or of the Roman Emperors, though we may fairly doubt particular incidents about them which ancient writers, relying upon popular tradition, may have reported. Finally, may we not modify a well-known aphorism, and safely venture the assertion that the ascription of miraculous powers has generally been the unconscious tribute which inferiority has paid to excellence?[20]

The translation fable as a stock epilogical decoration, therefore, developed as an elevated form of hero fabulation embroidering the exalted biography.

The culture understood the embellishment as the loftiest protocol in the nomination and canonization of antiquity's most celebrated iconic figures.

When specifically addressing the Roman apotheosis tradition, a Roman variation on the larger translation fable pattern, Simon Price has demonstrated that the tradition functioned as an honorific power for the senate of imperial Rome through the formal assembled act of *consecratio*. Price summarized:

> Given the close association of the living emperor with the heavenly powers, it would have been very difficult to remove the emperor from this context on his death and locate him firmly in the Underworld. Banishment in the Underworld was the punishment meted out to Claudius in the *Apocolocyntosis,* and when Carcalla killed his brother Geta he abolished his memory and instituted annual sacrifices to him in the Underworld. A place in the Underworld rather than among the gods was a fall from favour for which no other prize offered by the èlite could compensate. Deification was the fitting end of the good emperor. Such granting of deification allowed the senate to create an honourable role for itself. While the senate had gained some political authority over the citizen body of Rome, it had at the same time lost other authority to the emperor. The ceremony of apotheosis granted the senate symbolic supremacy over both populace and emperor.[21]

Cassius Dio related the speech of Gaius Maecenas before Augustus concerning the public understanding and function of this custom of deification:

ἀρετὴ μὲν γὰρ ἰσοθέους πολλοὺς ποιεῖ, χειροτονητὸς δ' οὐδεὶς πώποτε θεὸς ἐγένετο, ὥστε σοὶ μὲν ἀγαθῷ τε ὄντι καὶ καλῶς ἄρχοντι πᾶσα μὲν γῆ τεμένισμα ἔσται, πᾶσαι δὲ πόλεις ναοί, πάντες δὲ ἄνθρωποι ἀγάλματα ἐν γὰρ ταῖς γνώμαις αὐτῶν ἀεὶ μετ' εὐδοξίας ἐνιδρυθήσῃ, τοὺς δ' ἄλλως πως τὰ κράτη διέποντας οὐ μόνον οὐ σεμνύνει τὰ τοιαῦτα, κἂν ἐν ἁπάσαις ταῖς πόλεσιν ἐξαιρεθῇ, ἀλλὰ καὶ προσδιαβάλλει, τρόπαιά τέ τινα τῆς κακίας αὐτῶν καὶ μνημεῖα τῆς ἀδικίας γιγνόμενα· ὅσῳ γὰρ ἂν ἐπὶ πλεῖον ἀνταρκέσῃ, τοσούτῳ μᾶλλον καὶ ἡ κακοδοξία αὐτῶν διαμένει.

(52.5–6)

For, it is virtue that makes many equal to the gods. Nobody, however, has ever yet become a god by a show of hands. Inasmuch as you are good and rule well, the whole earth will be your sacred precinct, all cities your temples, and all people your offerings, since within their thoughts you shall ever be enshrined with glory. As for those, however, who administer their governance in a contrary fashion, not only does the building of such temples not exalt them, though they be placed in every city, but it also denigrates them, becoming the erection of monuments of their ill-repute and memorials of their injustice. For, the longer these temples last, the longer endures their notoriety.

Note that the opposite of deification, that is, *damnatio memoriae*, became the second option in the cultural assessment of prominent figures, just as Maecenas described.[22] Particularly in the political sphere of conquering generals, monarchs, and prefects, the threat of postmortem disgrace (*damnatio*) or the reward of postmortem honor (*exaltatio*) gave impetus to such powerful figures to govern with virtue and not tyranny. One must realize that this custom, along with triumphs and assassinations, arose out of necessity within a non-democratic, non-egalitarian world. These cultural protocols empowered the people through a form of postmortem referendum determining the prized patrimony or *Nachleben* of the ruler.

As Price has revealed, the Roman senate, of necessity, achieved some balance of power with the rise of the Principate through their decree or bestowal of such honors during funerary consecration, including the custom of providing eyewitness to the emperor's ascension to heaven, a custom following the tradition of Julius Proculus. Conversely, the senate also existed as an ever-present threat of assassination, following the conspiracy of Brutus. Thus, the desired aegis of the senate, through the hope of apotheosis and the threat of *damnatio*, placed the *princeps* under compulsion to act reasonably in accord with the senate and in keeping with republican *mos maiorum*, as Penelope J. E. Davies describes:

> The decision of apotheosis for a dead emperor rested with the Senate, who would judge the deceased on the basis of his virtues (or popularity). As L. Cerfaux and J. Tondriau aptly put it: "The Roman emperor is simply a candidate for apotheosis, and his reign constitutes an examination of his abilities." However, the illustrated *res gestae* seen on imperial tombs were an attempt to justify his deification, and, when apotheosis became the norm in the second century, they served to emphasize it. Apotheosis was in part a means of securing a personal afterlife, either with the gods or in men's memory and worship, but just as important, it was also a political move to further the dynasty, to ensure that kingship did not die with the passing of the king. Having identified this motive for the funerary monument's design, one perceives that the tomb was not simply a monument to a dead ruler, but, perhaps more significantly, an accession monument as well, erected either by an emperor for himself out of concern for his descendants or by an heir to validate his claim to the throne.[23]

The deification of Julius Caesar by Octavian and his own witness to his ascension in the form of a comet during the *ludi Veneris Genetricis* (44 B.C.E.; likely combined with Caesar's honorary *ludi funebres*), for example, served as an adroit political tactic aiding his claim to govern Rome in succession as *divi filius*.[24] The deification of Caesar had been met with much resistance prior to Octavian's effort, perhaps most notably by the successor to the consulship, the general Publius Cornelius Dolabella.

While the translation fable, as a distinct genus or kind of ending, did not serve to resolve fully all dissonance of plot—indeed, this ending type functioned more as a decorative epilogue to a biographic narrative than as a thematic *dénouement*—the embellishment did cast an exalted or idealized interpretation upon the βίος, whether in romanticized history, folklore, or mythopoeia. The fabulous coda operated as a biographical *deus ex machina,* redeeming, indeed dramatically reversing the disgraceful loss of such cultural luminaries. To be translated in literature and lore meant to be canonized publicly as one joining the ranks of persons of enduring and foremost significance. Where there concerned a missing body, the convention reversed the ignominy precipitated by lack of burial rite, vouchsafing a panegyrical tribute to an exceptional, culturally owned, and glorified persona. Even in the public sense of Roman political apotheosis, the body must not see decay, lest the remains demonstrate in perpetuity the mortal status of the hero. In narrative, as a stock feature on the storyboard of canonized figures, the translation fable served as the *conclusio* of emplotment, placing the icon as a metonym or emblem of classical virtue.

2.3 SAMPLES OF THE TRANSLATION FABLE

Through the sampling of instances, the following analysis aims to derive a general linguistic structure, underscoring its pliability, malleability, and resultant richness in variety. Although a qualified subset of the translation fable, Roman imperial apotheosis existed as a distinct conventional branch of the tradition and, as such, gains a special treatment deferred to follow this galleried assortment.

The Gallery

The following collection, while not exhaustive, provides a miscellany of instances of the Greek and Latin translation fable as a distinct type of biographic ending. The list follows an alphabetical order, with each entry including source(s), a brief précis of the fable, and the generic subtheme(s) applied. Note that each subtheme also functioned as a generic signal, further apprising the ancient reader of the convention's presence.

Acca Larentia

Source: Plutarch, *Rom.* 5.1–5; Augustine, *Civ.* 6.7.

Fable: Ancient lore held Larentia to have been the foster mother to the fabled founders of Rome, Romulus and Remus. The tale indicates that

Larentia, at life's end, disappeared near to where she had found the orphaned infants in the basket floating along the Tiber, namely, the Velebrum, between the Capitoline Hill and the Palatine Hill in Rome. Augustine freely intimates that this bestowal of divine honors arose due to her exemplary conduct.

Subthemes: Vanished / missing body; Translation associated with a river.

Aega, Daughter of Olenus

Source: Hyginus, *Ast.* 2.13; Antoninus Liberalis 36; Aratus, *Phaenomena* 150.

Fable: Aega (also referred to as Amalthea) was the storied nursemaid of Zeus. In some accounts she was a nymph, in others, a goat. In honor of her service, Zeus translated her into a goddess, to become the constellation Capella (or Capra, meaning "she-goat").

Subthemes: Catasterism.

Aeneas, Son of Aphrodite

Source: *Liv.* 1.2; Dionysius of Halicarnassus 1.64.

Fable: Legend had it that Virgil's epic hero and founding figure for the Roman peoples disappeared in battle near Latium along the river Numicius. The Latins built a shrine to him there with the inscription "To the father and god of this place, who presides over the waters of the river Numicius." They then henceforth bestowed upon him the appellation *Jovi Indigetes* and stated that he had been "translated to the gods."

Subthemes: Vanished / missing body; Translation associated with a river; Odious or dubious alternate account.

Alcmene, Princess of Mycenae and Tiryns

Source: Diodorus Siculus 5.58.6; Plutarch, *Rom.* 28.6; Antoninus Liberalis 33.

Fable: Perhaps most famous as mother to Heracles by almighty Zeus, Alcmene obtained a variety of tales concerning her life's end. Diodorus provided one such fable, writing that upon her return to Thebes she soon after vanished from sight (ἄφαντος γενομένη). The Thebans thus began to pay honor to her as a goddess. Both Plutarch and Antoninus, however, indicated that during her funeral procession, the gods snatched her corpse from her bier and, having translated her to immortality, replaced the body with a stone, that is, a κολοσσός.

Subthemes: Vanished / missing body; Postmortem translation.

Alcyone, Queen of Trachis

Source: Ovid, *Metam.* 650–749; Ps.-Apollodorus 1.7.3–4; Hyginus, *Fab.* 65.

Fable: Alcyone and King Ceÿx referred to themselves as Hera and Zeus. In anger, therefore, the father of the gods cast his thunderbolt at the king's ship, causing him to perish at sea. When the queen learned of this, she hurled herself into the sea out of unbearable grief and perished as well. The gods, having witnessed the tragedy, translated both of them into the eponymous "halcyon" birds.

Subthemes: Metamorphosis; Vanished / missing body; Eponymous etiology.

Alexander the Great

Source: Arrian, *Anab.* 7.27.3.

Fable: As the conqueror's premature death loomed close, and he rested in Babylon, he conceived the idea that he should perhaps take his own life by throwing himself into the Euphrates River, in order that, his body having disappeared, he might be numbered among the gods, thus sustaining his divine myth that he was a demigod, son of Ammon-Zeus.

Subthemes: Vanished / missing body; Translation associated with a river; Feigned translation.

Althaemenes, Prince of Crete

Source: Ps.-Apollodorus 3.2; Diodorus Siculus 5.59.1–4.

Fable: Althaemenes sought to avoid fulfilling the Cretan oracle that he would commit parricide against his father, King Catreus, by taking flight to Rhodes. There, nevertheless, he slew his father unwittingly, while the king was on an expedition to the region. Diodorus ends the fable with the prince dying of grief and receiving a hero's veneration by the Rhodians. Pseudo-Apollodorus, on the other hand, varies on the tale by stating that, when he realized what he had done, he prayed and disappeared into a chasm (εὐξάμενος ὑπὸ χάσματος ἐκρύβη).[25]

Subthemes: Vanished / missing body; Heinous or ignoble injustice rectified by translation.

Amphiaraus, King of Argos

Source: Pindar, *Nem.* 9.10–29; Ps.-Apollodorus, *Bibl.* 3.6.8; Euripides, *Suppl.* 925–9; Diodorus Siculus 4.65.8; Strabo 9.2.11; Pausanias 1.34.2, 2.23.2, 8.2.4; 9.19.4; Cicero, *Div.* 1.40.88.

Fable: While in battle against Thebes, the great commander and king slew the great Melanippus, son of Astacus, and fled along the river Ismenus on the road to Potniae from Poseidon's mighty son Periclymenus. Seeing his distress, Zeus saved Amphiaraus, sending his thunderbolt to the ground, thus creating a great fissure into which Amphiaraus and his charioteer Baton vanished. In this act, the king of Olympus had translated the king of Argos to immortality. At the place where Amphiarus disappeared, the city of Harma (ἅρμα, "chariot") was founded.

Subthemes: Heinous or ignoble injustice rectified by translation; Vanished / missing body; Translation associated with Zeus's thunderbolt; Translation associated with a river; Eponymous etiology.

Anaxibia, Queen of Thessaly

Source: Ps.-Plutarch, *De fluviis* 4.

Fable: While dancing upon Mt. Anatole ("the rising"), Helius saw the beautiful Anaxibia dancing and immediately became aroused with violent desire for her. With the god in pursuit, Anaxibia fled high into Mt. Coryphe along the river Ganges into the temple of Orthian Diana and therein vanished from this world.

Subthemes: Vanished / missing body; Eponymous etiology; Translation associated with a river; Translation associated with a mountain.

Anna Perenna, Sister of Dido

Source: Virgil, *Aen.* 4; Ovid, *Fast.* 3.523–656; Festus p. 194M.

Fable: Upon grieving the death of her beloved sister, Anna sailed for Italy. There, having been driven ashore by a storm, she found the camp of Aeneas in Lavinium. Soon enough, Anna fled Aeneas and the jealous plots of Lavinia, his wife. During the night, she fell into the river Numicius and there vanished. The fable tells that she, at that moment, was translated into a nymph, a Roman goddess of annual Roman festival (Ides of March).

Subthemes: Vanished / missing body; Translation associated with a river.

Antinous

Source: Dio Cassius 69.11.2–4; Pausanias 8.9.7–8; Aurelius Victor, *De Caesaribus* 14.5–7; Philostratus, *Vit. soph.* 1.25, 530–5; POxy. 31.2553, 50.3537, 63.43.52; Justin, *1 Apol.* 29; Clement of Alexandria, *Protr.* 4; Tertullian, *Marc.* 1.18; *Apol.* 13; *Cor.* 13; *Nat.* 2.10; Origen, *Cels.* 3.36–38, 5.63, 8.9; Athanasius, *C. Gent.* 1.9; *C. Ar.* 3.5; Eusebius, *Hist. eccl.* 4.8; Jerome, *Jov.* 2.7; *Vir. ill.* 22; Prudentius, *C. Symm.* 1.267–77.

Fable: Similar to Alexander's translation of his male lover Hephaestion, a topos seen in the eulogization of Achilles's Patroclus and Heracles's Hylas, the death of Hadrian's lover Antinous prompted his deification. The translation fable bestowed upon the cultural biography of Antinous indicated that he had mysteriously vanished in the Nile. An alternate account, however, circulated that Antinous had voluntarily submitted himself to human sacrifice in order to fulfill Hadrian's indulgence in Egyptian magical arts. Early Christian sources, of course, condemn Hadrian's deification of Antinous as a perverse expression of pederasty. The translation fable resulted in the founding of an eponymous city at the sacred site (Antinopolis), the placement, according to Dio, of innumerable cult statues (ἀγάλματα), and his own divine *cultus*. Mythographers declared a star to be the very ascended soul of Antinous.[26]

Subthemes: Vanished / missing body; Translation associated with a river; Odious or dubious alternate account; Catasterism; Eponymous etiology.

Apollonius of Tyana

Source: Philostratus, *Vit. Apoll.* 8.30.2–3.

Fable: The Neopythagorean thaumaturgist, according to epichoric fable, obtained two separate translation accounts. The Rhodians held that the sage, at the end of his career, entered the temple of Athena at Lindos and promptly vanished. The Cretans, however, told that he had been visiting the temple of Dictynna in the night. Having miraculously pacified the ferocious dogs guarding the τέμενος, Apollonius alerted the officials of the precinct. They apprehended him for witchcraft and put him in chains. At midnight, however, he miraculously loosed his bonds and, after calling for the guards, ran straightway into the temple. The very doors of the temple, according to the legend, opened and closed before him through some mysterious power. Once the itinerate sage had been enclosed within, the guards heard the sound of girls singing, calling the translated Apollonius heavenward. He was not seen again.

Subthemes: Vanished / missing body; Ascension; Post-translation appearance; Post-translation speech.

Ariadne

Source: Diodorus Siculus 5.51.4.

Fable: Having persuaded Theseus to abandon his elopement with Ariadne, princess of Crete, Dionysus retrieved Ariadne on the island of Naxos. The demigod led his lover to Mt. Drius, where the two famously disappeared.

Subthemes: Vanished / missing body; Translation associated with a mountain.

Aristaeus, Son of Apollo

Source: Diodorus Siculus 4.82.6; Pausanias 8.2.4–5; Athenagoras, *Leg.* 14.

Fable: While paying a visit to Dionysus in Thrace and being initiated into the secret rites, as the fable related, Aristaeus vanished near Mt. Haemus and was never again seen. Athenagoras wrote that the Ceans worshipped Aristaeus, "considering him equal to Zeus and Apollo."

Subthemes: Vanished / missing body; Translation associated with a mountain.

Aristeas of Proconnesus

Source: Pindar fr. 284; Herodotus 4.13–16; Plutarch, *Rom.* 28.4; Origen, *Cels.* 3.26–28.

Figure 2.1 Roman statue of Ariadne, Imperial Period second century C.E. Adaptation of Greek original of third or second century B.C.E. Metropolitan Museum of Art, New York City, NY. Photo courtesy of Mary Harrsch.

Fable: Originally an epichoric legendary tale of Proconnesus and Cyzicus (Propontic Mysia), the translation fable of Aristeas was made famous by Pindar and Herodotus. The legend stated that this divine man and poet had entered a fuller's shop in Proconnesus and there fell dead. The fuller then locked up his shop and went to notify the poet's relations. As the shopkeeper was out for quite some time (apparently days) with this task, a man reported to the town that, as he was on the road from Artake to Cyzicus, he had just met Aristeas, something impossible were Aristeas to have died as the fuller had reported.[27] The fuller and Aristeas's friends and family, therefore, returned to the fuller's shop only to find the body of Aristeas missing. Seven years later, as the tale states, Aristeas appeared again in Proconnesus and wrote his famous *Arimaspea* and again vanished. Another two hundred and forty years later, the Metapontes of Italy reported that Aristeas appeared to them as well and instructed them to build an altar to Apollo in their land and erect an adjacent statue of himself. Then, he again vanished.

Subthemes: Vanished / missing body; Postmortem translation; Post-translation speech; Post-translation appearance; Eponymous etiology.

Asclepius

Source: Hesiod fr. 109; Hyginus, *Astr.* 2.14; *Fab.* 251.2, 224.5; Lucian, *Dial. d.* 13; Minucius Felix, *Oct.* 23.7; Galen, *Commentary on the Covenants of Hippocrates* (extant in Arabic; Al-Bîrûnî, *Ta'rîkh al-Hind* 283); Origen, *Cels.* 3.24.

Fable: Asclepius was killed by Zeus's lightning and granted translation. After Asclepius's death, Zeus placed Asclepius's body among the stars as the constellation Ophiuchus ("Serpent Holder"). Galen (ca. 180 C.E.) instanced another tradition, indicating that, as happened with Heracles and Dionysus, Asclepius ascended to the gods in a column of fire. According to Celsus, Asclepius often appeared in a physical, postmortem form to perform many miracles of healing (Origen tacitly concurred that such accounts abundantly circulated). Hyginus reveals that the translated Asclepius became the constellation Ophiuchus.

Subthemes: Translation associated with Zeus's thunderbolt; Ascension; Postmortem translation; Post-translation appearance; Catasterism.

Aspalis of Pythia

Source: Antoninus Liberalis 13.

Fable: This beautiful young maiden of Melite caught the eye of the cruel tyrant king Tartarus. Upon learning that she had been ordered to his royal court to be his private concubine against her will, the virgin took her own life by hanging herself before the king could ravage her. Her brother Astygites, moreover, according to the fable, managed through his cunning to assassinate the king in order to avenge the memory of Aspalis. When the people, however, went to retrieve the body that hung from the tree, the corpse of Aspalis had vanished. Instead, a statue of the translated maiden (that is, a κολοσσός named the Ἀσπαλὶς Ἀμειλήτη Ἑκαέργη) appeared in the temple of Artemis.

Subthemes: Vanished / missing body; Heinous or ignoble injustice rectified by translation.

Astraea, Daughter of Zeus

Source: Hesiod, *Op.* 174–201; Aratus, *Phaenomena* 96–137; Ovid, *Metam.* 1.148–50; Hyginus, *Ast.* 2.25.

Fable: Of Hesiod's five epochs given in his *Works and Days,* Astraea (also named Justice and Nemesis) lived in the first, that is, in the Golden Age. In the conservatism of Hesiod, a deteriorationism prevalent in classical antiquity, the Golden Age closed with the dilapidation of ethical order. As the prior generation had passed, Astraea remained into the Silver Age. She became so discouraged, however, that eventually she disappeared, having flown away to the stars to become the constellation Virgo. According to Hyginus, she is sometimes identified as Parthenos.

Subthemes: Vanished / missing body; Ascension; Catasterism.

Aventinus, King of Alba Longa

Source: Augustine, *Civ.* 18.12.

Fable: Legend held that this king of archaic Italy, after whom the Aventine in Rome received its name, vanished in battle.

Subthemes: Vanished / missing body; Eponymous etiology.

Belus, King of Assyria

Source: Eusebius, *Praep. ev.* 9.41 (supposed originally in Euhemerus).

Fable: The late antique Christian historian provides a fragment from the Hellenistic historian Abydenus (ca. 200 B.C.E.) conveying a speech allegedly given by Nebuchadnezzar II, whom Abydenus described as "greater than Heracles." In the speech, the Neo-Babylonian king relates a prophecy given by King Belus. After this prophecy, according to Abydenus's Hellenistic portrayal, Nebuchadnezzar reports that Belus forever vanished.

Subthemes: Vanished / missing body.

Berenice, Queen of Ptolemaic Egypt

Source: Theocritus, *Id.* 17.34.

Fable: In Hellenistic Egypt, Queen Bernike, wife of Ptolemy Soter, died and, according to the bucolic poet, was rapt away before her exchange with the ferryman Charon; she was translated to become a Ptolemaic goddess for the people.

Subthemes: Postmortem translation.

Branchus, Son of Apollo

Source: Conon, *Narr.* 33; Scholia Statius, *Theb.* 8.198.

Fable: The Didymaean myth of Branchus indicated that the goatherd had been Apollo's pederastic beloved. Eventually, the god gave Branchus a magical crown and a wand by which the seer delivered profound oracles to the people. Not long after this, according to the fable, Branchus disappeared and the people, acknowledging his translation, immediately constructed a temple in his honor, the Branchiadon in Miletus.[28]

Subthemes: Vanished / missing body.

Britomartis, Cretan Huntress (Dictyna)

Source: Pausanias 2.30.3, 3.14.2; Antoninus Liberalis, *Metam*. 40.

Fable: Britomartis, the "good virgin," whose beauty allured King Minos, fled. After having eluded the king in a bundle of fishing nets, the maiden then escaped into a grove. Once Minos had discovered her there, she vanished into thin air, thus receiving the name Aphaia ("she who disappeared"). In the grove, the Cretans built a temple in her honor and, due to her translation, there appeared a statue (κολοσσός) in her image in the temple of Artemis.[29]

Subthemes: Vanished / missing body.

Canens, Daughter of Janus

Source: Ovid, *Metam*. 14.320–434.

Fable: The witch Circe had turned the husband of Canens, Picus, king of Latium, into a woodpecker.[30] Canens searched in vain throughout Latium for her missing Picus for six days and nights. She sang a final, enchanted song on the bank of the Tiber and vanished into thin air (*evanuit auras*). The location of her translation took the eponym "Canens."

Subthemes: Vanished / missing body; Translation associated with a river; Eponymous etiology.

Carya, Princess of Laconia

Source: Servius's scholia on Virgil, *Ecl*. 8.30; Athenaeus 3.78.

Fable: The virgin princess and her brothers sought to defend against the lustful advance of Dionysus. The god, in his fury, transformed the brothers into stone, but Carya into a gorgeous "nut tree" (her eponym). Due to this fabled metastasis, the Lady of the Nut Tree became identified with Artemis. The Athenians, therefore, established the cult shrine of Artemis Caryatis atop the sacred Acropolis.

Subthemes: Metamorphosis; Vanished / missing body; Eponymous etiology.

Ceÿx, King of Trachis

Source: Ovid, *Metam*. 650–749; Ps.-Apollodorus 1.7.3–4; Hyginus, *Fab*. 65.

Fable: Ceÿx and Queen Alcyone referred to themselves as Zeus and Hera. In anger, the father of the gods cast his thunderbolt at the king's ship, causing him to perish at sea. When the queen learned of this, she hurled herself into the sea out of unbearable grief and perished as well. The gods, having witnessed the tragedy, translated both of them into the eponymous "halcyon" birds.

Subthemes: Metamorphosis; Vanished / missing body; Eponymous etiology.

Castor, Son of Tyndareus

Source: Homer, *Od.* 11.301–4; Pindar, *Nem.* 10.55–59; Euripides, *Hel.* 191; Isocrates, *Archid.* 6.18; *Pyth.* 11.61–64; Virgil, *Aen.* 6.121; Ps.-Apollodorus 3.11.2; Lucian, *Dial. d.* 25; Hyginus, *Fab.* 80; *Ast.* 2.22.

Fable: With Idas having slain Castor in a tree, Zeus offered Castor's twin brother Pollux a share in his immortality with Castor, allowing them to alternate days on heavenly Olympus and days among the shades of Hades (Homer) or on earth at Therapne (Pindar). Pollux accepted the offer, and Zeus complied, adopting Castor as his demigod son, as was Pollux.[31] The Spartan twins thus become the two brightest stars of the ancient constellation Gemini.

Subthemes: Postmortem translation; Post-translation speech; Post-translation appearance; Catasterism.

Cheiron, Greatest of Centaurs

Source: Ovid, *Fasti* 5.379–89; Hyginus, *Ast.* 2.38;.

Fable: By accident, one of Heracles's poisoned arrows fatally wounded Cheiron (Chiron), first to invent the art of healing and mentor to many great figures of old. According to one tradition, Cheiron had dropped the arrow, thus piercing his hoof. In another, Heracles himself unwittingly fired the arrow at a group of centaurs, unaware of Cheiron's presence. The vicarious exchange of mortality and immortality between Prometheus and Cheiron complicates the latter myth, although Cheiron still, by several accounts, ascended to the stars (cf. Ovid, *Metam.* 2.633–75).

Subthemes: Heinous or ignoble injustice rectified by translation; Catasterism.

Cleomedes of Astypalaea

Source: Plutarch, *Rom.* 28.4–5; Pausanias 6.9.6–9; Origen, *Cels.* 3.36; Eusebius, *Praep. ev.* 5.34.

Fable: In the early fifth century B.C.E., legend had it that this Olympic champion boxer had killed a man with an illegal blow, after which he fled punishment. According to the tale, in his violence Cleomedes had pulled down the supporting pillar of a school, killing several children. The inhabitants chased the boxer into the temple of Athena, where Cleomedes closed himself within a box. When the citizens finally succeeded in opening the box, the pugilist had vanished mysteriously. The Delphic oracle instructed the people, despite his offense, to pay veneration to Cleomedes as a translated hero.[32]

Subthemes: Heinous or ignoble injustice rectified by translation; Vanished / missing body.

Croesus, King of Lydia

Source: Bacchylides Ode 3; Herodotus 1.85–92.

Fable: The Lydian king, upon inquiring of the oracle at Delphi, came to suppose that he should command his army to attack Cyrus, king of the Persians. His strategy, however, backfired, causing Cyrus to invade and seize Lydia. Croesus, his wife, and daughters had built a great pyric structure and climbed atop. As the vanquishing King Cyrus stood by, Croesus commanded that the pyre be set ablaze. The king cried out to Apollo regarding his unbearable tragedy. The two most embellished accounts both at this point include acts of divine intervention (*deus ex machina*), though with significant modal variance. The poet's ode indicates that Zeus sent rain upon the pyre, quenching its flames, and that Apollo then translated the king and his family to the mythic land of Hyperborea (to the far north). The historian, on the other hand, states merely that, after the king's prayer, rain came down upon the pyre, extinguishing its flames. King Cyrus saw this as a sign of divine favor, so he ordered the king and his family to be spared to become his personal servants.

Subthemes: Vanished / missing body; Heinous or ignoble injustice rectified by translation; Odious or dubious alternate account.

Cycnus, King of Kolonai

Source: Ovid, *Metam*. 7.350–403.

Fable: A hero of the Trojan War, Cycnus, son of Poseidon, fought the mighty Achilles on the battle field of Troy. When he was unable to pierce Cycnus with his spear, Achilles wrestled him to the ground and strangled him to death. Ovid indicated that at that moment the gods translated Cycnus, transforming him into the eponymous "swan" (*cycnus* in Latin), thus rendering the suit of armor empty of its corpse.[33]

Subthemes: Metamorphosis; Vanished / missing body; Postmortem translation; Eponymous etiology.

Daphne

Source: Parthenius, *Erot*. 15; Ovid, *Metam*. 1.525–600; Pausanias, *Descr*. 8.20.2–4; Hyginus, *Fab*. 190; Antoninus Liberalis, *Metam*. 17.

Fable: With Apollo in pursuit to rape the beautiful Daphne by the River Ladon, Daphne being nude from having bathed in the stream, the young maiden prayed to Zeus (to Peneus by some accounts) that she might evade the god. Zeus then transformed Daphne into the eponymous laurel tree (Δάφνη), a tree said to be endowed with her divine sentience. Veneration of Daphne became associated with Apollo and Artemis.[34]

Subthemes: Heinous or ignoble injustice rectified by translation; Metamorphosis; Translation associated with a river; Vanished / missing body; Eponymous etiology.

Diomedes, King of Argos

Source: Pindar, *Nem*. 10.7; Strabo, *Geogr*. 6.3.9.

Fable: Athena translated this great hero of the Trojan War, while he was on an eponymous island in the Adriatic. The goddess transformed his companions, moreover, into the birds that came to inhabit the island.

Subthemes: Vanished/missing body; Eponymous etiology; Metamorphosis.

Dionysus, Son of Zeus

Source: Diodorus Siculus 5.51.4; Nonnus, *Dion.* 40–48; Justin, *Dial.* 69.1.

Fable: Having persuaded Theseus to abandon his elopement with Ariadne, princess of Crete, the demigod retrieved Ariadne on the island of Naxos. Dionysus led his love to Mt. Drius, and the two disappeared.[35] Justin Martyr, however, conveyed the variant tradition that Dionysus had been "torn to pieces, died, rose again, and had ascended to heaven."

Subthemes: Vanished / missing body; Translation associated with a mountain; Heinous or ignoble injustice rectified by translation; Postmortem translation; Ascension.

Empedocles

Source: Diogenes Laërtius 8.68–69.

Fable: According to ancient lore, this pre-Socratic shaman-philosopher leapt into the volcano at Mt. Etna to confirm his divinity. The account states that "he set out on his way to Etna; then, when he had reached it, he plunged into the fiery craters and disappeared, his intention being to confirm the report that he had become a god." In an alternate account, Diogenes indicated that the philosopher vanished one evening from his party guests. One of these guests reported to the rest that he had heard an especially loud voice calling Empedocles in the night. Upon investigation, he saw only a bright light in the heavens. They consequently supposed that he had been translated to divinity.

Subthemes: Vanished / missing body; Feigned translation.

Epidius, Hero of Nuceria

Source: Suetonius, *Gramm.* 28; *Rhet.* 4.

Fable: Epidius, according to the *fabula*, fell into the Sarnus River and emerged with a bull's horns having sprouted from his head. Then, not long after, he mysteriously vanished. The Nucerians, therefore, established the worship of Epidius as one translated to divinity.

Subthemes: Vanished / missing body; Feigned translation.

Erechtheus, King of Athens

Source: Pausanias 1.26.4–5; Ps.-Apollodorus 3.15.4–5; Hyginus, *Fab.* 46.

Figure 2.2   Bacchus (Dionysus), Roman God of Wine, second century C.E. Musée du Louvre, Paris, France.

Photo courtesy of Mary Harrsch.

Fable: Zeus struck this archaic king, with an angered Poseidon in pursuit, with his divine bolt. Erechtheus thus became Διόβλητος, that is, "struck by Zeus," meaning he was to be honored as immortalized in Athenian cult.

Subthemes: Vanished / missing body; Translation associated with Zeus's thunderbolt.

Erigone, Daughter of Icarius of Athens

Source: Hyginus, *Fab.* 130; *Ast.* 2.4, 2.25, 2.36; Ps.-Apollodorus 3.14.7.

Fable: After Icarius of Athens was the first to learn the skill of wine-making from Dionysus, he shared his product with a group of shepherds. Once they had drunk their fill, the men turned on Icarius and killed him, believing he had given them some bewitched poison. Upon discovering her slain father, Erigone hanged herself from a tree. The gods, therefore, in light of such tragic injustice, translated Erigone to the stars; she became the constellation Virgo, according to Hyginus, her father became the constellation Arcturus, and their dog Maera became Procyon. The Greeks traditionally made sacrifices to Icarius and Erigone in propitiation during the festival Aiora.[36]

Subthemes: Vanished / missing body.

Euripides, Tragic Playwright

Source: Plutarch, *Lyc.* 31.3–4.

Fable: After his death in Macedonia, the people buried him at Arethusa. Legend had it that a great lightning bolt struck the tomb of Euripides, thus implying his translation to divinity.

Subthemes: Translation associated with Zeus's thunderbolt.

Europa, Princess of Phoenicia

Source: Lucian, *Syr. d.* 4.

Fable: Zeus, being enamored with the beauty of Europa, sister of Cadmus, transformed himself into a bull and carried the princess off across the sea to Crete. When she vanished with the god, the Sidonians built a temple in her honor. In Sidon, moreover, they stamped their coinage with an image of this sacred legend, namely, that of Europa upon the bull.

Subthemes: Vanished / missing body; Metamorphosis.

Euthymus, the Olympic Boxer

Source: Aelian, *Var. hist.* 8.18; Pausanias 6.6.4–11.

Fable: This fifth-century athlete, according to legend, vanished in the River Caecinus and thus was immortalized.[37]

Subthemes: Vanished / missing body; Translation associated with a river.

Gaius Flaminus

Source: Plutarch, *Fab.* 3.

Fable: During the second Punic War, the former consul to the Roman senate, Gaius Flaminus Nepos (a *novus homo*), commanded legions in Tuscany, defending against Hannibal's invasion. He himself fought heroically, it is written, but was slain in battle at Lake Trasimene. The famed Carthaginian commander and his men were unable to find the body of Flaminus, according to Plutarch; it had vanished.

Subthemes: Vanished / missing body.

Ganymede

Source: Homer, *Il.* 20.235–35.

Fable: Zeus transformed himself into an eagle and snatched away Ganymede and translated him to immortality to be his heavenly Olympian cup-bearer.

Subthemes: Vanished / missing body; Ascension.

Glaucus the Cretan

Source: Plato, *Resp.* 611d; Pausanias 9.22.7; Ps.-Apollodorus, *Bibl.* 3.3.1, 3.10.3; Apollonius of Rhodes, *Argon.* 1.1310–15; Ovid, *Her.* 18.160; *Metam.* 13.900–14.74; Statius, *Theb.* 7.335–9; Athenaeus, *Deipn.* 7.47–48; Scholia on Pindar, *Pyth.* 3.54; Hyginus, *Fab.* 49, 136, 146; *Ast.* 2.14.

Fable: Leonard Muellner wrote, "If the dramas of Sophocles, Euripides, and Aeschylus on the myth of Cretan Glaucus had survived intact, it is facile to suppose that, as three dramas on the same myth, they would have significantly affected the conventional view of Greek tragedy."[38] These works made famous the fable of this legendary fisherman and his metamorphosis into a sea-god. Athenaeus variously related in his *Deipnosophistae* that Glaucus had found quite accidentally a patch of immortalizing grass. As he chased a hare up the sea-side slopes of Mt. Oreia, the fisherman noticed the rabbit had died of exhaustion. He took his prey to a nearby spring and rubbed it with a handful of grass. The hare at once sprung back to life. Astonished by the resurrection, Glaucus then ate a bit of the grass himself and become overwhelmed by a divine madness compelling him to leap to his death from the sea-badgered cliffs into the ocean below. Both Ovid and Diodorus Siculus offer post-translation appearances of the deified Glaucus. As a sea-god, Glaucus had, instead of feet, a fish-tail. Stories varied wildly regarding the translation of Glaucus, including several that depicted his having been raised from the dead as a young boy (Cf. Ps.-Apollodorus).[39]

Subthemes: Vanished / missing body; Translation associated with a mountain; Post-translation appearance; Post-translation speech; Postmortem translation; Metamorphosis.

Harpalyce, Princess of Arcadia

Source: Parthenius, *Erot.* 15; Aeschylus, *Ag.* 1592–93; Euphorion 24; Hyginus, *Fab.* 206, 242; Homer, *Il.* 14.291.

Fable: Clymenous forces himself upon his daughter Harpalyce, the most beautiful of all young ladies in the realm, to engage an incestuous relationship. Eventually, however, he permits Alastor the Neleid to marry Harpalyce. After providing a splendid wedding for the young couple, however, Clymenous in his perversity had a change of heart and pursued Harpalyce, seizing her from Alastor and, after having returned home, lived openly with his daugther as his wife. In her bitter frustration, Harpalyce slew her younger brother Presbon, chopped him up, and, at an Argive festival, prepared his flesh as a dish, serving it to Clymenous as a meal. After this, she prayed to the gods that she might be removed from humankind, at which time the gods translated her to become a chalcis-bird. It is said that she then became Athena's personal attendant, an additional subtheme witnessed in translation legends, suggesting advocacy in divine petition.

Subthemes: Heinous or ignoble injustice rectified by translation; Metamorphosis; Vanished / missing body.

Helen, Daughter of Zeus

Source: Euripides, *Orest.* 1760–93, 1963–2015.

Fable: As a manifestation of the madness that afflicts the cursed house of Agamemnon after his unfaithful wife Clytemnestra murdered him upon his return from Troy, a meta-theme that the play-cycles unfold, their son Orestes sought the succor of King Menelaus. With this, Orestes slew his mother Clytemnestra to avenge his father, the Greek king, thereupon Menelaus distanced himself from Orestes, provoking his enmity. With his imminent execution, Orestes, along with his accomplices Pylades and Electra, thus plots to avenge the betrayal of Menelaus by killing his wife Helen and his daughter Hermione. Once he approached Helen, however, to slay her, she vanished into thin air. Apollo soon descended from heaven with Helen and declared that she had been translated at father Zeus's bidding to join the gods in immortality.

Subthemes: Vanished / missing body.

Heracles

Source: Lysias, *Funeral Oration* 11; Ps.-Apollodorus 2.7.7; Diodorus Siculus 4.38; Conon 17; Ovid, *Metam.* 9.132–3; 9.134–273; Pausanias 3.19.5; Seneca, *Herc. Ot.* 1840–996; Zenobius 1.33; Lucian, *Hermot.* 7.

Fable: Heracles slew the centaur Nessus with an arrow for attempting to rape Heracles's beautiful wife Deianira. As Nessus was dying and wishing vengeance upon the hero, Nessus instructed Deianira to collect his blood and semen. He indicated that, in order to prevent the virulent Heracles from further sexual infidelities, she should apply them to his raiments. As occasion would happen, Heracles become enamored with the allure of Iole, princess of Oechalia, at which point Deianira became jealous again. She applied

Figure 2.3 Marble Head of Heracles. Roman, Imperial Period, first century C.E., copy of a Greek statue of the second half of the fourth century B.C.E. attributed to Lysippos. Metropolitan Art Museum, New York City, NY. Photo © 2014 by Tracy Murphy.

the centaur's fluids to the hero's shirt. Once he put the shirt on, however, the garment began fiercely to burn Heracles's skin. Unable to stop the acidic consumption of his flesh, Heracles ascended Mt. Oeta and at once built a great wooden pyre, with himself secured at its center, and commanded Philoctetes that the pile be set ablaze. Zeus then sent a great lightning bolt down upon the pyre, utterly consuming the hero along with the wood. Some accounts state that a great cloud descended upon the pyre and snatched him away to Olympus. With his bones nowhere to be found amid the ash, the people declared that Heracles had been translated to divine immortality.[40]

Subthemes: Translation associated with a mountain; Heinous or ignoble injustice rectified by translation; Taken up by the winds or clouds; Vanished / missing body; Catasterism.

Heraclides Ponticus

Source: Diogenes Laërtius 5.89–91.

Fable: Diogenes related that the first-century B.C.E. biographer Demetrius of Magnesia wrote that Heraclides, pupil of Plato and Aristotle, instructed an attendant to assist in feigning his translation. His death being imminent, the philosopher asked that the attendant secretly remove his corpse from the bier and replace it with a snake, "that he might seem to have departed to the gods" (ἵνα δόξειεν εἰς θεοὺς μεταβεβηκέναι). Upon his master's death, the attendant did as Heraclides had asked. During the procession, however, the snake emerged from the bier quite unexpectedly, throwing the crowd into confusion. Soon after, the trick was found out and the memory of Heraclides became one of ridicule and disgrace over this incident. Diogenes chides the philosopher's folly: "You wished, Heraclides, to leave to all mankind a reputation that after death you became a living snake, but you were deceived, you sophist. For the snake was really an unruly serpent, and you were shown to be more an unruly serpent than a sage."

Subthemes: Vanished / missing body; Metamorphosis; Feigned translation.

Hesperus, Son of Eos

Source: Diodorus Siculus 3.60.1–3.

Fable: Diodorus described Hesperus as the most distinguished of the sons of Atlas "for his piety, justice toward those whom he governed, and his love of humanity" (εὐσεβείᾳ καὶ τῇ πρὸς τοὺς ἀρχομένους δικαιοσύνῃ καὶ φιλανθρωπίᾳ). Once the king had climbed to the top of Mt. Atlas to study the stars, great winds came and snatched him away, at which moment Hersperus vanished. The people granted him immortal honors and named the brightest of the stars after him.

Subthemes: Odious or dubious alternate account (suggested); Translation associated with a mountain; Taken up by the winds or clouds; Vanished / missing body; Catasterism.

Hieron, King of Syracuse

Source: Pindar, *Ol.* 1.

Fable: Poseidon snatched away Hieron, the son of Tantalus, in a tale similar to that written of the disappearance of Ganymede, thus taking the king to Olympus. The Ode suggests that Poseidon had a romantic desire for Hieron and, as such, made him his divine companion and Zeus's private cup-bearer in the heavenly court. Pindar offered an alternate account that Hieron was thought to have been chopped up and secretly served as a banquet dish.

Subthemes: Vanished / missing body; Odious or dubious alternate account.

Himera, Sister of Memnon, King of Ethiopia

Source: *Dictys Cretensis Ephemeridos belli Trojani* 6.10.

Fable: Himera (Hemera) vanished at Phalliotis while burying her brother. The account indicates that some thought she had been translated to be with her mother (also Himera, goddess of the day) at sunset. Alternatively, some said she had taken her own life, while others claimed the local people had killed her.

Subthemes: Vanished / missing body; Odious or dubious alternate account.

Horus, Son of Isis and Osiris

Source: Diodorus Siculus 1.25.6–7.

Fable: Following the Ptolemaic manner of *interpretatio graeca,* Diodorus offered a Hellenistic adaptation of the resurrection tale of the ancient Egyptian mythic king Horus. As with the analogous tale of the raising and immortalization of King Osiris passed down to us through Plutarch (*Isis and Osiris*), Isis administered a magic drug that raised her dead son, King Horus, and bestowed upon him immortal deification. The Greeks identified Horus as the Egyptian rendition of Apollo.

Subthemes: Vanished / missing body.

Hyacinthus, Beloved of Apollo

Source: Pausanias 3.19.3–5.

Fable: Hyacinthus of Amyclae as a youth became the pederastic beloved of Apollo. One day, while Apollo and Hyacinthus were throwing the discus together, Apollo's discus accidentally struck the young man, killing him. Pausanias described this hero's cultic burial site at Amyclae: "On the altar are also Demeter, the Maid, Pluto, next to them Fates and Seasons, and with them Aphrodite, Athena and Artemis. They are carrying to heaven Hyacinthus and Polyboea, the sister, they say, of Hyacinthus, who died a maid."

Subthemes: Heinous or ignoble injustice rectified by translation; Ascension.

Hylas, Son of King Thiodamas

Source: Apollonius of Rhodes, *Argon.* 1.1258–61, 1.1220–24; Valerius Flaccus, *Argon.* 4.22–57; Ps.-Apollodorus, *Bibl.* 1.9.18–19; Antoninus Liberalis 26.

Fable: Hylas, one of antiquity's famed Argonauts, gave himself as the youthful male beloved of Heracles while voyaging together on the Argo (Theocritus, *Id.* 13). Having come ashore at the narrows of the Black Sea (ὁ Εὔξεινος Πόντος) at Mysia, Hylas went to fetch water at the River Ascanius (at the spring of Pegae). Here he became seduced by nymphs, fell in love, and vanished. Heracles sought the young Hylas, in vain waiting by the water's edge. Valerius Flaccus included (Book 4) a post-translation appearance and speech of Hylas before the summoning Zeus. Apollonius Rhodius, however, provided the dreadful alternative account that Hylas had perhaps been mauled to death by wild beasts, while leaving the possibility of his abduction by river nymphs comparatively nebulous.[41]

Subthemes: Odious or dubious alternate account (suggested); Translation associated with a river; Vanished / missing body; Post-translation appearance; Post-translation speech.

Idmon, Son of Apollo

Source: Apollonius of Rhodes, *Argon.* 2.815–50.

Fable: While the Argonauts were guests of King Lycus in Bithynia, Idmon the soothsayer died, having been gored by a wild boar, while out gathering straw. They buried him at Heracleotes, and, upon his barrow, there grew an olive tree. Lore held this tree to have been the metamorphosed Idmon. Accordingly, Apollo commanded that the Boeotians and Nisaeans worship him at this thus sacralized site.[42]

Subthemes: Heinous or ignoble injustice rectified by translation; Metamorphosis; Postmortem translation.

Ino, Queen of Thebes

Source: Homer, *Od.* 5.333–53; Ovid, *Metam.* 4.512–63; Pausanias 1.42.7.

Fable: The Megarians alone claimed that Ino, daughter of Cadmus, was buried along their coast with a shrine, according to Pausanias. Elsewhere, however, it is said that she was translated into the fabled Leucothea (White Goddess). As this goddess of the sea, she gave divine aid to Odysseus on his homeward journey. Passed down by Ovid, legend stated that she had cast herself and her son Melicertes (to be called Palaemon) from a cliff into the churning sea below to their deaths, and they vanished there. Witnessing the tragedy, the gods—Venus prayed to Neptune, due to the severity of the tragedy—apotheosized them, translating them both into marine deities. The Theban women, being unaware of the translation of their queen and, thus, mourning her death and that of Melicertes, were about to follow her into the sea. Seeing this, Juno in an instant turned them all, high upon the cliff, to stone.

Subthemes: Odious or dubious alternate account; Vanished / missing body; Metamorphosis; Postmortem translation; Post-translation appearance; Post-translation speech.

Iphigenia, Daughter of Agamemnon

Source: Aristotle, *Poet.* 1455b; Pausanias 1.43.1, Lycophron, *Alexandra* .

Fable: Iphigenia was perhaps best known in the ancient world due to the famed plays of Euripides: *Iphigenia in Aulis* and *Iphigenia in Tauris*. Artemis, angered at King Agamemnon for having killed a deer in a sacred grove, stopped the wind behind his sails, leaving his ships adrift in the sea currents. The Homeric seer Calchis gave the oracle that Agamemnon must sacrifice his lovely daughter Iphigenia to appease the goddess. The tale indicated that Artemis snatched away the maiden before her sacrifice, leaving in her place a large deer, and transferred her to the land of Tauris. According to Pausanias, however, the now non-extant work of Hesiod *A Catalogue of Women* (known through Pausanias) indicated that Artemis had translated her to become the immortal goddess Hecate.[43]

Subthemes: Heinous or ignoble injustice rectified by translation; Vanished / missing body.

Leucippus, Son of Oenomaus

Source: Parthenius, *Erot.* 15; Pausanias 8.20.2–4.

Fable: In his love for Daphne (above), Leucippus would dress as a female in order to accompany the maiden on her hunting expeditions in the Laconian countryside. On one such occasion, while stopping to bathe at the River Ladon, Daphne's companions discovered Leucippus's gender. All of the women immediately took up javelins and plunged them into the young man (πᾶσαι μεθίεσαν εἰς αὐτὸν τὰς αἰχμάς).[44] The gods then took pity upon him and caused him to vanish; they had translated him.

Subthemes: Heinous or ignoble injustice rectified by translation; Translation associated with a river; Vanished / missing body; Postmortem translation.

Lycurgus, Lawgiver of Greece

Source: Plutarch, *Lyc.* 31.3–4.

Fable: When this great father of Hellenic law had died, the people brought his remains home to Sparta. Legend had it that, some time after Lycurgus had been buried, a great lightning bolt struck the tomb of Lycurgus, thus implying for the people his translation to divinity.[45]

Subthemes: Translation associated with Zeus's thunderbolt.

Figure 2.4 Head of Lycurgus, first century C.E. copy of a Greek original of the second half of the fourth century B.C.E. Museo Archeologico Nazionale di Napoli. Photo © 2014 by "* Karl *" (flickr.com).

Oedipus, King of Thebes

Source: Sophocles, *Oed. col.* 1645–66.

Fable: Creon finds Oedipus in the countryside outside of Athens and asks the former king to bless his son and successor, Eteocles. Oedipus instead utters a curse upon his sons for not having cared for him in his old age. The king then vanished. Sophocles offered with ambiguity that either he had been translated to immortality or had been peacefully escorted to the underworld.

Subthemes: Vanished / missing body.

Orion, the Hunter and Adventurer

Source: Euphorion fr. 65; Aratus, *Phaenomena* 636–46; Ovid, *Fasti* 5.493–536; Hyginus, *Fab.* 195.

Fable: Orion had been chasing Pleione or, in a variation, her children the Pleiades for seven years when Zeus intervened, translating the pursuing hero to the stars, thus to become the eponymous constellation.[46]

Subthemes: Vanished / missing body; Eponymous etiology; Catasterism.

Orithyia, Princess of Athens

Source: Pausanias 1.19.5, 5.19.1; Ps.-Apollodorus 3.15.2.

Fable: The Hellenic god of the cold north wind, Boreas, had fallen in love with the lovely daughter of King Erechtheus and, as she played along the Ilissus River just outside of Athens, the god swept her away to be his immortal wife. The Greeks, from then on, called upon Orithyia for divine assistance (e.g., Hdt. 7.189).

Subthemes: Vanished / missing body; Translation associated with a river.

Pamphilus, Philosopher of Amphipolis

Source: Anthologia Graeca 7.587.

Fable: An encomiastic epigram composed by one Julianus, prefect of Egypt, addressed the deified Pamphilus, stating, "The ground bore you; the sea destroyed you, and Pluto's chair did receive you, but you ascended from there to heaven. You did not perish in the depths as from a shipwreck, but only that you, Pamphilus, might lay hold of honor along with the rank of all immortals."[47]

Subthemes: Vanished / missing body; Odious or dubious alternate account; Post-translation appearance; Feigned translation.

Peisistratus, King of Orchomenus

Source: Ps.-Plutarch, *Parallela minora* 32.

Fable: The king ruled in Athens in the sixth century during the Peloponnesian War with Sparta. Peisistratus became hated by his own senators who consequently assassinated him, cutting their king to pieces to avoid the evidence of his corpse. The senators hid his chopped body parts in their robes and disassembled. They quieted the Athenians by giving them the tale that the king had vanished by translation and had subsequently appeared to them as a god.[48]

Subthemes: Vanished / missing body; Odious or dubious alternate account; Post-translation appearance; Feigned translation.

Peleus, Father of Achilles

Source: Euripides, *Andr.* 1256.

Fable: Peleus, prince of Aegina, and the goddess Thetis fell in love, married, and bore a son, the famed Achilles. At life's end, according to Euripides's artful embellishment, Thetis snatched away Peleus, granting him to share with her immortal life among the gods.

Subthemes: Vanished / missing body.

Phormion's Daughter

Source: Pausanias 3.16.2.

Fable: At their folkloric former residence of Tyndareus at Amyclae (Sparta), the immortalized Castor and Pollux, in an incognito translation appearance, visited the house's later occupant Phormion, while on their way from Cyrene. They asked, according to Pausanias, to lodge within their favorite room. Phormion received them hospitably, requesting only that they select another room, for his (nameless) maiden daughter resided there. The next day, the Dioscuri had vacated and the maiden daughter had vanished.

Subthemes: Vanished / missing body.

Proteus Peregrinus

Source: Lucian, *Peregr.* 40.

Fable: The second-century itinerate Cynic Peregrinus Proteus, according to Lucian of Samosata's satirical account, staged his own pyric death as a stunt during the Olympic games of 165 C.E. Following the tradition of Empedocles and Heracles, Proteus intended to be consumed utterly by the great pyre, thus leaving no skeletal remains. The account stated that "when the pyre was kindled and Proteus flung himself bodily in, a great earthquake first took place, accompanied by a bellowing of the ground, and then a vulture, flying up out of the midst of the flames, went off to Heaven, saying, in human speech, with a loud voice: 'I am through with the earth; to Olympus I fare.'" An old man of Athens subsequently stepped forward as a witness to the raised Proteus, having met Proteus in his translated state "in white raiment walking cheerfully in the Portico of the Seven Voices, and wearing a garland of white olive." Lucian intimated that Proteus's disciples had conspired with him to stage his translation in order to ensure an exalted *Nachleben*. Others, however, such as his former pupil Aulus Gellius, appear to have held Proteus in quite high esteem and presumably would have accepted such an account as a fitting embellishment for the man.[49]

Subthemes: Vanished / missing body; Postmortem translation; Ascension; Post-translation appearance; Feigned translation.

Ptolemy XIII Theos Philopator

Source: Appian, *Bell. civ.* 5.9.

Fable: The king, brother to Cleopatra, disappeared in the Nile while in battle with Caesar's soldiers.[50]

Subthemes: Vanished / missing body; Translation associated with a river.

Pythagoras

Source: Letter of Lysis to Hipparchus.

Fable: This ancient pseudepigraphon described the passing of Pythagoras as his having "disappeared from among men," demonstrating that such an expression suggesting translation had become something of an idiomatic euphemism for the death of particularly distinguished figures.[51]

Subthemes: Vanished / missing body.

Romulus, Son of Mars

Source: Ennius, *Ann.* 112–120; Cicero, *Resp.* 2.10; Ovid, *Metam.* 14.811–28; *Fasti.* 2.475–511; Horace, *Carm.* 3.3; Dionysius of Halicarnassus 2.56.2–6, 2.63.3–4; Livy 1.16.1–8; Plutarch, *Rom.* 27–28; *Num.* 2.1–3; *Fort. Rom.* 8; Florus, *Epit.* 1.1; Arnobius, *Adv. Gentes* 6.1.41; Augustine, *Civ.* 3.15.

Fable: The legendary founding king of Rome, while mustering troops on Campus Martius, was caught up to heaven when clouds suddenly descended and enveloped him. When the clouds had departed, he was seen no more. In the fearsome spectacle, most of his troops fled, but the remaining nobles instructed the people that Romulus had been translated to the gods. An alternate account arose that perhaps the nobles had slain the king and invented the tale to cover up their treachery.[52] Later, however, Julius Proculus stepped forward to testify before all the people that he had been eyewitness to the translated Romulus, having met him traveling on the Via Appia. Romulus, according to this tale, offered his nation a final great commission and again vanished.[53]

Subthemes: Vanished / missing body; Odious or dubious alternate account; Post-translation appearance; Post-translation speech; Eponymous etiology; Taken up by the winds or clouds; Metamorphosis; Catasterism.

Saturn, First King of Latium

Source: Ovid, *Fasti* 1.237–40; Macrobius 1.7.24.

Fable: This Golden Age king and fabled father of Jupiter vanished in the middle of his reign (Macrobius 1.7.24; *cum inter haec subito Saturnus non comparuisset, . . .*). Due to his translation, according to Ovid, Latium took its name (from *latente*, "hidden from sight").[54]

Subthemes: Ascension; Translation associated with Zeus's thunderbolt.

Semele, Daughter of Cadmus

Source: Pindar, *Ol.* 2.27; Diodorus Siculus 4.25.4, 5.52.2; Pausanias 2.37.1–5; Ps.-Apollodorus 3.5.3; Plutarch, *Sera.* 22; Philostratus, *Imag.* 1.14; Nonnus, *Dion.* 8.409–10.

Figure 2.5   Laureate Head of Romulus-Quirinus. C. Memmius C.f. 56 B.C. AR Denarius (19mm, 4.06 g, 4h). Rome mint. Image courtesy of Joe Geranio via cng-coins.com.

Fable: The demigod Dionysus, according to classical mythography, rescued the deceased Semele from the underworld and ascended with her to heaven.[55] In another tradition, Zeus had translated Semele through striking her with his immortalizing thunderbolt.

Subthemes: Ascension; Translation associated with Zeus's thunderbolt.

Semiramis, Queen of Assyria, Daughter of Atargatis

Source: Diodorus Siculus 2.20.1–2.

Fable: Diodorus's *Bibliotheca historica* includes the translation fable of this famous queen of Asia. The account states that Ninyas, her son, conspired against her to usurp the throne. Learning of this plot, in accordance with an oracle given by Ammon, the queen surrendered authority to the prince and thereupon vanished, just as the prophecy had foretold. It is said that she joined the company of the gods; others, however, say that she was transformed into a dove and had joined the company of the palace birds. Consequently, according to Diodorus, the Assyrians henceforth worshipped the dove as the deified Semiramis.

Subthemes: Heinous or ignoble injustice rectified by translation (suggested); Odious or dubious alternate account (suggested); Metamorphosis; Vanished / missing body.

Theseus, Founding King of Athens

Source: Pausanias 1.32.5; 1.15.4; Plutarch, *Thes.* 1.35.4–5.

Fable: Pausanias indicated that a "rustic man" vanished in battle, aiding in the Battle of Marathon against invading barbarians.[56] The oracle indicated this mysterious man's translated name was to be Echetlaeus and that he deserved divine, heroic honors. Plutarch, however, in his parallel with Romulus, indicated that the man was none other than the legendary Theseus. The biographer provided different accounts of his end, one by the treachery of Menestheus casting the king from a cliff, the other by his having slipped from a precipice, with his body then having mysteriously vanished. The Athenians thus erected a white stone statue of the man and were compelled "to honor Theseus as a demigod" (ὡς ἥρωα τιμᾶν Θησέα).

Subthemes: Vanished / missing body; Odious or dubious alternate account; Post-translation appearance.

Tithonus, Prince of Troy

Source: Homeric Hymn to Aphrodite 218–38.

Fable: Eos, goddess of the dawn, carried off the young Tithonus as her personal lover. She petitioned Zeus that he be translated to join the immortals. Zeus complied, but, since Eos had not specified that the prince should eternally retain his youth, the prince lived on with an aged appearance.

Subthemes: Vanished / missing body.

Trophonius, Son of Apollo

Source: Pausanias 9.37.4; 9.39.2–3.

Fable: After having slain his brother Agamedes, who had been caught in a trap while attempting to steal King Hyrieus's gold, Trophonius fled into a cave at Lebadeaea in Boeotia and there died. Another fable, however, held that the earth swallowed up the hero, thus translating him to divine rank. The cave at Lebadaea, therefore, became a site of pilgrimage for those seeking the oracle of Jupiter Trophonius.

Subthemes: Vanished / missing body; Odious or dubious alternate account; Postmortem translation; Post-translation speech.

Xisuthrus

Source: Eusebius, *Chron.* 25; Syncellus, *Chron.* 28.

Fable: The oriental Hellenist Berossus wrote in his *Babyloniaca*, the earliest fragments of which now survives in Eusebius (via Alexander Polyhistor), of the translation of Xisuthrus, last of the ten legendary (antediluvian) founding monarchs of Sumer. Having survived the great deluge in his vessel, he gave adoration to the gods and suddenly vanished; on account of his piety, Berossus wrote, he was translated to the gods. As he invisibly ascended, Xisuthrus briefly offered his people admonition and instruction. His wife and daughter likewise disappeared with him and thus obtained the same honors.

Subthemes: Vanished / missing body; Post-translation speech; Ascension.

Roman Imperial Apotheosis

Roman apotheosis, as a formal cultural and political custom, functioned as a subclass of the broader translation fable. The majority of the Principate emperors, that is, Roman emperors from 27 B.C.E. to 284 C.E., received the honor of deification as ritualized through the postmortem tradition of imperial apotheosis; those who did not, instead received *damnatio* for the perceived ignobility and tyranny of their reigns.[57] Simon Price accurately surmised that "the traditional models for imperial apotheosis were the ascension of Romulus and Hercules."[58] Roman propaganda, beginning with the mythologization of Julius Caesar and Augustus, drew heavily on these principal, archetypal figures as providing the protocols for translation to regnal divinity.

Julius Proculus and the "Eyewitness" Tradition

Scipio Africanus the Younger (via Cicero), Livy, Ovid, Dionysius of Halicarnassus, and Plutarch described the apotheosis of Romulus, the first Roman king, as a matter verified by the trusted Patrician Julius Proculus (Cicero, *Resp* 2.10; Livy 1.16.1–8; Ovid, *Fasti* 2.475–511; Dionysius of Halicarnassus, *Ant. rom.* 2.63.3–4; Plutarch, *Rom.* 27–28).[59] Livy *et alii* offered two primary accounts of the fate of Romulus, founder of Rome. First, the ancient accounts state that, while gathered for a muster on Campus Martius, a low-lying plain along the east side of the Tiber River in Rome, his senators slew him during an opportune moment. Various stories survive concerning the circumstances of his execution and the disposal of his body. Scholars have noted the clear similarities between the senatorial assassination of Julius Caesar and the elaborations on Ennius's "Romulus" tale found particularly in Livy and Plutarch as they reflected on the relatively recent death of the liminal Julius during the reign of Augustus just prior to the Common Era.[60] Second, the alternative tale arose that a thick cloud had settled upon the king and took him away into the sky to reside among the gods. According to these chronicles, the deified Romulus obtained the name "Quirinus" (a prior Sabine deity) at his assumption to heaven. As the study proceeds to demonstrate, both traditions variously combined and, as such, became essential for subsequent apotheosis accounts in Imperial Rome.

Describing the supposed dichotomy for the Roman people between these two accounts of the end of Romulus's mortal life, Dionysius of Halicarnassus narrated:

ἔτι γὰρ ἀγνοούντων τὸν ἀφανισμὸν αὐτοῦ Ῥωμαίων εἴτε κατὰ
δαίμονος πρόνοιαν εἴτ' ἐξ ἐπιβουλῆς ἀνθρωπίνης ἐγένετο, παρελθών
τις εἰς τὴν ἀγορὰν Ἰούλιος ὄνομα τῶν ἀπ' Ἀσκανίου γεωργικὸς
ἀνὴρ καὶ τὸν βίον ἀνεπίληπτος, οἷος μηδὲν ἂν ψεύσασθαι κέρδους
ἕνεκεν οἰκείου, ἔφη παραγιγνόμενος ἐξ ἀγροῦ Ῥωμαίων ἰδεῖν ἀπιόντα
ἐκ τῆς πόλεως ἔχοντα τὰ ὅπλα, καὶ ἐπειδὴ ἐγγὺς ἐγένετο ἀκοῦσαι
ταῦτα αὐτοῦ λέγοντος· "Ἄγγελλε Ῥωμαίοις, Ἰούλιε, τὰ παρ' ἐμοῦ,
ὅτι με ὁ λαχὼν ὅτ' ἐγενόμην δαίμων εἰς θεοὺς ἄγεται τὸν θνητὸν
ἐκπληρώσαντα αἰῶνα· εἰμὶ δὲ Κυρῖνος."

(*Ant. rom.* 2.63.3b-4)

For while the Romans were still unaware about his disappearance, whether it came about by divine providence or by human treachery, someone came along in the Agora by the name of Julius, one of those descended from Ascanius. He was a farmer, a faultless man, such that he would never have lied for the sake of domestic advantage. He said that as he was arriving from the field he saw Romulus departing from the city heavily armed. Being that he was near, it came about that he heard these things as [Romulus] was speaking, "Announce to the Romans, Julius, these things from me, [namely] that the genius assigned to me when I was born is carrying me off to the gods with my mortal life having transpired. I am Quirinus."

Offering a parallel account, Cicero conveyed the words of Scipio Africanus providing an apology for the historicity of such Roman etiological stories, seeking to distinguish the apotheosis of Romulus from "antiquated" tales produced by what he regarded as more primitive, prior cultures (e.g., the Greeks):

atque hoc eo magis est in Romulo admirandum, quod ceteri, qui dii ex hominibus facti esse dicuntur, minus eruditis hominum saeculis fuerunt, ut fingendi proclivis esset ratio, cum imperiti facile ad credendum inpellerentur, Romuli autem aetatem minus his sescentis annis iam inveteratis litteris atque doctrinis omnique illo fuisse cernimus.

(*Resp.* 2.10.18a)

And this is even more to be wondered at in the case of Romulus, because the rest who were said to have been made gods from humans came about during a less educated age of people, such that they were disposed to the making of [such] an account, and the naïve were easily driven to believe them. We, however, understand that the time of Romulus is now less than six hundred years ago when writing and education were long in existence and all those primitive misconceptions from uncultured society had come to an end.

Scipio Africanus curiously turned the argument, indicating that Julius Proculus was but a "peasant" (*homo agrestis*), thus presumably unaware of prior apotheosis legends and so politically disinterested as to be incapable of guile. Plutarch's account, however, referred to Julius as a "Patrician," that is, a member of the senatorial class during the legendary age of the Seven Kings. This later shift (ca. 100 C.E.) in his socio-political standing in the accounts likely corresponded with the prior, emergent senatorial tradition of the eyewitness to the apotheosis of the Roman emperors, often an extension to, and indeed a part of, their funerary consecration (elaborated below).[61]

The text continues:

> qui inpulsu patrum, quo illi a se invidiam interitus Romuli pellerent, in contione dixisse fertur a se visum esse in eo colle Romulum, qui nunc Quirinalis vocatur; eum sibi mandasse, ut populum rogaret, ut sibi eo in colle delubrum fieret; se deum sees et Quirinum vocari.
>
> (Cicero, *Rep* ii. 10.20b)

> [Proculus], with the prompting of the Senators so as to drive away from themselves the unpopularity of Romulus' demise, is said to have stated in the assembly that Romulus had been seen by him on the hill now called "Quirinal" and had ordered him to ask the people to make a shrine on that hill, and that he was now a god and that he be named "Quirinus."

One may observe the numerous analogies between the postmortem "hill" appearance in Cicero's text and the Synoptic Transfiguration narrative, as well as the postmortem appearances of Jesus in the Gospels and Acts, to be taken up in Chapter 4.

Livy's account (ca. 27 B.C.E.) furnished Romulus's "Great Commission" episode in the following passage:

> Et consilio etiam unius hominis addita rei dicitur fides. Namque Proculus Iulius, sollicita civitate desiderio regis et infensa patribus, gravis, ut traditur, quamvis magnae rei auctor, in contionem prodit. "Romulus" inquit, "Quirites, parens urbis huius, prima hodierrna luce caelo repente delapsus se mihi obvium dedit. Cum perfusus horrore venerabundus

adstitissem, petens precibus ut contra intueri fas esset, 'Abi, nuntia,' inquit, 'Romanis caelestes ita velle ut mea Roma caput orbis terrarum sit; proinde rem militarem colant, sciantque et ita posteris tradant nullas opes humanas armis Romanis resistere posse.' Haec," inquit, "locutus sublimis abiit." Mirum quantum illi viro nuntianti haec fides fuerit, quamque desiderium Romuli apud plebem exercitumque facta fide inmortalitatis lenitum sit.

(1.16.1–8)

And the counsel of one man is said to have added credence to the matter. For Proculus Julius, being a man weighty in counsel no matter how great the matter, when the citizenry was shaken by grief over the King and enraged at the Senators, proclaimed as follows: "Quirites," he said, "Romulus, [who is] Father of this City, at first light suddenly descended from the sky and confronted me. Filled with reverential fear, I stood there seeking by my entreaties if it might be acceptable for me to look upon him face to face. He said, 'Go. Announce that the deities above thus purpose that my Rome should be the capital of the world. Therefore, may they tend to the matter of war, and let them know and pass on to coming generations that no human power can resist Roman arms.' After saying this, he departed on high." It is amazing what trust there was in this man's tale, and how the grief at the loss of Romulus by the populace and the army was assuaged by the produced confidence of his immortality.

Following after Ovid's fanciful rendition of the heavenward assumption of the king in a horse-drawn chariot (*rex patriis astra petebat equis*), the *Fasti* depicts the scene:

> luctus erat, falsaeque patres in crimine caedis,
> haesissetque animis forsitan illa fides;
> sed Proculus Longa veniebat Iulius Alba,
> lunaque fulgebat, nec facis usus erat,
> cum subito motu saepes tremuere sinistrae:
> rettulit ille gradus, horrueruntque comae.
> pulcher et humano maior trabeaque decorus
> Romulus in media visus adesse via
> et dixisse simul "prohibe lugere Quirites,
> nec violent lacrimis numina nostra suis;
> tura ferant placentque novum pia turba Quirinum
> et patrias artes militiamque colant."
> iussit et in tenues oculis evanuit auras;
> convocat hic populos iussaque verba refert.
> templa deo fiunt, collis quoque dictus ab illo est,
> et referunt certi sacra peterna dies.

(*Fasti* 2.475–511)

There was lament, and the senators were falsely incriminated with his murder. That belief might have perchance stuck in their minds, but Julius Proculus was coming from Alba Longa. The moon was shining and he thus did not make use of a torch, when suddenly the hedges on his left shook with motion. He stepped back and his hair stood on end. Romulus, handsome and greater than a man, appeared standing in the middle of the road and at once said, "Let not the Quirites weep, nor let them violate my divinity by their tears. Let the devout crowd offer incense and appease the new Quirinus. Let them tend to the arts of their fathers and to war." Thus he commanded and vanished into thin air. Proculus called the people together and reported the words that he was commanded. Temples were built to the god, and a hill was even named after him, and sacred, ancestral rites are repeated on specific days.

Though composed with Ovid's ornate elegiac artistry, this account compares well with that of Livy and is roughly contemporaneous.[62] By the time of the Common Era, the story of Julius Proculus had become widespread and familiar. Most of the chief historians in the period were obliged to include the tale, indeed affording the account relatively large segments in their respective works. In the following section, the study explores the political function of the *imitatio* of the tale within early Imperial Rome or what Barbara Levick has termed the "high-tide of empire emperors" (14–117 C.E.).[63]

Either a King or a Fool

Seneca's political satire *Apocolocyntosis Divi Claudii* (ἀποκολοκύντωσις or *The Pumpkinification of the Divine Claudius*) began with the quotation of a popular, political proverb from the early empire: . . . *aut regem aut fatuum nasci oportere* ("[An emperor] must be born either a king or a fool"). This principle served as the fundamental subtext of Suetonius's *Vitae Caesarum*, as each emperor achieved either postmortem *exaltatio* or postmortem *damnatio*; the shame-honor binary allowed for no intermediate assessment. The *Apocolocyntosis* thus proceeded to lampoon and to profane the deceased emperor Claudius through the satirist's tale of Claudius's pathetic reception, after his death, among the gods in heaven. Caesar Augustus finally delivers a decisive rhetorical denunciation of Claudius's performance as emperor of Rome, whereupon the deities unceremoniously deject Claudius to Hades only for him to acquire a piteous, servile existence at the hands of those whom he had formerly oppressed.

The Romans applied the honorific title *rex* to those emperors who had achieved the highest political esteem, thus assigning them to the league of the Seven Kings of earliest Rome. With the rather severe attenuation of voting rights at the fall of the Republic, a public shame-honor system, along with assassination, became the most powerful means to keep the *princeps* in check.[64] Since the Senate and Roman citizenry held no formal vote over the installment or removal of the emperor, the puissant tradition of postmortem apotheosis or debasement gained popularity as an expression of public approbation or disapprobation toward the *princeps*.[65] If Caesar wished to obtain divine honors in his funerary consecration and later *Nachleben*, thus leaving behind a positive legacy for his successors, he needed to conduct himself in a manner befitting such obeisance. Seneca's work thus contrasted the lionization of Augustus with the derogation of Claudius; whereas the public had divinized the postmortem Augustus, most abased Claudius for his cruelties and ignominy, not to mention his having been a stuttering cripple, certainly not to be considered an exemplar of ἀρετή by vain Greco-Roman standards.

With regard to the emerging "eyewitness" tradition and the translated appearances of the Roman emperors, as with Romulus, the senators (as an act of *consecratio*), plebes, and successors assigned glory and deification to a deceased emperor through the process of formal "eyewitness" testimony to the monarch's translation. Perhaps the first such gesture came with the collapse of the Republic after Anthony and Cleopatra (31 B.C.E.). Octavian took power and enacted many reforms which resulted in unity and a Roman period of relative stability known as the *Pax Romana*. During this time, the Roman imperial cult arose. With the rather unpleasant realities of the conspired, senatorial assassination of Julius Caesar (March 15, 44 B.C.E.) still fresh in the minds of the citizens, Octavian was challenged as to how he might impress upon the Roman citizenry the formal legitimacy and supreme cultural significance of Caesar as his predecessor and thus presented him as apotheosized. Seizing a moment during the *ludi Victoriae Caesaris*, the commemorative games given in honor of Julius Caesar, Octavian pointed to a passing comet, announcing that this comet was in truth the apotheosized Julius, now *Divus Julius*. Pliny records the emperor's address to the people: "This comet, the people thought, indicated that Caesar's soul had been received among the immortal gods. For that reason this symbol is placed above the head of the statue of Caesar which I consecrated in the Forum soon after" (*Nat.*22.94). Ovid in his poetic fashion likewise made mention of this in his *Metamorphoses*:

> Caesar in urbe sua dues est; quem Marte togapue praecipuum non bella magis finite triumphis respue domi gestae properataque gloria rerum in sidus vertere novum stellamque comantem, neque enim de Caesaris actis alum maius opus, quam quod pater exstitit huius.
>
> (*Metam.* 15.746–51)

[Julius] Caesar is a god in his own city. Him, illustrious in war and peace, not so much his wars triumphantly achieved, his civic deeds accomplished, and his glory quickly won, changed to a new heavenly body, a flaming star; but still more his offspring deified him. For there is no work among all Caesar's achievements greater than this, that he became the father of this our Emperor.

Ovid later added:

> Vix ea fatus erat, medi cum sede sanatus constitit alma Venus nulli cernenda suique Caesaris eripuit membris nec in aera solvi passa recentem animam caelestibus intulit astris dumqeu tulit, lumen capere atque ignescere sensit emisitque sinu: luna volat altius illa flammiferumque trahens spatioso limite crinem stella micat antique videns bene facta fatetur esse suis maiora et vinci gaudet ab illo.
>
> (*Metam*. 15.843–51)

> Scarce had he spoken when fostering Venus took her place within the senatehouse, unseen of all, caught up the passing soul of her Caesar from his body, and not suffering it to vanish into air, she bore it towards the stars of heaven. And as she bore it she felt it glow and burn, and released it from her bosom. Higher than the moon it mounted up and, leaving behind it a fiery train, gleamed as a star. And now, beholding the good deeds of his son, he confesses that they are greater than his own, and rejoices to be surpassed by him.

Though Caesar's death and subsequent assumption imitated that of the mythic king Romulus, the converse observation may prove equally valid. Ennius's account, the only known source of the Romulean legend that predates Julius Caesar's assassination, no longer survives. In the politics of Roman literary production, the Romulean tale likely obtained added semblance to that of Caesar in an effort to associate Caesar more closely with the founding father of the Roman nation, especially regarding the matter of senatorial assassination (cf. Appian, *Bell. civ.* 2.114). Notice that Caesar's death and translation accounts do not draw close enough to the Romulean tales as to become identical. Rather, these stories were presumably devised to draw the pair into a compelling proximity of resemblance for the sake of political propaganda. No "eyewitness," for instance, ever met Julius Caesar on a road in his postmortem state. The constraints of actual historical events in the case of Caesar's death and the prior literary treatment of the Romulean legend certainly would have inhibited the possibility of a fully congruent crafting of the two accounts.

Observing the first century C.E., the panorama turns to the apotheosis of Julius Caesar's adopted son and heir, Octavian, who became emperor of Rome for forty-four years (31 B.C.E. to 14 C.E.). Regarding this towering figure in Roman history, M. Cary and H. H. Scullard assessed:

> The reign of Augustus was as much the turning-point of Roman History as Roman history was the pivot of ancient history in general. . . . The greatest testimonial to Augustus's work lay in its durability. His constitution remained the framework of Roman government for three centuries, and the general lines of his foreign policies were followed by

all but a few of his successors. No other Roman determined the future course of Roman history to a like degree.[66]

Discussing the eventual death of Caesar Augustus, Suetonius indicated that the Roman senators carried an effigy of his body in grand procession to Campus Martius, the location where Romulus had achieved apotheosis, to be "cremated" (*crematus*). Here Suetonius stated: *Nec defuit vir preatorius, qui se effigiem cremate euntem in caelum vidisse iuraret* (*Aug.* 99.4; "There was even an ex-praetor who took oath that he had seen the form of the Emperor on its way to heaven, after he had been reduced to ashes").

With Augustus, the tradition of the "eyewitness" thus began, having been mimetically derived from the prior Romulean tale of Julius Proculus. Dio Cassius made this genetic derivation quite explicit in his *Roman History*:

τότε δὲ ἀθανατίσαντες αὐτόν, καὶ θιασώτας οἱ καὶ ἱερὰ ἱερειάν τε
τὴν Λιουίαν τὴν Ἰουλίαν τε καὶ Αὔγουσταν ἤδη καλουμένην
ἀπέδειξαν, καὶ οἱμὲν καὶ ῥαβδούχῳ χρῆσθαι ἐν ταῖς ἱερουργίαις
αὐτῇ ἐπέτρεψαν· ἐκείνη δὲ δὴ Νουμερίῳ τινὶ Ἀττικῷ, βουλευτῇ
ἐστρατηγηκότι, πέντε καὶ ἐς τὸν οὐρανόν, κατὰ τὰ περί τε τοῦ
Πρόκλου καὶ περὶ τοῦ Ῥωμύλου λεγόμενα, ἀνιόντα ἑορακέναι ὤμοσε.
καὶ αὐτῷ ἔν τε τῇ Ῥώμῃ ἡρῷον ψηφισθὲν μὲν ὑπὸ τοῦ Τιβερίου
ἐποιήθη, καὶ αλλοθι πολλαχόθι, τὰ μὲν ἑκόντων δὴ τῶν δήμων τὰ
δὲ ἀκόντων οἰκοδομουμένων.

(56.46.1–2)

Then, after they declared August immortal, they assigned priests and ceremonies, and made Livia, who was already called Julia and Augusta, a priestess. They, moreover, entrusted to her a lictor to be used in the religious services. She then granted 250,000 [denarii] to one Numerius Atticus, a senator and ex-praetor, that he swear to have seen Augustus ascending to heaven just like what is said concerning Proculus and Romulus. A hero's shrine to [Augustus] voted for by the senate and built by Livia was erected both in Rome and in various other places, with some citizens willingly building these shrines and others unwillingly.

As "First Lady of Rome," Livia Drusilla instigated the immortalization of Caesar Augustus, her husband of fifty-one years, and largely instituted the Roman imperial cult throughout the broad, provincial empire upon his death. The candid history provided here by Dio records the first evidenced attempt at a comprehensive, mimetic application of Julius Proculus's "eyewitness" tradition in the Imperial Age. Though later resented by her son the Emperor Tiberius, the Empress nonetheless arguably achieved the highest power and honors of any single woman in Greco-Roman antiquity, holding supreme authority and influence over the Roman Senate during the height of the empire. Grether thus described the fullness of her prominence:

Preller, in introducing his discussion of the growth of the Roman imperial cult after the death of Augustus, wrote: "Under Tiberius, a great
part of the ceremonial dignity with which Augustus had surrounded
himself passed to Livia, who as Julia Augusta stood at the head both
of the *gens Julia* and of the cult of the deified Augustus." It is true that
after the death of Augustus Livia occupied a position of unique importance in the state, but this was not a sudden change. Even before his
death, during his long principate, she had shared increasingly in the
honors of her husband. She had the right of having her statues erected,
was allowed to administer her own property, and was endowed with
the sacred inviolability formerly characteristic of the tribune's office.
She, together with Augustus, had the privilege of dining in the temple
of Concordia, and her influence in the court was such that ambassadors
to Augustus often approached her to endeavor to make her an advocate
of their causes. Her share in the "ceremonial dignity" of the emperor
is, moreover, even more clearly seen in the cult honors and tributes of
a divine nature which were offered her and which she was permitted to
accept. These honors, beginning early in the principate of Augustus and
continuing throughout her long life and after her death, illustrate the
part played in the imperial cult by the wife of the reigning emperor, the
mother of the reigning emperor and priestess of Augustus, and, finally,
the deified ancestress of the Julian House. Chronologically, the history
of her cult extends from the early years of Augustus' principate down
into the period of the Antonine dynasty.[67]

Upon further assessment, Grether's appraisal may even appear to under-
state the sovereignty of Livia, later to be named *Diva Augusta* under the
reign of her grandson Claudius.

This brings the analysis back again to the resurrection of Claudius Caesar, who reigned from 41 to 54 C.E. Seneca indicated that Livius Geminus,
the senator who likewise testified concerning Drusilla's assumption, that is,
sister to Gaius, not to be confused with the aforementioned Julia Augusta,
offered himself eyewitness to the apotheosis of Claudius. He claimed to have
met the postmortem Claudius hobbling on the Via Appia. Describing the
tale, Seneca wrote:

> Quis unquam ab historico iuratores exegit? Tamen si necesse fuerit auc-
> torem producere, quaerito ab eo qui Drusillam euntem in caelum vidit:
> idem Claudium vidisse se dicet iter facientem "non passibus aequis." Velit
> nolit, necesse est ille omnia videre, quae in caelo aguntur: Appiae viae cura-
> tor est, qua scis et divum Augustum et Tiberium Caesarem ad deos isse.
>
> (Apoc. 1)

Who has ever demanded eyewitnesses from a historian? If there were,
nevertheless, a necessity to produce a witness, then ask the man who
saw Drusilla going into heaven. The same fellow will say that he had

seen Claudius traveling on the road with crippled steps. Whether he wants to or not, it is necessary for him to see everything that is translated into heaven. He is the Watchman of the Appian Way, along which you know that Divine Augustus and Tiberius Caesar went unto the gods.

Seneca thus has applied the imperial Roman tradition of meeting the postmortem king while traveling on the road, congruent with the legends of Julius Proculus. Before extensions by Trajan in the second century, the Via Appia stretched from the center of Rome, down the western coast of the Italian peninsula, ending at Beneventum.[68] One is able to identify the attestant based chiefly upon Dio's account of the ascension of Drusilla, daughter of Germanicus and sister to the Emperor Caligula, as the Senator Livius Geminus. Drusilla had been Caligula's incestuous lover; she died of an illness in 38 C.E. The ancient historian Dio Cassius wrote:

τότε οὖν Πάνθεά τε ὠνομάζετο καὶ τιμῶν δαιμονίων ἐν πάσαις ταῖς πόλεσιν ἠξιοῦτο, Λίουιός τέ τις Γεμίνιος βουλευτὴς ἔς τε τὸν οὐρανὸν αὐτὴν ἀναβαίνουσαν καὶ τοῖς θεοῖς συγγιγνομένην ἑορακέναι ὤμοσεν, ἐξώλειαν καὶ ἑαυτῷ καὶ τοῖς παισίν, εἰ ψεύδοιτο, ἐπαρασάμενος τῇ τε τῶν ἄλλων θεῶν ἐπιμαρτυρίᾳ καὶ τῇ αὐτῆς ἐκείνης· ἐφ᾽ ᾧ πέντε καὶ εἴκοσι μυριάδας ἔλαβε.

(59.12.3–4)

She was then, therefore, named Panthea and was deemed worthy of divine honors in every city. A certain Senator, Livius Geminus, swore that he had seen her ascending to heaven and conversing with the gods, invoking utter destruction both upon himself and his children if he should lie, by the witness of both the gods and of Drusilla herself. For this, he received 250,000 [denarii].

The "eyewitness" tradition had during the Julio-Claudian dynasty thus become the political protocol in the consecration of those most supremely honored in Roman government.

Heracles's Pyre and Caesar's Wax Effigy

As primitive and not in the least secondary, the archetypal benefactor of humankind, divine Hercules, provided the other of the two radices for the Roman imperial apotheosis tradition. With regard to this ideal of ruler benefaction, Pliny the Elder, under the auspices of the Emperor Vespasian, wrote:[69]

Deus est mortali iuvare mortalem, et haec ad aeternam gloriam via. hac proceres iere romani, hac nunc caelesti passu cum liberis suis vadit maximus omnis aevi rector Vespasianus Augustus fessis rebus subveniens. Hic est vetustissimus referendi bene merentibus gratiam mos, ut tales numinibus adscribant. Quippe et aliorum nomina deorum et quae supra retuli siderum ex hominum nata sunt meritis.

(*Nat.* 2.5)

A mortal who assists mortals is a god. This is the path to eternal glory, by which the most preeminent Romans have gone. By this path also with heavenward step, through coming to the aid of tired affairs, the greatest ruler of all ages, Vespasian Augustus, along with his sons, walks. To enroll such individuals among the gods is the most ancient manner of honoring them with gratitude for their benefactions. Indeed, all of the gods' names, as well as of the stars that I have mentioned above, have been derived from their services to humankind.

From the standpoint of ceremony, however, this connection with the legacy of Heracles became most explicit in the public *consecratio* of a deceased emperor through the formal practices of funerary custom. The transaction, for the historical person to fulfill the structured elements of "translation fable," required the ultimate absence of a body, lest the remains demonstrate in perpetuity the mortal status of the emperor. According to the Heraclean tradition, the witnesses must not find any charred bones, once the pyric flames have gone their course.

The bystanders, accordingly, bore witness both to a missing body and to the ascension of their deified king. Although the funerary procession from the Rostra traditionally ended at Campus Martius, the sacred location of Romulus's ascension, the ceremony culminated with the lighting of the grand, multi-tiered pyre, reenacting a Romanized, imperial adaptation of Heracles's pyric translation.[70] Of the two extant detailed sources of such events, both Cassius Dio and Herodian inform that the public funeral did not involve the actual corpse of the emperor, but a substituted wax effigy.[71] Besides the perhaps obvious benefit of logistical simplification in the planning and preparation of such a spectacle, not to mention the privacy given to the royal family in the actual cremation, the practice of applying the wax substitute ensured that no remains would be found.[72] For, as Dio indicated, honorific deification served as the burial ritual's chief purpose (75.5.5). The release of the eagle at the lighting of the pyre signaled the monarch's translated ascension to his immortal abode. This tradition persisted into the late second century and beyond, even despite the public Roman cultural shift toward inhumation, precisely on account of these essential semiotic protocols of deification in alignment with Heracles and the resultant Augustan legacy.

2.4 GENERIC MODALITY

In 1983, Paul Veyne asked, "*Les Grecs ont-ils cru à leurs mythes?*"[73] In answer to this, as Veyne himself similarly complicated, one must carefully unpack the polysemy of the two operative terms: myth and belief.

The gods, for the Greeks as with most all ancient civilizations, functioned both as sacred icons of cult and as fabulous figures of mythography, legend, and folklore. In ancient literature, one finds both modes variously present, with the latter being the more prevalent. Veyne's use of the term "myth," moreover, comes apart once one considers the ancient conscious awareness of mythopoesis in the production of art and literature. The rich embellishment of these sacred emblems of the classical world became the prolific occupation of Hellenistic cultures. One finds ample indication that Hellenistic and Roman culture comprehended and celebrated a burgeoning flourish of whimsical tales of such sacred and epichoric legends, at points quite analogous to the combined gravitas and enjoyment that modern culture assigns to the indulgence of film "entertainment." Veyne wrote:

On comprend, à lire Pausanias, ce que fut la mythologie : la moindre bourgade que décrit notre érudit a sa légende, relative à quelque curiosité naturelle ou culturelle locale; cette légende a été inventee par un conteur inconnu et, plus récemment, par un de ces innombrables érudits locaux que Pausanias a lus et qu'il appelle exégètes. Chacun de ces auteurs ou conteurs connaissait les productions de ses confrères, puisque les différentes légendes ont les mêmes héros, reprennent les mêmes thèmes et que les généalogies divines ou héroïques y sont, en gros, d'accord entre elles ou ne souffrent pas de contraditions trop sensibles. Toute cette littérature qui s'ignorait en rappelle une autre : les vies de martyrs ou de saints locaux, de l'époque mérovingienne à la *Légende dorée*; A. van Gennep a montré que ces hagiographies apocryphes, dont les Bollandistes ont eu de la peine à faire justice, étaient en réalité une littérature de saveur très populaire : ce ne sont que princesses enlevées, affreusement torturées ou sauvées par des saints chevaliers ; snobisme, sexe, sadisme, aventure. Le peuple s'enchantait de ces récits, l'art les illustrait et une vaste littérature en vers et en prose les reprenait.[74]

Reading Pausanias, one understands what mythology was: the most insignificant little village described by our author has its legend concerning some local curiosity, natural or cultural. This legend invented by an unknown storyteller, was later discovered by one of those innumerable local scholars whom Pausanias read (he called them "exegetes"). Each of these authors or storytellers knew the work of his colleagues, since the various legends have the same heroes and take up the same themes, and the divine or heroic genealogies are largely in agreement or at least do not suffer from blatant contradictions. This unknown literature recalls another one: the lives of the local saints and martyrs from the Merovignian era up to the *Golden Legend*. Arnold van Gennep has shown that these apocryphal hagiographies, which the Bollandists had so much trouble refuting, were in reality works of an extremely popular character. They abound with abducted princesses (horribly tortured or saved by saintly knights), along with snobbery, sex, sadism, and adventure. The people adored these accounts. Artists illustrated them, and an extensive literature in verse and prose took them up. (trans. Wissing)

With this, Veyne continues:

Ces mondes de légende étaient crus vrais, en ce sens qu'on n'en doutait pas, mais on n'y croyait pas comme on croit aux réalités qui nous entourent. Pour le peuple des fidèles, les vies de martyrs remplies de merveilleux se situaient dans un passé sans âge, dont on savait seulement qu'il était antérieur, extérieur et hétérogène au temps actuel ; c'était « le temps des païens ». Il en était de même des mythes grecs ; ils se passaient « avant », durant les générations héroïques, où les dieux se mêlaient encore aux humains. Le temps et l'espace de la mythologie étaient secrètement hétérogènes aux nôtres ; un Grec plaçait les dieux « au ciel », mais il aurait été non moins stupéfait de les apercevoir dans le ciel ; il aurait été non moins stupéfait si on l'avait pris au mot au sujet du temps et qu'on lui apprenne qu'Héphaïstos venait de se remarier ou qu'Athéna avait beaucoup vieilli ces derniers temps. Il aurait alors « réalisé » qu'à ses propres yeux le temps mythique n'avait guère qu'une vague analogie avec la temporalité quotidienne, mais aussi qu'une aspèce de lèthargie l'avait toujours empêché de se rendre compte de cette hétérogénéité. . . . Les générations héroïques se plaçaient de l'autre côté de cet horizon de temps, dans un autre monde. Voilà le mond mythique à l'existence duquel les penseurs, de Thucydide ou Hécatée à Pausanias ou saint Augustin, continueront à croire ; sauf qu'ils cesseront de le voir comme un monde autre et voudront le réduire aux choses du monde actuel. Ils feront comme si le mythe avait relevé du même régime de croyance que l'histoire.[75]

These legendary worlds were accepted as true in the sense that they were not doubted, but they were not accepted the way that everyday reality is. For the faithful, the lives of the martyrs were filled with marvels situated in an ageless past, defined only in that it was earlier, outside of, and different from the present. It was the "time of the pagans." The same was true of the Greek myths. They took place "earlier," during the heroic generations, when the gods took part in human affairs. Mythological space and time were secretly different from our own. A Greek put the gods "in heaven," but he would have been astounded to see them in the sky. He would have been no less astounded if someone, using time in its literal sense, told him that Hephaestus had just remarried or Athena had aged a great deal lately. Then he would have realized that in his own eyes mythic time had only a vague analogy with daily temporality; he would have thought that a kind of lethargy had always kept him from recognizing their hidden plurality. . . . The heroic generations are found on the other side of this temporal horizon in another world. This is the mythical world in whose existence thinkers from Thucydides or Hecataeus to Pausanias or Saint Augustine will continue to believe—except that they will stop seeing it as another world and will want to reduce it to the mode of the present. They will act as if myth pertained to the same realm of belief as history.

(trans. Wissing)

What Hesiod has delineated as a temporal partition between the world of myth and heroes and the world of the mundane present later predominantly became in Greek and Latin literature a purely modal partition. When applying a mode, to be clear, the *raconteur* must provide sufficient signals, thus directing the construction to a different mental *space* within the reader, either a *spatium historicum* or a *spatium mythicum*.[76] Writers applied translation legends quite liberally to a full array of characters ranging from historical to fabulous. In the case of the former, however, historiography and biography often provided transitional cues indicating the modal interlude.

Cicero divided up the ingredients of historiography into three modes: *historia, argumentum,* and *fabula:*

Ea, quae in negotiorum expositione posita est, tres habet partes: Fabulam, historiam, argumentum. Fabula est, in qua nec verae nec veri similes res continentur, cuiusmodi est: "Angues ingentes alites, inuncti iugo . . ." Historia est gesta res, ab aetatis nostrae memoria remota; quod genus: "Appius indixit Carthaginiensibus bellum." Argumentum est ficta res, quae tamen fieri potuit, huiusmodi apud Terentium: "Nam is postquam excessit ex ephebis, Sosia . . ."

(*Inv.* 1.27)

There are three divisions by which the exposition of accounts are delivered: fable, history, and plausible portrayal. A fable is that in which matters are composed that are neither true nor plausible, such as "gigantic winged serpents joined by a harness . . ." History is an account of matters that have transpired that are remote from our time of recollection, such as "Appius declared war on the Carthaginians." A plausible portrayal is an embellishment which could have occurred, such as given in Terence: "For, after he had matured beyond adolescence . . ."

Later, in the second century, Roman philosopher Sextus Empiricus divided up the stories of classical antiquity into these same three general modalities: ἱστορία, μῦθος, and πλάσμα, the last being functionally equivalent to Cicero's operative mode *argumentum,* that is, accounts that, while not often true, are given as plausible.[77] Most Greek and Roman historians allowed their histories to contain some patchwork of myth, though often presented with a disclaimer. This tradition extended back to Hecataeus and Herodotus and stood in contrast to the more strict historical method of, for instance, a Thucydides (Th. 1.21.1, 22.4). Despite his heterogeneous composition, Herodotus showed a sufficient ability to distinguish history from myth (Hdt. 1.5, 2.99).[78] A century later, Aristotle, in his classic treatment of mimesis in art and literature (*Poet.* 2–4), wrote of fundamental modal distinctions (διάφοροι) in literature, classified based upon the power or quality of the figure(s) being represented, ranging from the high mimesis of epic poetry and tragedy to the low mimesis of comedy and satire. Canadian literary theorist Northrop Frye, in the middle of the last century, took up Aristotle's paradigm as a model for understanding how the human psychology has processed works of literature within distinct modal spheres. In his essay "Historical Criticism: Theory of Modes," Frye proposed a list of five modes, each understood with respect to the story's hero (List 2.2):[79]

List 2.2: Frye's Hero Modalities

1. The hero is superior in kind both to humans and to the natural world.
2. The hero is superior in degree both to humans and to the natural world.
3. The hero is superior in degree to other humans but not to the natural world.
4. The hero is ordinary, like the reader.
5. The hero is inferior and thus provides a negative, ironic, or comedic example.

The "translation fable," therefore, as the coda (Lat. *cauda*, "tail") of a personal narrative, typically served as a closing modal flight, embroidering the storied qualities and achievements of the hero, elevating the final modality from *romance* (2–3) to *divinity* (1).

While later historiographers, such as Polybius and Tacitus, followed in the rigorous historical methods set down by Thucydides in their strict adherence to *spatium historicum*, other writers, such as Livy, Dionysius of Halincarnassus, and Diodorus Siculus, continued the less dry hybridic model established by Herodotus, namely, in weaving together *historia* and *fabula*. The Gallery of "translation fables" furnished in this chapter provides a more or less random sample, perhaps only peculiar as a sample by emphasizing the more famous instances of antiquity. Within which genres and modalities did the translation fable most comfortably reside (see Table 2.1)?

Table 2.1 shows the occurrences of the "translation fable," as catalogued in this chapter, indexed by author and sorted by number of instances. The tours of epichoric folklore, legend, and sacred history written by Pausanias, Ps.-Apollodorus, and Diodorus Siculus predictably provided a natural habitat for the "translation fable." The generic modality, moreover, of the principal mythographers of classical antiquity, such as Hyginus, Lucian, and Antoninus Liberalis, seamlessly articulated such tales without qualification or modal interlude. This observation holds equally for the mythopoetics of such listed composers as Homer, Hesiod, Pindar, Apollonius Rhodius,

Table 2.1 Translation Fables, Multiple Occurrences

Pausanias (19)	Parthenius (3)
Ovid (14)	Philostratus (3)
Hyginus (13)	Athenaeus (2)
Ps.-Apollodorus (12)	Cicero (2)
Diodorus Siculus (11)	Conon (2)
Plutarch (10)	Diogenes Laëtius (2)
Antoninus Liberalis (6)	Dionysius of Halicarnassus (2)
Pindar (6)	Euphorion (2)
Lucian (5)	Hesiod (2)
Euripides (4)	Livy (2)
Homer (4)	Nonnus (2)
Apollonius of Rhodes (3)	Ps.-Plutarch (2)
Aratus (3)	Virgil (2)

Aratus, Euphorion, Parthenius, Ovid, Virgil, and Nonnus. The playful homonymous works by Ovid, Apuleius, and Antoninus Liberalis underscore the prevailing preoccupation and sentimentality regarding such Hellenistic and Roman yarns of somatic metamorphosis. Indeed, not one of the above listed writers presents a "translation" account within any generic mode other than what one may best term a "sacred legend," even if, as in the case of Lucian's *Peregrinus* or even Seneca's *Claudius,* the author did lampoon the sacred through a lower genre of acerbic satire.

The histories and biographies containing a translation fable, on the other hand, tended to supply modal signals of interlude for the reader. Often, however, such markers were unnecessary inasmuch as the convention itself commonly implied the mode of fable. Such histories, nevertheless, typically provided modal signals if for no other reason than to assure the reader of the document's quality or integrity as history. Livy, for instance, in his *Ab urbe condita,* admitted to his readers that his etiological story of Rome and the seven earliest monarchs derived more from tales "adorned with poetic legends" (*poeticis fabulis decora*), than from "pure recollections of things done" (*rerum gestarum incorruptis monumentis*). As he stated in his introduction, Livy most fundamentally perceived this divide as between the divine and mundane, the latter providing the sphere of valid history (1.6–9). The promulgation of the Romulean translation myth, therefore, became for Livy not an endeavor to assert historical fact, but a gesture of Roman power as expressed through cultured *imperium* (1.7).[80] Plutarch, moreover, as has already been mentioned, was quite outspoken in his criticism of the convention, despite relating numerous "translation fables." The Middle Platonist wrote (*Rom.* 28.6): ὅλως πολλὰ τοιαῦτα μυθολογοῦσι, παρὰ τὸ εἰκὸς ἐκθειάζοντες τὰ θνητὰ τῆς φύσεως ἅμα τοῖς θείοις ("They tell many such fables, those who unreasonably deify the mortal elements of nature along with those that are divine"). As for the accounts given in Herodotus, Dionysius of Halicarnassus, and Diogenes Laërtius, each exhibited care to present their "translation fables" as epichoric legends, applying simple markers such as "they say . . ." (λέγουσι). Such was also the case with Cicero with respect to Amphiaraus. Though, concerning Romulus, the senator casts the greatest suspicion upon the tale delivered by Julius Proculus, writing that the treachery of the senators had put him up to the false testimony of the king's postmortem appearance (*Resp.* 2.10.20). Indeed, with the *consecrationes* of the Roman *principes*, these legends rose up immediately, within days of the emperor's death, falsifying the assumption that the production of legend requires the extensive lapse of time. To the contrary, cultural *exaltatio* in Hellenistic and Roman antiquity was deliberate and often immediate.

As has been discussed, the late ancient Christian writers struggled to renegotiate the modal lines. Augustine, for example, endeavored to distinguish between "fabulous theology" and "civic theology," the former affording no credence, with the latter, of course, legitimated and usurping as the rightful domain of Christian theism (*Civ.* 6.7). Philosophical attempts at systematization assisted with this shift, that is, the deliberate preference of many early Christian writers away from fabulous narrative toward theological treatises. The all but whimsical malleability of the "translation fable," and mythic narrative in general, made such traditions resistant to subsequent demands for higher degrees of modal credibility. As with all mythopoetics, getting the story straight never held much importance. Besides this variance in mythic accounts, the folklore behind such translated figures often prompted an alternate mundane explanation, as frequently evidenced in the Gallery (above). Despite a common modal understanding of such sacred legends, local communities or, in the case of the most prominent figures such as Heracles, entire empires nevertheless enjoyed such tales and indulged in some measure of belief, such as the πιστά of the fishermen with regard to the translated Glaucus (Pausanias 9.22.7), even while still relegating the story itself to the mental domain of legend.

NOTES

1. Jan Bremmer, *The Early Greek Concept of the Soul* (Princeton, NJ: Princeton University Press, 1983), 124; Cf. Emily Vermeule, *Aspects of Death in Early Greek Art and Poetry* (Berkeley: University of Californian Press, 1979), 1–82; Sarah Iles Johnston, *Restless Dead: Encounters between the Living and the Dead in Ancient Greece* (Berkeley: University of California Press, 1999), 1–35.

2. Regarding early Greek eschatological justice and this general hope, see Pindar, *Ol.* 2.55–75. Concerning the fate of heroes from the prior romanticized Heroic Age (the fourth generation) specifically, cf. Hesiod, *Op.* 156–73. Cf. Robert Garland, *The Greek Way of Death* (London, 1985), 60–66.

3. Regarding the Greek and Roman gods, n.b. that such physical interactions extended all the way to procreative intercourse with humans, another element underpinning the human-divine connection in classical myth.

4. Pindar, *O.* 2; fr. 133 *Dirges*. Rhadamanthys became associated with both the Isles of the Blessed and Elysium, or, seen the other way, the classical writers often conflate, confuse, or identify these two places with one another. The tradition of the preeminence of Rhadamanthys has its earliest known record in Homer, *Od.* 4.560–79.

5. *Ter conatus ibi collo dare bracchia circum, ter frustra comprensa manus effugit imago, par levibus ventis volucrique simillima somno.*

6. Cf. Aeschylus, fr. 50 *Europa;* Euripides, *Ba.* 1330–92; Apollonius Rhodius 4.811–16; Lycophron 1204–13; Strabo, *Geography* 3.2.13; Diodorus Siculus 5.81–82; Pausanias 3.19.11–13; 8.53.5; Antoninus Liberalis 33; Philostratus, *VA* 5.3; Quintus Smyrnaeus 2.549; 3.743; 14.223. Homer, *Od.* 1.235–51, moreover, shows that the "missing body" was not a topos in the Archaic Greek period of Homer. The poem credited Harpies (ἅρπυιαι means "snatchers"; cf. *Iliad* 16.150) for snatching away bodies that had gone missing. This, according to the epic, was a cause of grief, not celebration or praise, nor deification, despite the story of Ganymede.

7. Cf. Pindar, *O.* 13.87–90, *I.* 7.44; *Bibliotheke* 2.3.2; Homer, *Il.* 6.155–203, 16.328; Ovid, *Met.* 9.646.

8. Cf. Statius, *Silvae* 3.4.12–18; Herodianus Historicus 1.11.2. In the Roman imperial period, Ganymede had become a symbol for the hope of apotheosis often to be found in artistic rendition on the sides of Roman sarcophagi. See P. Hardie, "Another Look at Virgil's Ganymede," in *Classics in Progress: Essays on Ancient Greece and Rome* (ed. T. P. Wiseman; Oxford: Oxford University Press, 2002), 341–42; Michael C. J. Putnam, "Ganymede and Virgilian Ekphrasis," *AJP* 116, no. 3 (1995): 419–40; Josef Engemann, *Untersuchungen zur Sepulchralsymbolik der späteren römishen Kaiserzeit* (JAC-Erg.-Bd. 2; Munster, 1973), 1–41.

9. Vermeule, *Aspects of Death*, 120–28.

10. Jean-Pierre Vernant, "Mortels et immortels: Le corps divin" in *L'individu, la mort, l'amour: Soi-même et l'autre en Grèce ancienne* (Paris: Gallimard, 1989), 13.

11. Concerning ancient Greek burial rites and the cult of the dead, see Walter Burkert, *Greek Religion* (Cambridge, MA: Harvard University Press, 1985), 190–98; Erwin Rohde, *Psyche: The Cult of Souls and Belief in Immortality among the Greeks* (trans. W. B. Hillis; Routledge & Kegan Paul, 1925), 156–216.

12. Jean-Pierre Vernant, "Figuration de l'invisible et categorie psychologique du double: Le colossus," in *Mythe et pensée chez les Grecs: Etudes de psychologie historique* (Paris: François Maspéro, 1965), 2:65–78; in English translation as "The Representation of the Invisible and the Psychological Category of the Double: The Colossos," in *Myth and Thought among the Greeks* (London: Routledge, 1983), 305–20.

13. Deborah T. Steiner, *Images in Mind: Statues in Archaic and Classical Greek Literature and Thought* (Princeton, NJ: Princeton University Press, 2001), 6–7. This segment on the κολοσσοί is greatly indebted to Steiner's treatment in the first chapter of her monograph.

14. Steiner, 8 n. 17; see especially Joseph Fontenrose, "The Hero as Athlete," *California Studies in Classical Antiquity* 1 (1968): 73–104.

15. Penelope J. E. Davies, *Death and the Emperor: Roman Imperial Funerary Monuments from Augustus to Marcus Aurelius* (Cambridge: Cambridge University Press, 2000), 73.

16. Roland Barthes, "The Death of the Author," in *Image, Music, Text* (trans. Stephen Heath; New York: Hill and Wang, 1977), 147.

17. Cf. Hjalmar Wennerberg, "Der Begriff der Familienähnlichkeit in Wittgensteins Spätphilosophie," in *Ludwig Wittgenstein—Philosophische Untersuchungen*

(ed. Eike Savigny; Berlin: Akademie Verlag, 1998), 41–69; David Fishelov, *Metaphors of Genre: The Role of Analogies in Genre Theory* (University Park: Pennsylvania State University Press, 1993), 53–83.

18. Ludwig Wittgenstein, *Philosophische Untersuchungen/Philosophical Investigations* (New York: Macmillan, 1953), §66–67.
19. Lewis Richard Farnell, *Greek Hero Cults and Ideas of Immortality* (London: Oxford University Press, 1921).
20. Arthur Stanley Pease, "Some Aspects of Invisibility," *HSCP* 53 (1942): 35–36.
21. Simon Price, "From Noble Funerals to Divine Cult: The Consecration of Roman Emperors," in *Rituals of Royalty: Power and Ceremonial in Traditional Societies* (ed. David Cannadine and Simon Price; Cambridge: Cambridge University Press, 1987), 90–91.
22. The public disapprobation of a ruler as tyrant or official as scoundrel often resulted in the defacing or destruction of associated state images and inscriptions. See Eric R. Varner, *Mutilation and Transformation: Damnatio Memoriae and Roman Imperial Portraiture* (Leiden: Brill Academic Publishers, 2004); Harriet I. Flower, *The Art of Forgetting: Disgrace and Oblivion in Roman Political Culture* (Chapel Hill: University of North Carolina Press, 2006); Harriet I. Flower, "Rethinking 'Damnatio Memoriae': The Case of Cn. Calpurnius Piso Pater in A.D. 20," *CA* 17 (1998): 155–87; Friedrich Vittinghoff, *Der Staatsfeind in der Römischen Kaiserzeit: Untersuchungen zur 'damnatio memoriae'* (Berlin: Junker and Dünnhaupt, 1936).
23. Penelope J. E. Davies, *Death and the Emperor*, 74.
24. Cf. John T. Ramsey and A. Lewis Licht, *The Comet of 44 B.C. and Caesar's Funeral Games* (American Classical Studies 39; Atlanta: Scholars Press, 1997).
25. N.B., as so often happened with the translation fable, Ps.-Apollodorus did not bother to indicate what was meant by the disappearance of the prince. The bare signals of the epilogue proved sufficient to imply the theme of his veneration, just as Diodorus differently achieved with similar brevity.
26. Cf. Christopher Jones, *New Heroes in Antiquity: From Achilles to Antinoos* (Cambridge, MA: Harvard University Press, 2010), 75–83.
27. For a more detailed profile of this fascinating figure in classical antiquity, see J. D. P. Bolton, *Aristeas of Proconnesus* (Oxford: Oxford University Press, 1962).
28. Cf. Joseph Fontenrose, *Didyma: Apollo's Oracle, Cult, and Companions* (Berkeley: University of California Press, 1988), 106–8.
29. Apuleius (*Metam.* 11.5) revealed that the Cretans had identified Britomartis (Dictynna) with the goddess Artemis, referring to the former as "Diktynna Diana." Cf. Hdt. 3.59; Orphica, *Hymni* 36; Aristophanes, *Ranae* 1358–60; *Vespae* 367–9.
30. Lat., *picus*. The account in part functioned in Ovid as a myth of eponymity.
31. Exposing the honorific essence and the plasticity of the translation fable, Ps-Apollodorus (ref. above) related that Pollux had been translated as well: "Zeus smote Idas with a thunderbolt, but Pollux he carried up to heaven. Nevertheless, as Pollux refused to accept immortality while his brother Castor was dead, Zeus permitted them both to spend alternating days among the gods and among mortals."
32. Cf. Joseph Fontenrose, "The Hero as Athlete," 73–104.
33. Ovid, *Metam.* 12.143–45; *victum spoliare: arma relicta videt; corpus deus aequoris albam contulit in volubrem, cuius modo nomen habebat.* "He prepared to plunder his conquered enemy, but he saw the armor emptied. The gods had changed his body into the white bird whose name it even now bears."
34. Cf. the metamorphoses of Pitys into a pine tree (Nonnus, *Dion.* 2.108; Longus, *Daphn.* 2.7, 2.39; Lucian, *Dial. mort.* 22.4) and Syrinx into water reeds (Ovid, *Metam.* 1.689).

35. Bacchus likewise, according to Plutarch, snatched up his mother, Semele, and the two ascended to heaven (Plutarch, *Sera* 22). The tale of Dionysus harrying Hades in order to rescue Semele from the netherworld, though not a translation, compares well with adjacent tales of κατάβασις and the conquest of mortality (Cf. Pausanias 2.37.1–5 and Aristophanes, *Ran.*).

36. Cf. Aspalis (above).

37. For a rich historical analysis of this fascinating figure, see Ettore Pais, *Ancient Italy: Historical, and Geographical Investigations in Central Italy, Magna Graecia, Sicily, and Sardinia* (trans. C. Densmore Curtis; Chicago: University of Chicago Press, 1908), 39–52.

38. Leonard Muellner, "Glaucus Redivivus," *HSCP* 98 (1998): 1–30.

39. See Sir George James Frazer, "Resurrection of Glaucus," appendix 7, pp. 363–70 in *Apollodorus, The Library*, vol. 2 (Loeb Classical Library; Cambridge, MA: Harvard University Press, 1921). Regarding the ancient tradition of ornithomancy as relates to the translation of Glaucus, see Emilio Suárez de la Torre, "The Portrait of a Seer" in *Antike Mythen: Medlen, Transformation und Konstruktionen* (ed. Christine Walde and Ú Dill; Berlin: Walter de Gruyter GmbH & Co., 2009), 171–72.

40. Cf. H. A. Shapiro, "*Heros Theos*: The Death and Apotheosis of Herakles," *CW* 77, no. 1 (1983): 7–18. Contrast the archaic tale of Odysseus gazing upon the phantom of Heracles in Hades (Homer, *Od.* 11.601–16). Hesiod, however, appears to describe the postmortem hero as having joined the immortals (*Theog.* 950–5; see also Pindar, *Nem.* 1.69–72). Regarding his constellation, see Dionysius of Halicarnassus 1.41.

41. Paul Murgatroyd has provided an in-depth philological-comparative analysis of the Hylas story as conveyed in the Greek and Latin epics (i.e., those by Apollonius of Rhodes and Valerious Flaccus, respectively). The development of the translation fable in this instance, as manifest in nearly all diachronic, comparative studies of instances of a given translation fable, reveals the malleable nature of mythography as well as the progressive fascination with and development of specific themes related to the generic "translation fable" tradition. Paul Murgatroyd, *A Commentary on Book 4 of Valerius Flaccus' Argonautica* (Leiden: Brill, 2009), 31–58.

42. For further critical discussion of the pliability of this etiological tale, see William G. Thalmann, *Apollonius of Rhodes and the Spaces of Hellenism* (Oxford: Oxford University Press, 2011), 110.

43. Cf. Antonius Liberalis's mythographon on Iphigenia (*Metam.* 27), where she is both transferred to the Isles of the Blessed and translated to become the immortal deity Orsilochia, house-mate to Achilles. This account is especially noteworthy because of the conflation of these two typically disparate Hellenic traditions (i.e., transference and translation). The text also tacitly indicates that Achilles had been translated to immortal divinity. Compare his cult on the Island of Leuke and his divine epithet Ποντάρχης, Ruler of the Black Sea.

44. μεθίημι can mean "to throw" (as given in Lightfoot's Loeb translation; Parthenius, *Erot.* 15.3), but, with the pronominal phrase εἰς . . . , the verb tends to mean "to stab" or "to plunge," particularly with weapons of piercing.

45. See also Euripides.

46. As with nearly every fable in the Gallery, the translation myths applied to Orion exhibited an all-but-whimsical variety, exemplifying the nearly limitless quality of plasticity and malleability typical of ancient mythology.

47. Χθών σε τέκεν, πόντος δὲ διώλεσε, δέκτο δὲ θῶκος Πλουτῆος· κεῖθεν δ' οὐρανὸν εἰσανέβης. οὐχ ὡς ναυηγὸς δὲ βυθῷ θάνες, ἀλλ' ἵνα πάντων κλήροις ἀθανάτων, πάμφιλε, κόσμον ἄγῃς.

48. This story shares uncanny relationships with both the alternative story of treachery applied to Romulus and the infamous senatorial assassination of Julius Caesar. Cicero appears to have been aware of the Athenian king's notoriety (*Resp.* 1.44).

49. Aulus Gellius, *Noct. att.* 12.11.1

50. The conventional signals of Appian's account are suggestive, though perhaps semiotically insufficient to qualify as a translation fable. Ptolemy XIV likewise went missing, not long after the assassination of Julius Caesar, never to be seen again (Plutarch, *Caes.* 49.5). Scholars suppose that he had been poisoned by Cleopatra, who then, along with her son Caesarion, assumed the throne. One may reasonably speculate that these Ptolemaic "disappearance" stories served to cover over the treachery of the ambitious, redoubtable queen.

51. Other similar phrases included catasterisms, such as being "set among the stars." Diogenes Laërtius (8.41) related that Pythagoras had made a subterranean dwelling and later re-emerged from the cave reporting that he had descended to Hades and had returned to tell of it. To this, the local Italians responded by granting the philosopher divine honors. This story was identical to that of Zalmoxis and may even have been (falsely) assimilated to Pythagoras or, just as likely, this kind of tale became a rather developed topos in classical culture. According to Herodotus, Zalmoxis purported to have been a manumitted slave of the famed Pythagoras. Having returned to his homeland of Thracia, Zalmoxis came to be seen as a divine sage. He taught his people that they were in fact immortal, like the gods. In an effort to demonstrate this by feigning his own κατάβασις similar to Odysseus's famous descent into the netherworld (*Od.* 11), Zalmoxis dug an underground chamber. Eventually, he disappeared into the cave. The sage hid there for three years only to re-emerge and appear before the Thracians as proof of his claim to immortality. Herodotus himself offered skepticism about this epichoric Geto-Dacian tale. Herodotus 4.93–96; Strabo, *Geogr.* 7.3.5; see also Yulia Ustinova, *Caves and the Ancient Greek Mind: Descending Underground in the Search for Truth* (Oxford: Oxford University Press, 2009), 100–105, 186–90.

52. Cf. King Orchomenus. The alternate account may have been a late republican embellishment, tacitly evoking the senatorial assassination of Julius Caesar. Alternate accounts, typically proposed as dubious, though often approximating accurate history, demonstrate the implied honorific and political function of the translation fable. Greek and Roman culture did not tolerate well the ignobility of tragic death when closing the narratives of their most storied heroes, the compendiums of such celebrated tales ultimately constituting the larger cultural narratives of the Hellenistic and Roman civilizations.

53. N.B., the translation fable of Romulus extended back as early as Ennius, ca. 200 B.C.E. The Archaic Latin poem, for instance, states: *Romulus in caelo cum dis genitalibus aevum degit* (*Ann.* 115; "Romulus lives eternally in heaven with the gods who bore him.").

54. In an alternative account supplied by Patrocles of Thurian, Saturn died and received a hero's tomb in Sicily (Arnobius, *Adv. Nationes* 4.25).

55. Concerning the harrying of Hades, cf. Aristophanes, *Ranae.*

56. Cf. Oibotas who, legend held, fought along with the Greeks some two hundred years after his death. Pausanias 6.3.8. In consideration of other phantom heroes, see Pausanias 1.4.4, 1.32.5, 10.23.2; Herodotus 8.38–39.

57. For perhaps the clearest attestation to the regularity of the apotheosis custom, see Herodian 4.2.

58. Simon Price, "From Noble Funerals to Divine Cult," 73.

59. Cf. Florus 1.1.18; Ps.-Aurelius Victor, *De viris illustribus* 2.13.

60. Simon Price, "From Noble Funerals to Divine Cult," 72–75. Cf. Walter Burkert, "Caesar und Romulus-Quirinus," *Historia* 11 (1962): 356–76; Jean Gage, "Le Témoignage de Julius Proculus (sur l'Assomption de Romulus-Quirinus) et les Prodiges Fulguratoires dans l'Ancien 'Ritus Comitialis,'" *L'Antiquité Classique* 41 (1972): 49–75.

61. Plutarch, *Romulus* 28.

62. Both authors were said to have died in the year 17 C.E. in the reign of Tiberius.

63. Barbara Levick, *The High Tide of Empire: Emperors and Empire AD 14–117* (London: London Association of Classical Teachers, 2002).

64. E. S. Staveley, *Greek and Roman Voting and Elections* (Aspects of Greek and Roman Life; ed. H. H. Scullard (Ithaca, NY: Cornell University Press, 1972), 217–26.

65. Cf. Lactantius, *Inst.* 1.15.

66. M. Cary and H. H. Scullard, *A History of Rome down to the Reign of Constantine* (3d ed.; New York: Palgrave, 1975), 349–50.

67. Gertrude Grether, "Livia and the Roman Imperial Cult," *AJP* 67, no. 3 (1946): 222–23.

68. Trajan's extension, the Via Traiana, ended in Brindisium, along the Adriatic coast (on the "heel" of Italy, the ancient region of Calabria), extending the Via Appia an additional two hundred and five miles.

69. Regarding this theme, cf. Cicero, *Nat. d.* 2.62; Horace, *Carm.* 3.3.

70. Regarding the protracted spectacle and theatrics of the imperial funeral, see Geoffrey S. Sumi, "Impersonating the Dead: Mimes at Roman Funerals," *AJP* 123 (2002): 559–85.

71. Dio Cassius 56.34–46, 75.4–5; Herodian 4.1–2. Ovid's apotheosis of Julius Caesar seems unclear regarding the nature of his postmortem state, whether having an immortal body or a bodyless soul. The poem only makes clear the shedding of his assassinated, mortal body as Venus bears him upward to join the celestial host (Ovid, *Metam.* 15.843–51). This possible exception may imply an accommodation of Platonizing conceptions of the body or may simply represent one of many instances of mythic incoherence. The mythic exaltation of the deceased, not systematic coherence, provided the subtext of such presentations. Ovid thus emphasized the shedding of Caesar's disgraced body, a body that immediately became inconsequential to his eternal station as divine overseer of the *Imperium Romanum*.

72. Cf. Elias J. Bickermann, "Die römische Kaiserapotheose," *AR* 27 (1929): 1–34; Elias J. Bickermann, "*Consecratio*," in *Le culte des souverains dans l'empire romain* (ed. Elias J. Bickermann and W. den Boer; Entretiens sur l'antiquité classique 19; Genève: Hardt, 1973), 3–25; and Florence Dupont, "The Emperor-God's Other Body," in *Fragments for a History of the Human Body* (ed. Michel Feher; New York: Zone, 1989), 396–419.

73. Paul Veyne, *Did the Greeks Believe in Their Myths? An Essay on the Constitutive Imagination* (trans. Paula Wissing; Chicago: University of Chicago Press, 1988).

74. Paul Veyne, *Les Grecs ont-ils cru à leurs mythes? Esssai sur l'Imagination* (Paris: Seuil, 1983), 28.

75. Ibid., 28–29.

76. Such distinctions between history and myth held, despite the occasional verisimilitude decorating a given narrative. One may, at least in part, attribute this seeming interest to blur the line between myth and reality to what Larry Levin astutely referred to as "that willed tendency of art to approximate reality." Larry Levin, *The Gates of Horn: A Study of Five French Realists* (Oxford: Oxford University Press, 1986), 3.

77. Sextus Empiricus, *Adversus mathematicos* 253.

78. Cf. Peter G. Bietenholz, *Historia and Fabula: Myths and Legends in Historical Thought from Antiquity to the Modern Age* (Leiden: Brill, 1994), 21–61.
79. Northrop Frye, "Historical Criticism: Theory of Modes," in *Anatomy of Criticism: Four Essays by Northrop Frye* (Princeton, NJ: Princeton University Press, 1957), 33–70.
80. Cf. Bietenholz, *Historia and Fabula*, 48–51.

BIBLIOGRAPHY

Barthes, Roland. "The Death of the Author." Pages 142–48 in *Image, Music, Text.* Translated by Stephen Heath. New York: Hill and Wang, 1977.

Bickermann, Elias J. "Das leere Grab." *Zeitschrift für die neutestamentliche Wissenschaft und die Kinde der älteren Kirche* 23 (1924): 281–92.

———. "Die römische Kaiserapotheose." *Archiv für Religionswissenschaft* 27 (1929): 1–34.

Bieler, Ludwig. "Consecratio." Pages 3–25 in *Le culte des souverains dans l'empire romain*. Edited by Elias J. Bickermann and W. den Boer. Entretiens sur l'antiquité classique 19. Genève: Hardt, 1973.

Bietenholz, Peter G. *Historia and Fabula: Myths and Legends in Historical Thought from Antiquity to the Modern Age*. Leiden: Brill, 1994.

Bolton, James D. P. *Aristeas of Proconnesus*. Oxford: Oxford University Press, 1962.

Bremmer, Jan. *The Early Greek Concept of the Soul*. Princeton, NJ: Princeton University Press, 1983.

Burkert, Walter. "Caesar und Romulus-Quirinus." *Historia* 11 (1962): 356–76.

———. *Greek Religion*. Cambridge, MA: Harvard University Press, 1985.

Cary, M. and H. H. Scullard, *A History of Rome down to the Reign of Constantine*. 3d ed. New York: Palgrave, 1975.

Davies, Penelope J. E. *Death and the Emperor: Roman Imperial Funerary Monuments from Augustus to Marcus Aurelius*. Cambridge: Cambridge University Press, 2000.

Dupont, Florence. "The Emperor-God's Other Body." Pages 396–419 in *Fragments for a History of the Human Body*. Edited by Michel Feher. New York: Zone, 1989.

Engemann, Josef. *Untersuchungen zur Sepulchralsymbolik der späteren römishen Kaiserzeit*. Jahrbuch für Antike und Christentum-Erg.-Bd. 2. Munster, 1973.

Farnell, Lewis Richard. *Greek Hero Cults and Ideas of Immortality*. London: Oxford University Press, 1921.

Fishelov, David. *Metaphors of Genre: The Role of Analogies in Genre Theory*. University Park: Pennsylvania State University Press, 1993.

Flower, Harriet I. "Rethinking 'Damnatio Memoriae': The Case of Cn. Calpurnius Piso Pater in A.D. 20." *Classical Antiquity* 17 (1998): 155–87.

———. *The Art of Forgetting: Disgrace and Oblivion in Roman Political Culture*. Chapel Hill: University of North Carolina Press, 2006.

Fontenrose, Joseph. "The Hero as Athlete." *California Studies in Classical Antiquity* 1 (1968): 73–104.

———. *Didyma: Apollo's Oracle, Cult, and Companions*. Berkeley: University of California Press, 1988.

Frazer, George James. "Resurrection of Glaucus." Pages 363–70 in *Apollodorus, The Library*. 2 vols. Loeb Classical Library. Cambridge, MA: Harvard University Press, 1921.

Frye, Northrop. "Historical Criticism: Theory of Modes." Pages 33–70 in *Anatomy of Criticism: Four Essays by Northrop Frye*. Princeton, NJ: Princeton University Press, 1957.

Gage, Jean. "Le Témoignage de Julius Proculus (sur l'Assomption de Romulus-Quirinus) et les Prodiges Fulguratoires dans l'Ancien 'Ritus Comitialis.'" *L'Antiquité Classique* 41 (1972): 49–75.

Garland, Robert. *The Greek Way of Death*. Ithaca, NY: Cornell University Press, 1985.

Grether, Gertrude. "Livia and the Roman Imperial Cult." *American Journal of Philology* 67, no. 3 (1946): 222–52.

Hardie, Philip. "Another Look at Virgil's Ganymede." Pages 333–61 in *Classics in Progress: Essays on Ancient Greece and Rome*. Edited by T. P. Wiseman. Oxford: Oxford University Press, 2002.

Johnston, Sarah Iles. *Restless Dead: Encounters between the Living and the Dead in Ancient Greece*. Berkeley: University of California Press, 1999.

Jones, Christopher. *New Heroes in Antiquity: From Achilles to Antinoos*. Cambridge, MA: Harvard University Press, 2010.

Levick, Barbara. *The High Tide of Empire: Emperors and Empire AD 14–117*. London: London Association of Classical Teachers, 2002.

Levin, Larry. *The Gates of Horn: A Study of Five French Realists*. Oxford: Oxford University Press, 1986.

Muellner, Leonard. "Glaucus Redivivus." *Harvard Studies in Classical Philology* 98 (1998): 1–30.

Murgatroyd, Paul. *A Commentary on Book 4 of Valerius Flaccus' Argonautica*. Leiden: Brill, 2009.

Pais, Ettore. *Anicent Italy: Historical, and Geographical Investigations in Central Italy, Magna Graecia, Sicily, and Sardinia*. Translated by C. Densmore Curtis. Chicago: University of Chicago Press, 1908.

Pease, Arthur Stanley. "Some Aspects of Invisibility." *Harvard Studies in Classical Philology* 53 (1942): 1–36.

Price, Simon. "From Noble Funerals to Divine Cult: The Consecration of Roman Emperors." Pages 56–105 in *Rituals of Royalty: Power and Ceremonial in Traditional Societies*. Edited by David Cannadine and Simon Price. Cambridge: Cambridge University Press, 1987.

Putnam, Michael C. J. "Ganymede and Virgilian Ekphrasis." *American Journal of Philology* 116, no. 3 (1995): 419–40.

Ramsey, John T. and A. Lewis Licht. *The Comet of 44 B.C. and Caesar's Funeral Games*. American Classical Studies 39. Atlanta: Scholars Press, 1997.

Rohde, Erwin. *Psyche: The Cult of Souls and Belief in Immortality among the Greeks*. Translated by W. B. Hillis. London: Routledge & Kegan Paul, 1925.

Shapiro, H. Alan. "*Heros Theos*: The Death and Apotheosis of Herakles." *Classical World* 77, no. 1 (1983): 7–18.

Staveley, E. Stuart. *Greek and Roman Voting and Elections*. Aspects of Greek and Roman Life. Edited by H. H. Scullard. Ithaca, NY: Cornell University Press, 1972.

Steiner, Deborah T. *Images in Mind: Statues in Archaic and Classical Greek Literature and Thought*. Princeton, NJ: Princeton University Press, 2001.

Suárez de la Torre, Emilio. "The Portrait of a Seer." Pages 158–88 in *Antike Mythen: Medlen, Transformation und Konstruktionen*. Edited by Christine Walde and Ü Dill. Berlin: Walter de Gruyter GmbH & Co., 2009.

Sumi, Geoffrey S. "Impersonating the Dead: Mimes at Roman Funerals." *American Journal of Philology* 123 (2002): 559–85.

Thalmann, William G. *Apollonius of Rhodes and the Spaces of Hellenism*. Oxford: Oxford University Press, 2011.

Ustinova, Yulia. *Caves and the Ancient Greek Mind: Descending Underground in the Search for Truth*. Oxford: Oxford University Press, 2009.

Varner, Eric R. *Mutilation and Transformation: Damnatio Memoriae and Roman Imperial Portraiture*. Leiden: Brill Academic Publishers, 2004.

Vermeule, Emily. *Aspects of Death in Early Greek Art and Poetry*. Berkeley: University of Californian Press, 1979.

Vernant, Jean-Pierre. "Figuration de l'invisible et categorie psychologique du double: Le colossus." Pages 2:65–78 in *Mythe et pensée chez les Grecs: Etudes de psychologie historique*. Paris: François Maspéro, 1965.

———. "The Representation of the Invisible and the Psychological Category of the Double: The Colossos." Pages 305–20 in *Myth and Thought among the Greeks*. London: Routledge, 1983.

———. "Mortels et immortels: Le corps divin." Pages 7–39 in *L'individu, la mort, l'amour: Soi-même et l'autre en Grèce ancienne*. Paris: Gallimard, 1989.

Veyne, Paul. *Les Grecs ont-ils cru à leurs mythes? Esssai sur l'Imagination*. Paris: Seuil, 1983.

———. *Did the Greeks Believe in Their Myths? An Essay on the Constitutive Imagination*. Translated by Paula Wissing. Chicago: University of Chicago Press, 1988.

Vittinghoff, Friedrich. *Der Staatsfeind in der Römischen Kaiserzeit: Untersuchungen zur 'damnatio memoriae.'* Berlin: Junker and Dünnhaupt, 1936.

Wennerberg, Hjalmar. "Der Begriff der Familienähnlichkeit in Wittgensteins Spätphilosophie." Pages 41–69 in *Ludwig Wittgenstein—Philosophische Untersuchungen*. Edited by Eike Savigny. Berlin: Akademie Verlag, 1998.

Wittgenstein, Ludwig. *Philosophische Untersuchungen/Philosophical Investigations*. New York: Macmillan, 1953.

3   Critical Method and the Gospels

Tout discours, même une phrase poétique ou oraculaire porte en elle un dispositif, des règles pour produire des choses analogues et donc une esquisse de méthodologie.

Every discourse, even a poetic or oracular sentence, carries with it a system of rules for producing analogous things and thus an outline of methodology.

[Jacques Derrida, 1987][1]

In the year 1977, humankind launched two extraordinary spacecraft, *Voyager 1* and *Voyager 2*, aimed at exploring Earth's solar system and beyond. Having officially entered interstellar space as of September 2013, these two probes now constitute the farthest human-made objects ever to have left Earth's atmosphere. NASA charged renown cosmologist Carl Sagan, one of the principal visionaries behind these missions, to produce a communiqué representing human civilization, in case another intelligent life form may perchance intercept one of these space vehicles at some distant point in the cosmic future. Professor Sagan assembled a team of experts from various fields to aid in creating what came to be known as the Golden Record, a gold-coated copper phonograph containing salutations in over sixty human languages, an audio essay, numerous photographs, and over ninety minutes of music.[2] Had Sagan consulted an expert linguist, however, he may have faced a rather insoluble problem. According to the most basic findings of linguistic theory, language, culture, and society indelibly interlock. How could one wholly unconditioned by the social conventions of human language even make a start at decoding the record's message?

The New Testament records traverse across millennia to this present time from a substantially distant place in human cultural history, the urban cultural hubs of classical Mediterranean society. One must ask, "What, of necessity, does the mental process of 'reading' entail, both for the ancient consumer of Greek prose and for the modern philologist, if one is correctly to comprehend such documents?" As this chapter explores, in order to comprehend the original significance of these documents, one must cultivate familiarity with the lively inferential world of antique Hellenistic and Roman society. Such an immersion requires the application of a rich tapestry of historical, literary, and cultural critical methodologies. For this study, a method qualifies on a purely pragmatic scale; expressly stated, to what extent does a given application elucidate the matter to be demonstrated (Q.E.D.)? While one may fruitfully bring to bear a broad array of methodological voices, of first priority must be to comprehend the linguistic, cultural, and social implied significance or impressive sense governing these ancient New Testament narratives. Accordingly, while certain methods prove vital to the analysis, others may provide mere dubious or marginal service. Albeit, the present study in no way promises to exhaust its subject matter or the methodological voices that may fruitfully come to bear within a deservedly broadening discourse on the topic.

3.1 SEMIOTICS AND THE SOCIOLOGY OF INFERENCE

Operating within the urban contexts of the Roman provincial Greek East, the New Testament Gospels functioned and flourished as acts of counter-cultural language, potent media that early Christian communities rehearsed, sacralized, and ritualized. While these texts applied many ideological, mythical, and literary elements from early Judaism, their traction as counter-cultural vehicles prevailed in the flanking sophistication of their linguistic and cultural relation to the dominant codes and structures of the Hellenistic world. The explosive, growing movement promulgated an orientalist metaphor, contesting through its proud alterity the very order of classical antiquity. As such, these texts strategically adapted, orientalized, and transvalued many of the most potent and canonized elements of Hellenistic culture. Beyond simply having been composed in Greek, the Gospels spoke to and from the cultural grammar of the Greek Levant, appropriating, leveraging, confronting, and rivaling many of its most cherished cultural and linguistic structures. A radicalized mode of cultural identity negotiation in these turbulent urban contexts furnished the creative semiotic strategy behind the Gospels. The applied cultural and linguistic methods of this study, therefore, afford a greater measure of clarity and insight in assessing the alleged application of the translation fable in the Gospels, greater than, for example, a mere nebulous study by comparison, thereby delimiting the field of justifiable inference.

Connotation, Not Denotation

In the parlance of semiotic theory, Magritte's painting conveys a sign composed of the signifier, the image of a "pipe," and the signified, that which the image meant or conveyed. The surrealistic representation of the signifier, the painted image of the "pipe," indexes a connotative rather than denotative meaning. Such constitutes the fundamental point of artistic rendition, namely, to provide a vehicle to suggest or invoke significant connotations.

The larger-than-life cartoon "pipe" image conveyed exclusivity, proposing a potent symbol of gentlemanly luxury in twentieth-century France, by association romanticizing, celebrating, and thus reinscribing the delineation or semiotic "code" of social classification in urban French society. As French literary theorist and semiotician Roland Barthes has reminded us, the connotative and not the denotative significance truly constitutes the meaning of an expression.[3] This efficacy emerges all the more in the *poiesis* of artistic and literary signs and sign structures.

Remarkably, Michel Foucault's clever essay on René Magritte's painting *La trahison des images* (1928–1929) did not discuss the matter of connotative identity. Foucault instead addressed the perhaps more (absurdly) obvious observation that the painting is indeed not a "pipe," but a representation of a pipe. Yet, as Harkness describes, both the painter and the essayist shared a common linguistic intent:

> As cartographers of Heterotopia, both Foucault and Magritte engage in a critique of language—the former historico-epistemological, and the latter visual. Each in his way concurs with the linguist Ferdinand de Saussure in asserting the arbitrariness of the sign—that is, the essentially circumstantial, conventional, historical nature of the bond between the signifier (e.g., a word) and the signified (the object or concept represented).[4]

Figure 3.1   La trahison des images by René Magritte (1928–1929) © 2014 C. Herscovici / Artists Rights Society (ARS), New York.

From this semiotic standpoint, one begins to perceive the distance between "rendition" and "mundane object," appreciating the potent meaning that the former is capable of conjuring within the interpreter.

Such a distance becomes all the more pronounced when considering the charged textualizations of Jesus in earliest Christian literature. The historical person has been altogether lost to us, indeed utterly irrelevant behind a bricolage of potent semiotic structures meant to invoke, confront, and menace many of the most powerful conventions, figures, and institutions of antique Mediterranean culture. Volumes by numerous well-intended historians have dealt considerable violence to the Gospel texts, pressing and interrogating them in the hope that an authentic historical Jesus would somehow step forward and present himself. While such a task is not entirely futile, however bleak its prospects, the matter eschews the primary value and significance of these texts for the modern historian and cultural critic of antiquity. Early Christian prose provides a wealth of data toward answering a perhaps more vital question, namely, how might these documents inform scholars about the dispositions and designs of the early Christian communities that produced, utilized, and celebrated them? Jesus, in these romanticized, mythic, textualized forms, became the emblem and literary-rhetorical vehicle of the earliest Christian movement(s). As shall be taken up toward the end of this chapter, the societies behind the earliest Christian literary traditions appear strangely disinterested in the authentic historical person, Jesus (e.g., consider Paul's lack of quotation of or reference to the mundane figure and the absence of historical argumentation throughout the Gospel narratives).

The subversive, often esoteric nature of the Gospels, moreover, directs attention to a more critical reading, an "infrapolitical" reading, as political scientist James C. Scott has coined the term. In his *Domination and the Arts of Resistance: Hidden Transcripts*, Scott introduces his critical insight, taking Plato's *Symposium* as his heuristic case:

> In a social science already rife—some might say crawling—with neologisms, one hesitates to contribute another. The term *infrapolitics*, however, seems an appropriate shorthand to convey the idea that we are dealing with an unobtrusive realm of political struggle. For a social science attuned to the relatively open politics of liberal democracies and to loud, headline-grabbing protests, demonstrations, and rebellions, the circumspect struggle waged daily by subordinate groups is, like infrared rays, beyond the visible end of the spectrum. That it should be invisible, as we have seen, is in large part by design—a tactical choice born of a prudent awareness of the balance of power. The claim made here is similar to the claim made by Leo Strauss about how the reality of persecution must effect our reading of classical political philosophy: "Persecution cannot prevent even public expression of the heterodox truth, for a man of independent thought can utter his views in public and remain unharmed, provided he moves with circumspection. He can even utter

them in print without incurring any danger, provided he is capable of *writing between the lines.*" The text we are interpreting in this case is not Plato's *Symposium* but rather the veiled cultural struggle and political expression of subordinate groups who have ample reason to fear venturing their unguarded opinion. The meaning of the text, in either case, is rarely straightforward; it is often meant to communicate one thing to those in the know and another to outsiders and authorities. If we have access to the hidden transcripts (analogous to the secret notes or conversations of the philosopher) or to a more reckless expression of opinion (analogous to subsequent texts produced under freer conditions) the task of interpretation is somewhat easier. Without these comparative texts, we are obliged to search for noninnocent meanings using our cultural knowledge—much in the way an experienced censor might![5]

Applying a Foucauldian critical orientation regarding the political performance of texts, Scott's methodology assists the careful reader in remaining ever mindful in discerning the furtive subtext variously imbedded in the literary expression of subjugated, subaltern, or persecuted peoples. A superficial reading would not tend to yield the primary significance or function of such texts. Scott insists that one first must find the "hidden transcript" of the oppressed community, in order to unlock the latent, often subversive, message of a given literary work.

Though the findings of an academician presumably unacquainted with the study of early Christian literature, Scott's methodological insight transposes with promising elegance into the sphere of Gospel studies. Every stratum of the Gospel tradition arose out of a milieu of turbulent political oppression vis-à-vis early Jewish sectarian and institutional power and Roman regional occupation in the Levant. From its inception, the early Christian movement(s) self-identified as the oppressed and persecuted counter-culture, the "true" divine kingdom. The written etiological myths of the early Christians, that is, τὰ εὐαγγέλια, celebrated the founding icon of their movement, a scandalously executed political *provocateur*, tacitly embodying a disquieting critique of both Jewish and Roman authority. Under the Principate (27–248 C.E.), by publishing anything that would undermine the grandeur of the empire, its people, and perhaps especially its *princeps*, a group or individual could, once having been reported by the *delatores*, face the severest charge under Roman law: *maiestas minuta populi Romani*. Such oppressive contexts gave rise to the flanking critical disposition of the Cynic philosopher, as well as the political crypticism of the apocalypticist, to name but two traditions that proved particularly relevant to the composition of the earliest strata of the Gospel texts, namely, those within Matthew's λόγια or "Q" material.[6] In an unprecedented moment of early Christian candor, did Justin drawn back the veil and provide an explicit gaze at that "hidden transcript" in his admission at *1 Apology* 21, thus allowing us a vital key to unlock the *roman à clef* of the Gospel narratives? This prescribed degree of methodological poise, along with the previously mentioned considerations, supplies the careful reader with yet another reason to suppose that the historical Jesus was not present in the Gospel texts.

Composers, Not Authors

Not only is the historical person indeed not the object of the New Testament Gospels, just as Magritte's "pipe" is not a pipe, but also the supposed "authors" of these texts must, upon further scrutiny, receive a career change. Roland Barthes was unerring, if somewhat hyperbolic, in his funerary tribute to the "textual author."[7] The assertion that more knowledge of the author of a given text promises to offer no additional insight as to the text's meaning may appear as absurd existential subjectivism at first glance. Such an approach may strike one as superimposed, a contrived effort by New Critical literary theorists and at odds with the conventional "introductions" given in most contemporary biblical commentaries. This interest in the Gospels' authors as the presumed *loci* of textual meaning, however, proves all the more useless when the best academic attempts at identifying such authors have proven futile. One simply does not know who wrote them. Perhaps the Gospel of John's admitted authorial plurality in the epilogue of its final redaction should point us toward comprehending these texts more as community projects than as single-author, static publications: Οὗτός ἐστιν ὁ μαθητὴς ὁ μαρτυρῶν περὶ τούτων καὶ ὁ γράψας ταῦτα, καὶ οἴδαμεν ὅτι ἀληθὴς αὐτοῦ ἡ μαρτυρία ἐστίν (Jn 21.24).[8]

Barthes's proposal, however, sprang from a very different, indeed more expedient source of reasoning, namely, that of literary structuralism. Barthes wrote:

> We know that a text is not a line of words releasing a single 'theological' meaning (the 'message' of the Author-God) but a multi-dimensional space in which a variety of writings, none of them original, blend and clash. The text is a tissue of quotations drawn from innumerable centres of culture. Similar to Bouvard and Pécuchet, those eternal copyists, at once sublime and comic and whose profound ridiculousness indicates precisely the truth of writing, the writer can only imitate a gesture that is always anterior, never original. His only power is to mix writings, to counter the ones with others, in such a way as never to rest on any one of them.[9]

Within the grand semiotic system, that is, the *langue*, as Swiss linguist Ferdinand de Saussure originally applied the term, the conditioned reader draws upon a variegated complex of common linguistic codes and structures, a procedure that, when coupled with a subject's social disposition, delimits a text's possible range of meaning. One literary critic describes:

> Barthes conceives the author as chef, the text as food, and the reader as ingesting and digesting that which the chef has prepared. In Barthes's

opinion, only in entering the reader's mouth does the food take on any flavor, and only in his stomach does it release any energy. Moreover, Barthes relentlessly reminds us that the author did not create (in the sense of bringing into existence) any of the ingredients in his dishes, and that the chef would cease to have any real purpose without his patrons, that it wouldn't really do him much good to prepare meals that would merely sit on a table until they rotted away. Barthes deconstructs the binary of "Author / reader" to show that the reader is the necessary supplement and then privileges the reader: a necessary corrective in the flow of literary interpretation, to be sure.[10]

So, while one may better regard Barthes's "author" as "editor," "compiler," or "composer," this individual has not "died," but has obtained a more accurate job description. The signifying indices of a work derive not from the inner parts of an "author," but from a broader, exterior semiotic grammar of culture(s) and literature(s) being variously referenced and invoked by Barthes's "composer."[11] Apprehending the common semiotic system, not the textual author, therefore, prevails as the prime requisite in accurately discerning the original language of the Gospels.[12]

Semiotics and *La Ressemblance*

The relevance of association between semiotics and *la ressemblance* for the present study arises from Saussure's comprehension of his category "language" as divided into *langue* and *parole*. The *langue* is the grand semiotic system, that is, the language minus *parole* ("speech"). *Parole*, therefore, exists in the instantiation(s) of the *langue*, namely, in the presentation of signifiers, whether by audible, visible, or any other sensible means. Once having illuminated this distinction, Saussure then added the vital denotation: *La langue est une institution sociale.*[13] This step serves as the fundamental basis for the field of structural linguistics as postulated and founded by Saussure himself.[14] The study at hand applies a structuralist and post-structuralist methodological approach following these fundamental tenets of linguistic and literary critical theory. The ancient Greek and Latin narrative thus now becomes intelligible insofar as the philologist comprehends the complex of conventions, semiotic structures, and cultural codes inherent to classical Mediterranean written culture. Michel Foucault describes the pre-modern Western literary tradition:

> Jusqu'à la fin du XVIe siècle, la ressemblance a joué un rôle bâtisseur dans le savoir de la culture occidentale. C'est elle qui a conduit pour une grande part l'exégèse et l'interprétation des textes; c'est elle qui a organisé le jeu des symboles, permis la connaissance des choses visibles et invisibles, guidé l'art de les représenter. Le monde s'enroulait sur lui-même : la terre répétant le ciel, les visages se mirant dans les étoiles, et l'herbe enveloppant dans ses tiges les secrets qui servaient à l'homme. La peinture imitait l'espace. Et la

représentation—qu'elle fût fête ou savoir—se donnait comme répétition : théâtre de la vie ou miroir du monde, c'était là le titre de tout langage, sa manière de s'annoncer et de formuler son droit à parler.[15]

Up to the end of the sixteenth century, resemblance played a construc-tive role in the knowledge of Western culture. It was resemblance that largely guided exegesis and interpretation of texts; it was resemblance that organized the play of symbols, made possible knowledge of things visible and invisible, and controlled the art of representing them. The universe was folded in upon itself: the earth echoing the sky, faces see-ing themselves reflected in the stars, and plants holding within their stems the secrets that were of use to man. Painting imitated space. And representation—whether in the service of pleasure or of knowledge— was posited as a form of repetition: the theatre of life or the mirror of nature, that was the claim made by all language, its manner of declaring its existence and of formulating its right of speech.[16]

While, from a semiotic and structuralist standpoint, all human communi-cation, not just classical and medieval literature, relies upon what Foucault termed *la ressemblance*, the Hellenistic cultures of antiquity especially and consciously applied archetypal mimesis in most every sphere of representa-tion. A cultural communication became intelligible insofar as its mimetic signals were present and legible. While this is true of modernity, *mélange* and interplay with *la ressemblance* became the measured quality of Helle-nistic expression. One is not surprised then to find the early Christian Jesus fashioned as the consummate emblem of the figured world of Hellenistic and Roman power. Nothing less would suffice to embellish this candidate of a new transcendent order of cultural dominion, that is, the proposed divine *rex regum* of earliest Christian ideology.

Deluding Discursive Restraints

Four fundamental discursive restraints have impeded the above-stated step in logic, and these, it is to be suggested, derive from the politics behind the Christian Bible, the long-standing sacred canon of Western civilization.

First, the Christian West has supposed that the narratives themselves are of divine origin. Scholars have, therefore, despite appearances to the contrary, all too often been reluctant to contextualize fully the biblical texts within mun-dane antiquity, instead tacitly accounting for interpretive difficulties or the "strangeness" of the text by assigning the Bible a distinct, revelatory character. From a meta-critical standpoint, this obsession with discerning the uniqueness of the biblical text has served to isolate and recontextualize the Gospels, thus allowing for readings that promote standing ecclesiological interests.

The assigned "sacred" nature of the text in this way has served as a license, whether entirely or more subtly by degree, to segregate these texts from the ancient literary domain(s) of which they were indeed a part. This segregation has constituted the second discursive restraint. The new *langue* became the theological lexicon instead of the classical lexicon. Students through the history of the Western academy have studied "Biblical Greek," as though such a thing had ever existed or the New Testament authors had ever shared any distinctive use of the language, whether grammatically or lexically. This artificial bifurcation has served to partition discursive authority, relegating supreme interpretive powers into the hands of elite theological institutions, thus ensuring and governing the hegemony of Western ecclesiastical power. Early Christian literature emerged from classical antiquity, was indeed a product of classical antiquity, and, as such, wholly resides within the domain of classical studies. There can be no academically honest impetus or excuse to extricate New Testament or early Christian studies from this larger disciplinary context.

A similar artificial divide has existed between the classifications "early Christian literature" and the "New Testament," as though the latter ought in any sense not to be fully subsumed under the former. Just as the previous distinction between classical and early Christian studies, this homologous distinction has served as a discursive partition regulating who is authorized to grant proper interpretations for society. Michel Foucault's criticisms of Western institutional powers, particularly regarding discursive restriction, appear to find their most flagrant example in this very instance.

Analogous to this discursive restriction, we find a fourth, equally problematic, contrived tendency, subsuming earliest Christian literature under early Jewish Studies. While several vital antecedents to earliest Christian writing resided in early Jewish literature (e.g., the "Son of Man," references and intertextuality with the Septuagint, apocalypticism, *et cetera*), the writings themselves arose out of the urban, Hellenistic cultural hubs of antique Mediterranean society, appealing to public converts from every quarter of the Hellenistic metropolis. With the possible exceptions of the Letter to the Hebrews, Matthew's λόγια or "Q" material, and perhaps John's Apocalypse, these were outward-facing texts with a broad implied readership ranging well beyond converts from Hellenistic Jewish society. Yet, even these texts show the abundant markings of Hellenization. Allowing for this hybridic nature of the New Testament *corpus*, the fundamental semiotic domain or *langue* behind these works decidedly presents itself as that of the Greek Levant, with creative antecedents also drawn from Hellenistic Judaism.

Scholars have tendentiously understated such creolization in the Gospels, it would appear, due to persistent myths in Western historiography, namely, concerning "paganism" and its obsolescence in the evolution of a Christian Western civilization. The designation *pagani*, a derogatory socio-religious trope deployed in the late antique Roman Christianization of the remaining empire, conveyed similar connotations to those of "heathen," "savage," "hick," and "philistine."[17] The term, therefore, has no place as a legitimate category in professional academic discourse, as it reinscribes that rhetorical hegemony and bias of a Christianized West. There was nothing "pagan" about Cicero, Plato, Virgil, or Herodotus, and not one of these figures would have accepted the indignity of such socially deprecatory terminology being applied to them or those of similar classical society. The New Testament documents, as complex acts of counter-culture, interfaced and played upon the common codes and conventions of the thought world of Hellenistic Roman culture perhaps as much as with regard to any Jewish subculture. The tendency, therefore, to relegate the Gospels to such low literary station as to deny them significant intercourse with classical literature and culture, particularly when contrasted with the measure of sophistication that some presently allow vis-à-vis the classical Hebrew texts, appears to reflect more a modern ignorance of classical written culture than any evident lack of familiarity on the part of early Christian converts in these ancient cities of the Greek East.

In this way, just demonstrated in but a few examples, the very language that has framed the field customarily titled "New Testament studies" has wrought obscurant violence upon the content of the discourse.

Identification of the Semiotic Domain

The present book then, duly having thrown off the menace of such constraints, immediately identifies the semiotic structure of classical culture(s) as the proper discursive nexus in the study of the New Testament Gospels. This *langue*, moreover, provided the social agreement, an interpretive contract delimiting the valid range of possible meaning to be read from the text, just as Umberto Eco has reminded us.[18] Roland Barthes further describes:

> [The *langue*] is therefore, so to speak, language minus speech: it is at the same time a social institution and a system of values. As a social institution, it is by no means an act, and it is not subject to any premeditation. It is the social part of language, the individual cannot by himself either create or modify it; it is essentially a collective contract which one must accept in its entirety if one wishes to communicate. . . . The institutional and the systematic aspect are of course connected: it is because a language is a system of contractual values (in part arbitrary, or, more exactly, unmotivated) that it resists the modification coming from a single individual, and is consequently a social institution.[19]

From a structuralist standpoint, all cultural expression essentially and naturally exists by common assent and shared signification, because culture arises most fundamentally as a social institution and not anything else.

The *parole* given in the earliest Christian gospels becomes intelligible insofar as we identify its *langue*, that is, the commonly shared cultural grammar of the implied readership of these documents. Inasmuch as these texts may represent a counter-cultural, socio-religious movement, the binary values or code governing the narrative must exist vis-à-vis the dominant code(s) of the classical Mediterranean world. One should expect, therefore, the early Christian text to have been no less mimetically reliant upon the literary cultural forms of the day, while transvaluing and contesting these dominant codes through distinct methods of innovation.

While, as a starting point, the present study accepts the synchrony of Saussurean linguistic theory, in post-structuralist fashion, one complicates the method with a more nuanced awareness of the genetic diachrony visible in the evolution of all semiotic expression. A sign is never static, even if one would impose upon it such a state for the sake of dissection. Although Saussure, Barthes, *et alii* appear to have been quite aware of this, this complication has all too often seen neglect, even if more carefully considered in Post-structural criticism. In keeping with the spirit of this work, the Soviet semiotician and cultural historian Yuri Lotman has, for instance, brought together a broader, more comprehensive methodological system.[20] In like manner, the present book seeks to combine a plurality of methodological considerations most closely approximating or recognizing the interpretive phenomena of the human mind of the ancient implied reader, attempting to avoid any reductionistic pitfalls or methodological blind spots that may otherwise exist.

3.2 CULTURAL PATTERNS AND ARCHETYPAL MIMESIS

Semiosis occurs not only at the level of individual words, phrases, or gestures; semiosis occurs within larger linguistic and cultural structures or patterns. Specific signature elements alert the subject to the presence of such a sign. One recognizes complexities of variation through the common faculties of analogical discernment. Awareness, therefore, of mimetic interplay constitutes a specific kind of semiotic cognizance, whether conscious, semiconscious, or subconscious.

Derivation as Legibility

Familiarity, association, and resemblance in early Christian literature served various purposes. Most fundamentally and earliest in the mythopoeic processes of literary production, recognizable semiotic patterns made these writings legible, just as the prior segment of this chapter has sought to explain. The application of generic markers, modal markers, and conventional motifs, imagery, and language drew upon the standing semiotic system. There is no other way to achieve sentient communication. For this reason, Carl Sagan's Golden Record should prove incomprehensible to any receiving intelligent life-form, inasmuch as an alien decoder will have no shared or conditioned semiotic domain. All signs are arbitrary and thus require a common grammar of interpretation.

Having placed all literature, indeed all practiced expression (*parole*) under a most penetrating scrutiny, one must confess that the human mind indeed only achieves by modest graduation, and that quite rarely, any genuine moment of noteworthy innovation or creativity. Our practiced comprehension of history tends to cherry-pick particular figures or "starting points" within the larger flow of semiotic discourse. Such a process of decontextualizing extraction or dissociation has the deluding result that such icons or labelled moments in history appear to have achieved quantum bursts of creativity in stark relief to the crude sketch of history that such myopia tends to yield. Albert Einstein, for all of his intellect, appears far more human and modest in careful intellectual history when juxtaposed with his closest discursive contemporaries (e.g., Lorentz, Hilbert, and Poincaré). With popular history having removed him from that complex context, a cultural myth of Einstein has become credited with the collective results achieved by his broader disciplinary discourse. His actual measure of innovation, when seen instead in an up-close fashion, appears shockingly minor and contiguous within his broader socio-discursive trajectory. The processes of evolution or fluctuation of the human semiotic system occur so gradually that the semiotician has tended to view the structure as a static, synchronic system. Upon conscious examination, the earliest Christian writings propose nearly nothing that had not already entered the cultural systemic stream. Regarding this content, only within its recombination and reconstitution, does one find the valued innovative moment that curiously grew to revolutionize the cultural-ideological order of classical antiquity over the course of centuries.[21]

This patent phenomenological observation has historically eluded so many New Testament scholars or, rather, scholars have eluded this observation, due to the deluding will to perceive a divine breach into the cultural-religious affairs of history, namely, with the "advent of Christ" or what Karl Barth *et alii* termed "the in-breaking of the kingdom of God" (*der Anbruch des Reiches Gottes*) into classical antiquity. With the rise of Western critical biblical scholarship, for decades now, indeed for nearly two centuries, the student of the Bible need not posit a special divine act to account for either the New Testament documents or the movements whence the Christian religion did emerge. The early nineteenth century works of H. E. G. Paulus and D. F. Strauß should have proved sufficient to close any serious considerations to the contrary, were the field purely the outworking of careful historical and literary inquiry.[22] Such fundamental conclusions required no further data, only refinement in detail and method. Bearing the grand legacy of Strauß, the present book modestly sets out to provide such refinement specifically with regard to the legibility of the mythological signals of the New Testament postmortem disappearance, appearance, and ascension narratives.

By "legibility" we mean "intelligibility," that is, a narrative applying sufficient semiotic conventionality to render such a story *type* reasonably comprehensible for a Mediterranean readership during the cultural period of the Roman Principate. The question arises: Can such a linguistic logic allow for uncoventionality or the "miraculous" in fact to have occurred in antiquity? The careful historian must acquire the seemingly less ambitious disposition and instead settle upon the more fundamental question, specifically, what did the earliest Christian documents seek to communicate? For, if the literary evidence demonstrates that the earliest Christian documents did not convey an historical resurrection-ascension, then the question of the possibility of the miraculous becomes moot, at least in this case. Notwithstanding, the present study does allow that the earliest Christians and most Mediterranean inhabitants held a worldview that included the possibility of divine intervention or intrusion into the mundane operations of the world. Thus, within the prescribed methodology, the scholar's worldview concerning the inclusion or exclusion of the "miraculous" in world history obtains no particular importance or consequence to the present region of study. One merely seeks to grasp the connotative tenor and impressive sense that the resurrection narratives of the four Gospels would have conjured within the mind of the implied ancient reader.

The Anthropological Pattern of the Hero

In 1909 in Vienna, one of Sigmund Freud's closest collaborators Otto Rank published his influential treatise *Der Mythus von der Geburt des Helden*, in which Rank pioneered a psychoanalytic theory behind heroic birth narratives. Rank, in keeping with Freud's work with Oedipus and dream theory, sought to describe a pattern recurrent in such stories and an underlying, inherent psychological value for that pattern in human literature through the ages. Inasmuch as Rank's pattern(s) transcended the processes of cultural interaction across civilizations and epochs, Rank indeed succeeded in demonstrating a non-genetic phenomenology that properly relocates the analysis toward a psychoanalytic and anthropological explanation.

While much of Freud's conceptual theory regarding subconscious psychological patterns is now outdated, having been replaced in the field by models better validated, Freud's basic thesis that the patterned phenomena that constitute our dreams and the most curious, transcendent features that form our cultural stories subconsciously address our mental needs and processes has proven altogether valid.[23] Since the discovery of REM sleep in the 1950s, researchers have developed new models to explain the function of sleep within both animals and humans. Until recently, such studies have not yielded adequate results. From an evolutionary standpoint, theorists have been forced to answer, what vital function must sleep serve such that its benefits outweigh the patent risks of being rendered unconscious and vulnerable for many hours every day? What happens during sleep that is vital for survival? Current breakthroughs have lead the way at finally answering these perplexing questions. Sleep researchers Robert Stickgold, Pierre Maquet, Carlyle Smith, and Patrick McNamara have demonstrated that sleep is essential for healthy brain plasticity:

Brain plasticity refers to the ability of the brain to persistently change its structure and function according to the genetic information, in response to environmental changes or to comply with the interaction between these two factors (Chen and Tonegawa 1997; Kolb and Whishaw 1998). By facilitating brain plasticity, sleep would allow the organism to adapt its behavior to the circumstances, within the constraints set by species-specific genetic material.[24]

Patrick McNamara at the Evolutionary Neurobehavior Laboratory at Boston University, moreover, has fruitfully explored the subconscious features of human "dream" psychology and their significance in the human plight for survival and special success.[25] Contrary to prior understandings, dream content is not the product of arbitrary mental exercises, a meaningless stream of mental forms; dream content arises out of the subconsciously discerned survival and adaptive needs of the individual in relation to its social and physical environment. These "myths" apply and strengthen advantageous patterns within the human mind and reference our deepest psychological needs.

In many ways following the footsteps of James George Frazer, Claude Lévi-Strauss established the field of structural anthropology in the mid-twentieth century. Prefiguring and congruent with the aforesaid findings in dream theory, Lévi-Strauss demonstrated that the mythic dimensions of cultural stories, rather than being the mere arbitrary product of a supposed whimsical human imagination, arise out of the innate anthropological, psychic disposition of the peoples who produce and value them. The cultural myth thus emerges as a bricolage of patterns addressing the transcendent, subconscious (often primal) needs of the human mind. As psychoanalytic theorist Jacques Lacan and his successors have shown, such mythic structures recur, driving the narrative imagination, due largely to this common anthropological service, not merely as an innocent function of cultural tradition or "entertainment."[26]

In a similar vein and following in the tradition of Rank, Lord Raglan's 1936 publication, *The Hero: A Study in Tradition, Myth, and Drama* succeeded in identifying a recurring pattern in "hero" narratives across times in civilizations, in this case not merely limited to distinctive "birth narrative" motifs. In this significant work, Raglan set out a cluster of twenty-two features that constitute the "hero" pattern (178–79) (List 3.1):

List 3.1: Elements of Raglan's Hero Pattern

- The hero's mother is a royal virgin;
- His father is a king, and
- Often a near relative of his mother, but
- The circumstances of his conception are unusual, and
- He is also disputed to be the son of a god.
- At birth an attempt is made, usually by his father or his maternal grandfather, to kill him, but

- He is spirited away, and
- Reared by foster-parents in a far country.
- We are told nothing of his childhood, but
- On reaching manhood he returns or goes to his future kingdom.
- After a victory over the king and/or a giant, dragon, or wild beast,
- He marries a princess, often the daughter of his predecessor, and
- Becomes king.
- For a time he reigns uneventfully, and
- Prescribes laws, but
- Later he loses favour with the gods and/or his subjects, and
- Is driven from the throne and city, after which
- He meets with a mysterious death,
- Often at the top of a hill.
- His children, if any, do not succeed him.
- His body is not buried, but nevertheless
- He has one or more holy sepulchers.

Having established this list of heroic pattern features, Raglan then proceeded to score a variety of heroic figures: Oedipus, Theseus, Romulus, Heracles, Perseus, Jason, Bellerophon, Pelops, Asclepius, Dionysus, Apollo, Zeus, Joseph, Moses, Elijah, Watu Gnung, Nyikang, Sigurd (or Siegried), Llew Llawgyffes, Arthur, and Robin Hood, to which Berkeley folklorist Alan Dundes has properly since added Jesus (who scored seventeen out of the Raglan's above-listed twenty-two elements).[27]

Twentieth-century Swiss psychologist Carl Jung postulated the notion of a human "collective unconscious," a set of archetypal, conceptual forms common to all human psychology. In his final work before his death in 1961, Jung expounded his theory of "archetypes":

Dreams serve the purpose of compensation. This assumption means that the dream is a normal psychic phenomenon that transmits unconscious reactions or spontaneous impulses to consciousness. Many dreams can be interpreted with the help of the dreamer, who provides both the associations to and the context of the dream image, by means of which one can look at all its aspects.

This method is adequate in all ordinary cases, such as those when a relative, a friend, or a patient tells you a dream more or less in the course of conversation. But when it is a matter of obsessive dreaming or of highly emotional dreams, the personal associations produced by the dreamer do not usually suffice for a satisfactory interpretation. In such cases, we have to take into consideration the fact (first observed and commented by Freud) that elements often occur in a dream that are not individual and that cannot be derived from the dreamer's personal experience. These elements, as I have previously mentioned, are what Freud called "archaic remnants"—mental forms whose presence cannot be explained by anything in the individual's own life and which seem to be aboriginal, innate, and inherited shapes of the human mind.

Just as the human body represents a whole museum of organs, each with a long evolutionary history behind it, so we should expect to find that the mind is organized in a similar way. It can no more be a product without history than is the body in which it exists. By "history" I do not mean the fact that the mind builds itself up by conscious reference to the past through language and other cultural traditions. I am referring to the biological, prehistoric, and unconscious development of the mind in archaic man, whose psyche was still close to that of the animal.[28]

Freud's "archaic remnants" and Jung's "collective unconscious" appear to be the modern conceptual successors to Plato's noetic Forms as, for instance, presented by Socrates's Parable of the Cave (*Republic* 514a–520a). Lending continuity to these observed phenomena, the aforementioned research in analytic "dream" psychology allows that many recurrent, psychic features arise out of innate genetic predisposition.

While such theory when applied to transcendent cultural motifs may often prove, at least in part, quite valid, one may wonder if this principle need be enlisted as an explanation of the manifest, universal aspects of the "hero" narrative. Should one wonder that cultures universally produce superhuman projections, avatar figures who transcend the most severe and grievous limitations of the human condition? Should one become astonished that the principal, defining features of such mythopoeic biographies contain superhuman birth and death / translation narratives as grand, framing book-ends, despite the cultures whence these arise? A superhuman source and destination for the hero appears to be a rational pattern of embellishment, not necessarily suggesting the presence of Jungian archetypes.

Regardless of the extent to which Jung's "archetypes" or Freud's "archaic remnants" may yet provide useful insights into the survival patterns and social impulses of the lower brain, the study of generic anthropological structures in hero fabulation across the span of time and cultures has shown to be a compelling methodological enterprise of great promise. Perhaps Joseph Campbell's popular 1949 study *The Hero with a Thousand Faces* would better have resided under this methodological rubric, rather than his more narrow reliance upon the work of Jung. The insight of dream theorists within analytic psychology assists the present study, perhaps above all else, by reminding that cultural production, in this case the mythopoeic produc-tion of heroic stories in classical antiquity, is not a mere innocent fashioning of aesthetic entertainment. If dreams fundamentally cultivate the patterns of human-conditioned adaptation, and thus are vital to the effort to process the challenges of an ever-changing world, then story, literature, and film serve the same ends, only within consciously governed media. This seemingly whimsical process accrues insights, values and modeled skills toward the fulfillment of the instincts of the lower brain, and the negotiation of social power, within our semi- and subconscious psychology, and as such provides what one experiences as the pleasure of "entertainment." Myth and fiction are not, therefore, mere superfluous *hominum desiderata*, but are integral necessities of the human plight.[29]

Archetypal Mimesis in Classical Antiquity

After taking a more high-resolution look, however, at the heroic patterns of classical Mediterranean antiquity, a different picture arises. The Hellenistic and Roman cultures consciously, and not merely subconsciously, imitated the Hellenic and Hellenistic archetypal forms, in this case specifically, their heroic figures. One finds such conscious archetypal mimesis operative and ubiquitous in Hellenistic and Roman art, coins, and literature. Indeed, ὁ ἑλληνισμός precisely entailed *imitatio graecorum* as its single, essential characteristic in classical Mediterranean cultures from the time of Plato and Aristotle onward.[30]

When considering, more specifically, the heroic and political portraits of the Hellenistic and Roman periods of the Greek East, the Hellenic demigods served as the archetypal heroic patterns, each having one human and one divine parent (Table 3.1).

Within the comprehensive hierarchical Greek and Roman worlds, a ladder of gradation or a continuum existed ranging from mundane to divine.[31] The theological chasm present in modern monotheistic religious thought between divinity and humanity did not exist. The self-conscious comprehension of the mythic quality of the divine in antiquity provided one prominent reason (or result) related to this difference, accounting for the open-ended and often nebulous catalogue of demigods in classical antiquity.[32] In most instances, this was not a scientific taxonomy; assigning an individual the rank of "demigod" became a function of honorific embellishment for kings, founders, sages, and sacred figures, elevating them to superhuman station, thus distinguishing and signifying such persons as fantastic or exceptional. Indeed, the Euhemerist tradition, that is, the practice of comprehending the Greek and Roman pantheon as apotheosized humans of a distant, archaic past, extended from the time of Alexander in the late fourth century and the writing of the Euhemerus's Ἱερὰ ἀναγραφή well into Roman late antiquity, serving as evidence of the prominent influence that the custom of deification came to hold, even to the extent of subsuming the classical divine cast under the tradition.[33]

The philosophical criticism set forth by Plutarch, however, sought to press this "soft," nonliteral phenomenon into the more difficult place of hard factuality. In this revealing excerpt, he criticized the "ascension" subtheme of deification through the critical lens of Middle Platonism, rejecting the ascension of the human σῶμα:

οὐδὲν οὖν δεῖ τὰ σώματα τῶν ἀγαθῶν συναναπέμπειν παρὰ φύσιν εἰς οὐρανόν, ἀλλὰ τὰς ἀρετὰς καὶ τὰς ψυχὰς παντάπασιν οἴεσθαι

Table 3.1 Prominent Hellenic Demigods

	Sired by Zeus / Jupiter	
Demigod(dess)	Description	Mortal Mother
Achilles	Lydian boy who contested Aphrodite	Lamia
Aethlius	King of Elis	Calyce
Alexander	King of Macedon, conqueror of the East	Olympias
Amphion	King of Thebes	Antiope
Argus / Pelasgus	King of Argos	Niobe
Atymnius	Worshipped on Crete	Cassiopeia
Castor	One of the epic "Gemini" heroes	Leda
Corinthus	Eponymous founder of Corinth	?
Crinacus	Father of Macareus	?
Dardanus	Founded the city Dardania	Electra
Emathion	King of Samothrace	Electra
Endymion	King of Elis	Calyce
Epaphus	King of Egypt	Io
Graecus	Grecian king	Thyia
Helen	Queen of Sparta	Leda
Hellen	Grecian king	Pyrrha
Hercules	Foremost hero of strength and skill	Alcmene
Hercules	Hero of Thebes	Lysithoë
Herophile	First sibylline priestess of the Greeks	Lamia
Iasion	Demigod of the Samothracian mysteries	Electra
Latinus	King of Latium	Pandora
Macedon	Eponymous first king of Macedonia	Thyia
Magnes	Eponymous first king of Magnesia	Thyia
Minos	King of Crete	Europa
Myrmidon	King of Phthiotis	Eurymedusa
Perseus	Founder of Mycenae	Danaë
Pirithous	King of the Lapithia tribe, Thessaly	Dia
Pollux	One of the epic "Gemini" heroes	Leda
Rhadamanthus	Wise ruler of Crete	Europa
Sarpedon	King of Lycia	Europa
Sarpedon	King of Lycia (later)	Laodamia
Tityus	Boeotian giant	Elara
Zethus	King of Thebes	Antiope

(*Continued*)

Table 3.1 (Continued)

Sired by Apollo		
Demigod(dess)	Description	Mortal Mother
Amphiaraus	King of Argos	Hypermnestra
Amphissus	King of Dryopia	Dryope
Amphithemis	Libyan king	Acacallis
Anius	King of Delos	Rhoeo
Argeus	Ruler of Diphys	Euboea
Asclepius	Demigod of healing	Coronis
Branchus	Founded a clan of prophets	Woman of Miletus
Chaeron	Eponymous hero of the city Chaeronea	Thero
Coronus	King of Sicyon	Chrysorthe
Cycnus	Prince of Hyria	Hyria
Delphus	Ruler / Founder of Delphi	Celaeno
Dorus	Founder of the Dorians	Phthia
Epidaurus	King of Epidaurus	?
Eriopis	Princess of Messenia	Arsinoe
Erymanthus	Ruler of Arcadia	?
Hilaeira	Princess of Messenia	Philodice
Hilaeira	Priestess of Athena and Artemis	Wife of Leucippus
Iamus	Founded an order of Olympian priests	Evadne
Idmon	Argonaut seer	Asteria
Ion	Founded Helike; Founded the Ionians	Creüsa
Laodocus	Aetolian king	Phthia
Linus	Prince of Argos	Psamathe
Lycomedes	King of Scyros	Parthenope
Melaneus	Founded Oechalia	?
Miletus	King of Melitus	Areia
Mopsus	Seer and ruler of Cilicia	Manto
Oncus	King of Arcadia	?
Orpheus	Archaic Greek bard and prophet	Daughter of Pierus
Parthenos	Princess of the island of Naxos	Chrysothemis
Philammon	Bard and king of Phocis	Chione
Phoebe	Priestess of Athena and Artemis	Wife of Leucippus
Polypoetes	King of Aetolia	Phthia
Pytheaus	Founded the cult of Apollo in Argos	?
Tenerus	Priest of Apollo on Mt. Ptous	Melia
Tenes	King of the island of Tenedos	Proclia
Troilus	Trojan prince	Hecuba
Trophonius	Prince of Minyan Orchomenus	Wife of Erginus

κατὰ φύσιν καὶ δίκην θείαν ἐκ μὲν ἀνθρώπων εἰς ἥρωας, ἐκ δ' ἡρώων
εἰς δαίμονας, ἐκ δὲ δαιμόνων, ἂν τέλεον ὥσπερ ἐν τελετῇ καθαρθῶσι
καὶ ὁσιωθῶσιν ἅπαν ἀποφυγοῦσαι τὸ θνητὸν καὶ παθητικόν, οὐ
νόμῳ πόλεως, ἀλλ' ἀληθείᾳ καὶ κατὰ τὸν εἰκότα λόγον εἰς θεοὺς
ἀναφέρεσθαι, τὸ κάλλιστον καὶ μακαριώτατον τέλος ἀπολαβούσας.

(*Vita Romuli* 28.8)

On account of being against the natural order, it is necessary, therefore, not to send off to heaven the bodies of good individuals, but instead to suppose that, according to natural order and divine justice, their virtues and souls altogether be translated from being men to being heroes, and from being heroes to being demigods, and finally, provided they have been purified and made holy, having escaped mortality, from being demigods to being gods, not by civic custom, but in alignment with reality and sound reason; in this way, the lives of such individuals obtain the best and most blessed conclusion.

Notice that the standing convention, that of which Plutarch was critical, arose out of civic or social custom. While specific archetypal figures served as mimetic templates in the biographical embellishment of the array of such individuals, both fictive and historical, whom society elevated via these processes, the tradition itself took on a predominantly political and aristocratic function. Of those promoted, moreover, most were rulers, often founding figures located in etiological narrative (see Table 3.1, for examples), some were priests, and a few were exceptional athletes, poets, or philosophers.[34]

From a semiotic standpoint, the convention or custom of deification relied upon the display of mimetic signals related to specific archetypal figures established early in the tradition. Of these, a select few served as archetypal demigods, supplying the semiotic narrational patterns of the tradition. This special list typically included Heracles, Dionysus, Castor and Pollux, Asclepius, and Romulus, the premiere iconic figures of classical antiquity whom Anton Elter described as *"ein bestimmter Kanon von Halbgöttern."*[35] In his *de Natura Deorum*, Cicero explicitly explained the policy, listing the archetypes:[36]

Suscepit autem vita hominum consuetudoque communis ut beneficiis excellentis viros in caelum fama ac voluntate tollerent. Hinc Hercules hinc Castor et Pollux hinc Aesculapius hinc Liber etiam . . . hinc etiam Romulus, quem quidem eundem esse Quirinum putant, quorum cum remanerent animi atque aeternitate fruerentur, rite di sunt habiti, cum et optimi essent et aeterni.

(2.24)

Human manner and community custom have established that they, as regards fame and disposition, raise up to heaven persons of distinguished benefaction. Thus, Hercules, Castor and Pollux, Aesculapius, Liber (i.e., Dionysus), . . . and Romulus, the same one whom they regard as Quirinus, with their souls enduring and enjoying eternal life, are fittingly regarded as gods, since they are the very best and are immortal.

Cicero's description affords striking clarity, particularly given his role as the prominent Roman senator during the tumultuous transition from *res publica* to *imperium* in the first century B.C.E., a position interior to the institution of the imperial "apotheosis" tradition under Octavian. Deification was, as Cicero plainly wrote, honorific, not literal. That the "translation" tradition, from its very inception, functioned as "fable" obtains special attention throughout the book, informing the fundamental matter of modality and the cultural, narrative function invariably implied by the convention's use.

The most emphatic instances of deification drew mimetically upon the signature characteristics of these inceptive, archetypal figures. Yet, for the Romans, the relation to the Hellenic archetypal demigods often visibly shifts from *imitatio* to *aemulatio* or even to *rivalitas* particularly with the liminal figures of the late Republic and early Principate. Leading into this period, with the Roman government then faced with the dilapidation of the *res publica* in the first century B.C.E., Rome saw the rise of singular potent figures. These were polarizing, charismatic military and political leaders who divided her regions east and west, first Pompeius Magnus and Julius Caesar (of the First Triumvirate), then Marcus Antonius and Octavian (of the Second Triumvirate). Of these, Pompey the Great and Mark Antony engaged most vigorously in acts of *imitatio deorum*, following the imperial tradition of governance over the former Hellenistic kingdoms of the Levant. These acts, as we shall consider, were to be rendered as excessive and immodest by Julius Caesar's and Octavian's respective regimes in the Latin West.

In classical antiquity, mimetic associations may exist in either of two directions: (1) by stylizing or rendering one figure with the signature qualities of an archetypal figure or, (2) by refashioning an archetypal figure with the distinctive features or narrative of a given, associated person. Describing these two aspects with respect to visual representation, John Pollini has written:

An important feature of religious belief and political rhetoric in the late Republic and the principate is the special relationship that individual leaders claimed to enjoy with the gods, an idea which served to enhance the leader's position in the state and to validate his acts. In the visual arts an association with the divine could be expressed most directly through assimilation or imitation of a divinity. Divine assimilation comprises either the alteration of an individual's portrait so that he looks like a god, or the representation of a god with some degree of physiognomic resemblance to a specific individual. In either case, there may be ambiguity as to whether a man is portrayed like a god, or a god like a man.[37]

Broadening Pollini's scope, however, these two strategies of association should expand to include "historical" archetypal figures (e.g., Alexander the Great, Socrates, or Caesar Augustus) and should apply equally to visual as to literary rendition. In both cases, moreover, the "figure" should connote the persona conceived in cultural or popular myth, not merely a "raw" historical person or even the detailed rendition of a specific divine or fictive figure, unlike direct textual, syntagmatic mimesis. With archetypal mimesis, the semiotic relationship exists first as an order of associated images, often culturally sketched in the form of mental caricatures and simple, well-trodden narratives that come to conjure or embody the iconic persona, *le beau idéal*, in the public imagination. In Livy's alternative account of the disappearance of Romulus, for instance, instead of his ascension to heaven, Romulus suffers cruel betrayal and assassination at the hands of his own senators (1.16.4); thus, the Augustan writer renders the great Roman founding figure in imitation of Julius Caesar. In similar fashion, as Clifford Weber has elucidated for us, did Virgil's Aeneas imitate the Dionysian association of Mark Antony, not to mention Aeneas's additional *imitatio* of both Apollo and Augustus to be noted elsewhere and throughout the epic.[38]

In their mimesis, what traits did these archetypal images invoke? From the field of classical studies, several prominent works have emerged specifically related to this notion of archetypal figures in ancient Mediterranean culture(s), culling data from a wide array of primary sources. Arthur Darby Nock's 1928 article "Notes on Ruler-Cult, I–IV" (*Journal of Hellenic Studies* 48:1 [1928], 21–43) described the language and nature of such associations, particularly as related to Hellenistic and Roman ruler imagery. Nock, for instance, provided a substantive section on the appellation νέος Διό νυσος, a title applied to such figures as Mithridates IV, Ptolemy XII, Ptolemy XIII, Mark Antony, Gaius, Trajan, Hadrian, Antinous, Antoninus Pius, and Commodus. *Imitatio Bacchi*, particularly when applied to the Hellenistic and Roman rulers, by extension likewise signaled candidacy for the imperial legacy of Alexander, that is, *imitatio Alexandri*, as oriental conqueror and world-ruler. The designation "νέος" expands, however, to include the full range of archetypal figures and may apply, in substitution, a variety of interchangeable terms, such as καινός, ἕτερος, ἄλλος, δεύτερος, and ὁπλό τερος. Nock's article, moreover, likewise becomes instructive in recalling that the *imitatio* of these archetypal figures did not imply an ontological identification or equivalency. After careful survey and analysis, Nock concluded: "There is not, therefore, in general a definite popular belief that a particular ruler is in a strict sense the reincarnation of a particular deity" (p. 35).

Andrew Runni Anderson's 1928 article "Heracles and His Successors: A Study of a Heroic Ideal and the Recurrence of a Heroic Type" (*Harvard*

Studies in Classical Philology 39, pp. 7–58) stands as the first substantive treatment of archetypal mimesis in classical studies and has provided a scrupulous introduction to this towering icon and his pervasive, mimetic presence as antiquity's most prominent emblem of power. Anderson's survey exposes *en clair* that the figure of Heracles invoked two distinct, potent images: that of κοσμοκράτωρ (world-ruler) and that of σωτήρ (deliverer and liberator). Concerning the former role, the first-century Bithynian historian Dio Chrysostom closed his first essay on "proper kingship" with the following familiar myth:

κἀκεῖνος ἐπέτρεψεν αὐτῷ βασιλεύειν τοῦ σύμπαντος ἀνθρώπων
γένους, ὡς ὄντι ἱκανῷ τοιγαροῦν ὅπου μὲν ἴδοι τυραννίδα καὶ
τύραννον, ἐκόλαζε καὶ ἀνήρει παρά τε Ἕλλησι καὶ βαρβάροις· ὅπου
δὲ βασιλείαν καὶ βασιλέα, ἐτίμα καὶ ἐφύλαττεν. καὶ διὰ τοῦτο τῆς
γῆς καὶ τῶν ἀνθρώπων ἔφη Σωτῆρα εἶναι, οὐχ ὅτι τὰ θηρία αὐτοῖς
ἀπήμυνεν—πόσον γὰρ ἄν τι καὶ βλάψειε λέων ἢ σῦς ἄγριος;—ἀλλ'
ὅτι τοὺς ἀνημέρους καὶ πονηροὺς ἀνθρώπους ἐκόλαζε καὶ τῶν
ὑπερηφάνων τυράννων κατέλυε καὶ ἀφηρεῖτο τὴν ἐξουσίαν. καὶ νῦν
ἔτι τοῦτο δρᾷ, καὶ βοηθός ἐστι καὶ φύλαξ σοι τῆς ἀρχῆς ἕως ἂν
τυγχάνῃς βασιλεύων.

(*Or.* 1.84)

[Due to the excellent qualities of Heracles,] Zeus entrusted Heracles to rule over all of humankind. And so, on account of his being suitable for the task, wherever Heracles discovered a tyranny and a tyrant, he punished and destroyed them, among Greeks and barbarians alike; but wherever he found a kingdom and a king, he gave honor and protection. This . . . was what made him Liberator of the earth and of humankind, not the fact that he protected them from the savage beasts—for how little damage could a lion or a wild bear inflict?—no, it was the fact that he chastised untame and evil people, and destroyed and took away the authority of insolent tyrants. And now, even to this day, Heracles continues this work and you have him as a helper and protector of your realm for as long as you may reign.

Also tracing the political function of *imitatio Herculis*, though with much greater depth, Ulrich Huttner's *Die politische Rolle der Heraklesgestalt im greschishen Herrschertum* (Stuttgart, Franz Steiner Verlag, 1997) focused on the sustained, traditional role that archetypal mimesis of Heracles played in the Hellenistic period beginning with Alexander, particularly as evident in the Seleucid and Ptolemaic monarchies. Throughout the period of the Roman Principate, as Simon Price has well elucidated and as this study has discussed, the funerary custom of the apotheosis "pyre" ascension mimetically followed the translation fable of this most preeminent archetypal hero.[39]

The archetypal figure "Romulus" arose out of the etiological myths of Naevius, Fabius Pictor, Ennius, and the historians of the late Republican and Principate periods, with likely antecedents in archaic Roman oral culture. Considering the nature of etiological narrative generally, Peter Green astutely observes that "crucial to social stability had to be the function of myths in providing explanations, authorization or empowerment for the present in terms of origins: this could apply, not only to foundations or charter myths and genealogical trees (thus supporting family or territorial claims) but also to personal moral choices."[40] As with all *aitia*, these founding myths proved quite malleable in their creative, fabulous content and typically arose out of and were configured to the weighty performative concerns of a text's present historical, socio-political location. This observation of modal constitution and function prevails as much for the etiological stories of the Christians, namely, the Gospels, as for the creative narrations of the regal period of the Roman nation. The liberal, near-whimsical variance between the early Christian foundation tales, not to mention their myriad of conventional fictive signals, indicated for the ancient reader a mythopoeic modality, however nuanced to form a distinctive "early Christian" brand. Matthew Fox has detailed the variance in the legends of the early Roman monarchs as rendered in service to the different designs of the Roman historians.[41] The literary "Romulus" of the early Principate came to resemble the signature attributes of Julius Caesar or Augustus, just as, conversely, these figures in turn came to emulate their founding patron and monarch.[42] Although a full treatment of *imitatio Romuli* has yet to emerge, Jane DeRose Evans's *The Art of Persuasion: Political Propaganda from Aeneas to Brutus* provides a substantive survey of the political role and the function that the "Romulus" legends served from the time of the Punic Wars through to the age of Augustus. From Cossus to Scipio Africanus to Caesar and Augustus, imitation of Romulus sought to legitimate these towering liminal figures of Roman political history. As this study has explored and as Simon Price likewise has briefly noted, the funerary custom of the "apotheosis" eyewitness mimetically followed the translation fable of the signified monarchical icon of Roman origins, the exalted Romulus.[43]

Imitatio Alexandri became the standard royal pattern among the βασιλεῖs Ἑλληνισταί of the Antigonid, Ptolemaic, Seleucid, and Attalid dynasties, upon the division of Alexander's oriental conquests. With the Second Punic War, through the propagandized figures of Hannibal and Scipio Africanus, respectively, both the rising empires of Carthage and Rome vied for the crowning imperial legacy of Alexander.[44] With the emerging Roman interest in extending and sustaining the empire in the eastern Mediterranean, moreover, archetypal mimesis of the emblems of the Greek East took a central place in Roman imperial propaganda.[45] As far back as Alexander, the precedence for mythologized cultural-political imagery and propaganda had already been well established, extending forward into the Hellenistic kingdoms and imperial Rome. Deborah Steiner comments:

> With Alexander (and to a lesser extent, his father Philip), official control of information and media develops into an important function of autocracy. This means that the way in which historians recorded their actions became an integral function of their reigns. The high level of control over his own image that Alexander appears to have achieved became formalized in the Hellenistic kingdoms, developing into a significant element in the burgeoning propaganda machines of these emerging states.[46]

In a very real sense, all such propaganda of ruling figures following Alexander stood as the most fundamental expression of *imitatio Alexandri*.

Non-literary Hellenistic and Roman archetypal mimesis often took the form of distinctive physical attributes, raiment, or other signature symbols and imagery. The chosen mimetic traits logically depended upon those qualities which one wished to assign emphasis. While focusing, as one of numerous vivid examples, on Q. Pompeius's *imitatio Alexandri*, Diana Spencer writes:

> As becomes clear, the power figures that dominated Rome in the first century did not exist in isolation, and each was closely involved with his older contemporaries. Pompey was born c. 105 BCE, into an influential equestrian family from Picenum. He had the foresight to side with Sulla when he landed at Brundisium in 83 BCE, and after success in fighting against the Marian veterans he was acclaimed *Magnus* by his troops. This, together with Pompey's supposed cultivation of Alexandrian appearance, emphasizes the developing association between 'Alexander' and potential Roman greatness. He was already a sufficiently significant figure in the Roman consciousness for his appropriation of Pompey to be useful, and the main associations must still have been positive. A second associative level is invoked by the story that Pompey's *'magnus'* (The Great) was awarded to him 'spontaneously' by his soldiers. This idea of the general as 'one of the men', a commander who had the complete and utter loyalty of his troops and who shared their dangers and triumphs, tied him directly to images of Alexander the Great as an all-conquering general and ruler. These two areas of comparison are completed by the tradition that Pompey deliberately cultivated an Alexander-style image, longish curling hair, and an upward tilt of the head, in his portraiture. In this development of attributes of Alexander as ultimate eastern conqueror, favored by the gods, is coming an important model for Roman power-seekers. It is not until the end of Caesar's life and the propaganda battle between Antony and Octavian that we find the negative comparisons with Alexander being brought into play, for example: drunkenness,

tyrannous monarchy, obsession with personal glory, and aspiration to divinity.[47]

Comparing the range of numismatic and statued portraiture, in like manner, Karl Galinsky observes concerning Pompey:

> There is a "citation" of Alexander by means of the parted hair over the right forehead. It is reminiscent of the youthful world conqueror's tossed-back hair, which Pompey deliberately affected in imitation of Alexander (Plut., *Pomp.* 2) and which appears in Pompey's portraits in combination with his placid, kindly mien.[48]

Following the defeat of Mithridates the Great and Tigranes the Great, Pompey eventually established Roman provincial rule over the former Seleucid regions of Anatolia and Syria, and, aiding the Hasmonean king Hyrcanus II in his siege on Jerusalem in 63 B.C.E. to defeat the Hellenists under Aristobulus II, the general secured Roman supremacy in Palestine. These exploits in the Greek East placed Pompey under the shadow of the principal emblem of the Hellenistic world, divine Alexander himself, such that the saying arose on the streets of Athens hailing Pompey and his fame: "The more you know you are a man, the more you become a god" (ἐφ' ὅσον ὦν ἄνθρωπος οἶδας, ἐπὶ τοσοῦτον εἶ θεός; Plutarch, *Pomp.* 27.3). Appian of Alexandria, Roman historian during the Antonine Dynasty, recorded the inscription given at Pompey's burial monument: "What a pitiful tomb for one bestowed with so many temples" τῷ ναοῖς βρίθοντι πόση ἀπάνις ἔπλετο τύμβου.[49] As with Alexander *et alii*, at stake in all of these mimetic echoes was not an actual claim for Pompey to ontological divinity *qua* "divine"; supreme cultural-political legitimacy and significance were at stake as registered through the most potent iconic symbolisms, that is, legible cultural themes invoking the legacy of Hellenistic power.[50] The postmortem renditions of Pompeius Magnus, as, for instance, provided by Plutarch, fashioned this historic figure within the signature, structural qualities of Alexander in order to signify the Roman general as bearer of that most exalted legacy in the Greek East.[51]

After Pompey's defeat by Julius Caesar and his subsequent death in Egypt at the hands of Ptolemy XIII in 48 B.C.E., Caesar, so it would appear, failed to secure fully the divine monarchical legacies of the eastern provinces; this is evidenced in part by the continued polarization between East and West, as witnessed between Antony and Octavian during the institution of the *triumviri rei publicae constituendae*, that is, the Second Triumvirate. These contests were as much a battle of cultural image and propaganda as they were a matter of military skill. Where Julius Caesar failed in the former, Octavian, soon to be Caesar Augustus, did illustriously succeed.

Regrettably, the powerful Augustan and subsequent periods did not allow for a fair, positive historical or biographical treatment of Antony, particularly with respect to his apparent successes in projecting a divine, royal image as emergent ruler in the Hellenistic provinces of the Levant.[52] All that survives as direct evidence of such protracted success, namely, the setting forth of a mythic, "divine" Antony, are various numismatic images, inscriptions, and statuary.[53] Antony fashioned himself as the new Osiris, the new Dionysus, the new Heracles, and, by extension, the new Alexander. Octavian, however, successfully turned all of these attempts at political *imitatio* against Antony. With regard to Antony's extensive *imitatio Alexandri* in the Greek East, Diana Spencer writes:

> Going East means traveling into a world defined as much by myth and fiction as by hard fact. To journey eastwards is to take a trip into a region dominated by stories of excessive consumption, of luxury and wantonness, of sexual profligacy, and decadent refinement. A place where men are made effeminate and gender roles are turned upside down, where kings rule as despots over their people, and magic and superstition are rife. This is the kind of world that Roman Alexander narratives invoke, and the seductive, aggressively degenerative characteristics of the storied East are apparent throughout all of the versions of 'Alexander'. Suetonius represents Antony degenerating in Alexandrian terms: he fails to conduct himself as befits a Roman (for which we might read in 'Macedonian'; *Aug.* 17.1), and his adoption of the roles of new-Dionysus, new-Helios, and descendant of Hercules bolster the comparison with Alexander and its increasingly problematic overtones. Curtius' use of the slogan *'uindex publicae libertatis'* (defender of the public freedom; 8.5.20, 10.2.6–7), in conjunction with a growing, though ineffectual series of challenges to Alexander's authority transforms this changed, orientalized Alexander into an enemy within. Curtius' emphasis on the Macedonian inability to shake off Alexander's increasing orientalism is comparable to popular distaste for Antony's supposed enslavement by the 'barbarian Queen,' Cleopatra. A connection between the above slogan and the motif of *dominatio* (essentially an expression of tyranny: government by a Lord or Master) in propaganda against Antony is evident in the particular hostility shown by Augustus to the term. The negative implications of the word make it easy to see how a contemporary inference could be drawn from the use of *uindex publicae liberatis* as an epithet for an opponent of Alexander's orientalization. Plutarch describes how Antony sought to play up through his dress a supposed likeness to Hercules in features, but in the end, subdued by the spells of Cleopatra, his similarity was more akin to Hercules disarmed by Omphale. Imitation of Hercules and Dionysus leads to Alexander, a line traced directly by Plutarch in his 'Life of Antony' (*Ant.* 4, 24, 54, 60). If Antony was descended from Hercules and became a new Dionysus in life, then his *imperium* still had aspirations to Alexander's universal empire, with its centre at the symbolic capital of Alexandria. Buying into this imagery, Antony opened himself

to charges of luxury, orientalism, and *dominatio* from Octavian, who had difficulty in convincing the Senate of the dangers of such an orientalizing course. The convergence of terms applied to Antony and Alexander encompass not only these 'dangers,' but also the 'threat' of enchantment by a barbarian wife.[54]

To this, Richard Stoneman adds:

Dietmar Kienast (1969) . . . built on the more wide-ranging discussion by Alfred Heuss (1954), to show how Augustus' own use of Alexander in his propaganda attempted rather successfully to reconcile two quite incompatible views. On the one hand, Mark Antony had already associated himself strongly with Alexander, as an oriental potentate, using Dionysiac imagery to colour his own self-presentation as Alexander had also done. Augustus had to use his 'oriental' representation of Antony to damage his opponent. On the other hand, the figure of Alexander as a world ruler had also been current in Roman thought for some time, not least in the legends that surrounded Scipio Africanus, whose birth was alleged to have been as miraculous as Alexander's. To establish his authority in the east, it suited Augustus to present himself as a new Alexander, visiting the latter's tomb in Alexandria and honouring the city. He also used an image of Alexander as his personal seal. His plan for a Parthian War is part of this Alexander imitation. In Rome, however, he had to be more cautious; as Kienast puts it, there was no room for Alexander in the world of the *Ara Pacis*.[55]

Especially in these cases, imperial propaganda in the Greek East sought to appropriate, eclipse, and even demote the crowning figures of Hellenistic culture. Consider the words of the leading court lyric poet to his emperor, Augustus. Horace wrote:

Cum tot sustineas et tanta negotia solus,
res Italas armis tuteris, moribus ornes,
legibus emends, in publica commoda peccem,
si longo sermone morer tua tempora, Caesar.
Romulus et Liber pater et cum Castore Pollux,
post ingentia facta deorum in templa recepti,
dum terras hominumque colunt genus, aspera bella
componunt, agros assignant, oppida condunt,
ploravere suis non respondere favorem
speratum meritis, diram qui contudit hydram
notaque fatali portenta labore subegit,
comperit invidiam supremo fine domari,
urit enim fulgore suo, qui praegravat artis
infra se positas; exstinctus amabitur idem.

praesenti tibi maturos largimur honores,
iurandasque tuum per numen ponimus aras,
nil oriturum alias, nil ortum tale fatentes.
Sed tuus hic populus sapiens et iustus in uno,
te nostris ducibus, te Grais anteferendo,
cetera nequaquam simili ratione modoque
aestimat et, nisi quae terris semota suisque
temporibus defuncta videt, fastidit et odit.

(Ep. 2.1.1–22)

I would be violating the public welfare, O Caesar, were I to waste your time with a long discourse, since you alone handle such great affairs, guarding Italy with armies, furnishing its code of conduct, reforming its laws. Romulus, Father Liber, and Castor and Pollux were granted deities' temples after their remarkable deeds, inasmuch as they cared for the earth and humankind and resolved harsh wars, allocated lands, and founded cities. They disparaged that the favor they received for themselves did not match their merits, even the one who destroyed the horrible Hydra, overcame in his fated Labours the famous monsters, and exposed his envy which was to be subdued in his ultimate death. Indeed, with a great flash of lightning he incinerated himself, that one who surpasses the abilities of those beneath him, and only after being deprived of life was he to be loved. Yet, while you are still with us, we bestow upon you fitting honors, and we erect altars at which to swear oaths by your divine majesty, confessing that such a one has never arisen nor will arise. But, your people are so wise and right in one matter alone, namely in placing you above our leaders and the Greeks, and they do not regard anyone else with a comparable reckoning or standard, but, with the exception of those whom they've seen being removed from the earth and finishing their time here, the people loath and disregard them.

From a Roman standpoint, the appropriation of the Hellenic iconic figures meant a kind of plundering or usurpation of Greek *imperium* in the East inasmuch as these potent symbols were so inextricably entrenched in the Mediterranean Orient.[56] With that appropriation, however, came a tacit acknowledgment of Hellenic cultural and political puissance dominating the legacy of Mediterranean rule throughout classical antiquity. As Horace did famously write, "*Graecia capta ferum victorem cepit et artis intulit agresti Latio.*"[57] The complexities of such appropriation, however, as Simon Price incisively has described, arose in the confluence of numerous cultural tributaries giving way to the pride of a distinctly Roman mythology.[58] This same measure of complexity came to characterize the heterogeneity of the Gospel traditions, distinctly Christian amalgams of Hellenistic, Roman, oriental, and specifically early Jewish cultural forms.

To make any claim or challenge to that Hellenistic legacy required the appropriation of its foremost symbols and images. To surpass or eclipse that legacy meant the mimetic production of consummate figures, that is, the proposition of new icons that embodied the best and greatest of the Greek heroic tradition. Aeneas must be greater than Odysseus, Romulus than Theseus, Augustus than Alexander. This process of *consummatio*, however, often entailed more than simply a one-to-one mimetic one-upmanship; *consummatio* meant the cultural proposition of singular figures comprising a bricolage of Hellenic / Hellenistic iconic themes and the absorption of related divine figures (e.g., the Egyptian Isis and the Roman Sol Invictus). Roman propaganda sought to elevate the profile, and thus the *auctoritas*, of the *princeps senatus*, by setting forth, for example, Caesar Augustus as not merely the new and improved Alexander, but at once the Roman embodiment of Heracles, Castor, Romulus, Mercury, Apollo, Aeneas, Julius Caesar, and the office of the empire's High Priest (*pontifex maximus;* conferred in 12 B.C.E. as the epigraphic calendar *Feriale Cumanum* reveals, "[eo die Caesar Pontifex Ma]ximus creatus est, supplicat[i]o Vestae").[59]

The success of Augustus lay not only with his oriental archetypal mimesis, but also with his claim to an occidental legacy of power. While one may accurately describe the career of Augustus as the highest ascension of power in the history of Western civilization, one finds upon closer examination a complex liminality, an ambition often modulated by Roman conservatism (*mos maiorum*), displays of modesty, and the legitimation of traditional, senatorial governance.[60] As Duncan Fishwick has detailed, the tradition of emulating the heroes, demigods, and deities of classical civilization arose not out of Italy, but out of Greece and Hellenistic Orient.[61] One would be severely mistaken, therefore, to confuse the emergence and presence of divine archetypal emulation by Roman political figures with a mere matter of "comparative cultures" or cultural borrowing or influence. The tacit function of such mimesis often served imperialistic ends through the claim to the legacies of these towering symbols of culturally entrenched Mediterranean authority. A part of the brilliance of the reign of Augustus resided in his success in appropriating this oriental practice, while not unduly upsetting the Roman aristocracy, a balance-beam walk perhaps especially visible in his romanized subsumption of the practice in his sought-after association with Romulus. Dio has provided a window into the extent of this volition:

Ὁ δ' οὖν Καῖσαρ πολλὰ μὲν καὶ πρότερον, ὅτε τὰ περὶ τῆς ἐξωμοσίας τῆς μοναρχίας καὶ τὰ περὶ τῆς τῶν ἐθνῶν διανομῆς διελέχθη, ἔλαβε· καὶ γὰρ τό τε τὰς δάφνας πρὸ τῶν βασιλείων αὐτοῦ προτίθεσθαι, καὶ τὸ τὸν στέφανον τὸν δρύινον ὑπὲρ αὐτῶν ἀρτᾶσθαι, τότε οἱ ὡς καὶ ἀεὶ τούς τε πολεμίους νικῶντι καὶ πολίτας σῴζοντι ἐψηφίσθη. καλεῖται δὲ τὰ βασίλεια παλάτιον, οὐχ ὅτι καὶ ἔδοξέ ποτε οὕτως αὐτὰ ὀνομάζεσθαι, ἀλλ' ὅτι ἔν τε τῷ Παλατίῳ ὁ Καῖσαρ ᾤκει καὶ ἐκεῖ τὸ στρατήγιον εἶχε, καί τινα καὶ πρὸς τὴν τοῦ Ῥωμύλου

προενοίκησιν φήμην ἡ οἰκία αὐτοῦ ἀπὸ τοῦ παντὸς ὄρους ἔλαβε· καὶ
διὰ τοῦτο κἂν ἄλλοθί που ὁ αὐτοκράτωρ καταλήῃ, τὴν τοῦ παλατίου
ἐπίκλησιν ἡ καταγωγὴ αὐτοῦ ἴσχει. ἐπεὶ δὲ καὶ τῷ ἔργῳ αὐτὰ
ἐπετέλεσεν, οὕτω δὴ καὶ τὸ τοῦ Αὐγούστου ὄνομα καὶ παρὰ τῆς
βουλῆς καὶ παρὰ τοῦ δήμου ἐπέθετο. βουληθέντων γάρ σφων
ἰδίως πως αὐτὸν προσειπεῖν, καὶ τῶν μὲν τὸ τῶν δὲ τὸ καὶ
ἐσηγουμένων καὶ αἱρουμένων, ὁ Καῖσαρ ἐπεθύμει μὲν ἰσχυρῶς
Ῥωμύλος ὀνομασθῆναι, αἰσθόμενος δὲ ὅτι ὑποπτεύεται ἐκ τούτου τῆς
βασιλείας ἐπιθυμεῖν, οὐκέτ' αὐτοῦ ἀντεποιήσατο, ἀλλὰ Αὔγουστος
ὡς καὶ πλεῖόν τι ἢ κατὰ ἀνθρώπους ὢν ἐπεκλήθη· πάντα γὰρ τὰ
ἐντιμότατα καὶ τὰ ἱερώτατα αὔγουστα προσαγορεύεται.

(53.16.4–8)

Caesar, therefore, received many honors, even earlier, when the matters
concerning refusal of monarchy and the distribution of the ethnic provinces were being discussed. For the right to place the sacred laurels in
front of his kingly abode and to hand the oaken crown above them was
then voted upon, these things showing that he was always victor over
his enemies and savior of the citizenry. His royal abode was called the
Palatium, not because it was ever determined that it should be named
as such, but because Caesar resided on the Palatine Hill and there also
was his military headquarters. His house, of no little fame, was the
place where Romulus had once lived. Thus, should the emperor live in
another residence, that place nevertheless receives the name "Palatium."
Once, by his labor, he had fulfilled his promises, the name "Augustus"
was bestowed upon him by the Senate and the people. For as they were
deciding what distinct title by which to address him, and people were
proposing and selecting various possibilities, Caesar strongly desired
that he be named "Romulus." But, after perceiving that they were sus-
pecting him to be desirous of kingship, he no longer laid claim to it, but
he was named "Augustus," since he was greater than men; for, all of the
most precious and sacred things are termed "augustus."

Not only did Octavian often dress like the imaged Romulus, he lived in
his house, sought to take on his name as his *agnomen*, and, as Suetonius
indicates, instead took the name "Augustus," providing an added association with Romulus as the *augustum augurium* (Suet., *Aug.* 7).[62] Considering
Octavian's method of deification in relation to Hellenistic and Roman tradition, Karl Galinsky writes:

Another notion that developed from early on, therefore, was that of
Octavian the savior. Soteriology was a common concept (and business)
in Hellenistic Greece, and until his accession as Augustus we find Octavian looking to both Greek and Roman traditions as he was building up
his divine aura in Rome. As previously mentioned, he belonged, unlike

any Roman leader before him, to all four major priesthoods. The numerous dreams, oracles, and portents linking him with divine parentage and providence also had their genesis in this period. One of them was that upon the assumption of his first consulate on August (still called Sextilis) 19, 43 B.C., twelve vultures appeared to him just as they had to Romulus when he founded Rome. It was what Ennius had called the *augustum augurium* and Octavian eventually opted for taking that epithet as his name, but only after giving some serious attention to Romulus. Vergil's Tityrus hailed Octavian as savior and *deus* in his first *Eclogue*, and so did many Italian cities after he and Antony seemingly patched up their differences in 40 B.C. (Appian, *BC* 5.314). Episodes like these and Vergil's fourth *Eclogue* demonstrate that after many grim decades, the world of Italy and Rome was rife with soteriological expectations and even the faintest hope could be greeted with enthusiastic excess.[63]

As with Julius Caesar, in the *exaltatio memoriae* of Augustus after his death, a matter powerfully enacted by his surviving wife, Livia Drusilla (then named Julia Augusta), the emperor's image did achieve the height of embellished honors. These contests of propaganda set in motion the patterns and protocols that followed in the Julio-Claudian dynasty and subsequent monarchies of the Principate period. Archetypal mimesis, however, included the imitation of a wide array of "lesser" figures; Pythagoras, Socrates, the Dioscuri, Asclepius, Aeneas, even Caesar Augustus himself also frequently functioned as iconic figures for imitation.[64] Since archetypal mimesis had become the standard protocol (*comme il faut*) in cultural production, consciously more so then than perhaps in any other context, the genetic resemblance between stories of figures of "power" in antique Mediterranean civilization achieved an unspoken clarity in their implied interpretation. This single topic, namely, the study of archetypal mimesis in classical antiquity, is deserving of its own comprehensive treatment well beyond this provided cursory sketch.

Excursus: Archetypal Mimesis and Matthew's Divine Birth Myth

As a subset of the larger rubric "archetypal mimesis," fictive archetypal embellishment, particularly with regard to divine birth and divine translation, often functioned to embroider the beginnings and endings of biographic narrative, tacitly invoking these same powerful associations. Perhaps the most vivid manner to describe such literary phenomena is by way of example. An apropos *excursus* allows for the application and observation of the methodologies herein proposed, namely, a look into the archetypal patterns applied in the divine birth myth found in the Gospel of Matthew.[65]

It is indeed striking that the Romans have composed most every extant ancient source on the life of Alexander the Great. From the time of Scipio Africanus through the late ancient emperors, the textualization of Alexander served to calibrate Roman imperialism, just as previously discussed. Each great general or emperor measured himself against Alexander, seeking through propaganda and *imitatio* to match his achievements while avoiding his degeneracy. Alexander's legacy had so determined Hellenistic governance in the Levant and Egypt that all aspiring rulers of the region were invariably measured by the looming stature and strategic disposition of the man. Matthew's divine king affords no exception.

Classicists have typically neglected the details of this phenomenon, instead interrogating the ancient sources with the pointed hope that the historical Alexander would eventually show himself. While, as with the quest for the historical Jesus, such an enterprise may appear quite worthy and alluring, scholars of both spheres have often overlooked the promise that these narratives hold for enriching our understanding of the contexts in which and for which they were produced. In both cases, readers endeavor to see beyond the mythic figure to some flesh-and-blood person, all the while failing to note that such texts deliberately favored the myth to the real, and for good reason. The conscription of these cultural-political icons served the pressing social needs of later contexts to such a degree that any historical person becomes elusive, perhaps even irrelevant. What mattered was the fabulation, that is, how the textualized, mythologized Jesus or Alexander functioned culturally, socially, and politically. While this is certainly the case with our extant sources for Alexander, it becomes all the more visible with the charged mythopoeic renditions of Jesus in early Christian literary production.[66]

Plutarch and Arrian serve as the two chief sources for Alexander the Great. Plutarch's *Vita Alexandri*, a work precisely contemporaneous with Matthew's final redaction, displays the following birth narrative for the king:

Ἀλέξανδρος ὅτι τῷ γένει πρὸς πατρὸς μὲν ἦν Ἡρακλείδης ἀπὸ Καράνου, πρὸς δὲ μητρὸς Αἰακίδης ἀπὸ Νεοπτολέμου, τῶν πάνυ πεπιστευμένων ἐστί. λέγεται δὲ Φίλιππος ἐν Σαμοθράκῃ τῇ Ὀλυμπιάδι συμμυνθεὶς αὐτός τε μειράκιον ὢν ἔτι κἀκείνης παιδὸς ὀρφανῆς γονέων ἐρασθῆναι καὶ τὸν γάμον οὕτως ἁρμόσαι, πείσας τὸν ἀδελφὸν αὐτῆς Ἀρύμβαν. ἡ μὲν οὖν νύμφη, πρὸ τῆς νυκτὸς ᾗ συνείρχθησαν εἰς τὸν θάλαμον, ἔδοξε βροντῆς γενομένης ἐμπεσεῖν αὐτῆς τῇ γαστρὶ κεραυνόν, ἐκ δὲ τῆς πληγῆς πολὺ πῦρ ἀναφθέν, εἶτα ῥηγνύμενον εἰς φλόγας πάντη φερομένας διαλυθῆναι. ὁ δὲ φίλιππος ὑστέρῳ χρόνῳ μετὰ τὸν γάμον εἶδεν ὄναρ αὐτὸν ἐπιβάλλοντα σφραγῖδα τῇ γαστρὶ τῆς γυναικός· ἡ δὲ γλυφὴ τῆς σφραγῖδος, ὡς ᾤετο, λέοντος εἶχεν εἰκόνα. τῶν δὲ ἄλλων μάντεων ὑφορωμένων τὴν ὄψιν, ὡς ἀκριβεστέρας φυλακῆς δεομένων τῷ Φιλίππῳ τῶν περὶ τὸν γάμον, Ἀρίστανδρος ὁ Τελμησσεὺς κύειν ἔφη τὴν ἄνθρωπον, οὐδὲν γὰρ ἀποσφραγίζεσθαι τῶν κενῶν, καὶ κύειν παῖδα θυμοειδῆ καὶ λεοντώδη τὴν φύσιν. ὤφθη δέ ποτε καὶ δράκων κοιμωμένης τῆς Ὀλυμπιάδος παρεκτεταμένος τῷ σώματι· καὶ τοῦτο μάλιστα τοῦ Φιλίππου τὸν ἔρωτα καὶ τὰς φιλοφροσύνας ἀμαυρῶσαι λέγουσιν, ὡς μηδὲ φοιτᾶν ἔτι πολλάκις παρ' αὐτὴν ἀναπαυσόμενον, εἴτε δείσαντά τινας μαγείας ἐπ' αὐτῷ καὶ φάρμακα τῆς γυναικός, εἴτε τὴν ὁμιλίαν ὡς κρείττονι συνούσης ἀφοσιούμενον.

(Alex 2.1)

That Alexander, with regard to his lineage, on his father's side was a descendent of Heracles through Caranus and on his mother's side was a descendent of Aeacus through Neoptolemus, is among those things entirely trusted. And it is said that Philip, after being initiated into the mysteries on Samothrace together with Olympias, and while he was but a youth and an orphan, fell in love with her and so betrothed her, having persuaded her brother Arymbas. Then, the night before they were to consummate the marriage, the bride thought, while there was lightning, that a thunderbolt had fallen upon her womb. From the blow, a fire was ignited; thereby, as it broke into flames, the fire scattered in all directions. Later after the wedding, Philip saw himself in a dream placing a signet impression on his wife's womb. The emblem of the signet, as it seemed, had the image of a lion. While the other diviners were distrusting the vision, namely that they needed a more careful guard for Philip of those who attended the wedding, Aristander of Telmessos said that she conceived a man, for nothing seals those things that are empty, and that she conceived a child who was courageous and as a lion by nature. There then appeared a serpent, as Olympias slept, stretched out alongside her body. They say that this most of all quenched Philip's love and fondness [for her] such that with her he did not often have sexual relations as he lay with her, either because he feared that some of his wife's spells and enchantments may come upon him, or because he avoided the curse of intercourse, since she was joined to one greater than himself.

One notes the similarities between this account and Matthew 1.1–25 now enumerated for clarity (List 3.2):

List 3.2: Plut., *Alexander* 2.1–4 and Matthew 1.1–25 Compared

Both contain. . .

- A parental genealogical description placed at the beginning, aimed at signifying the respective hero via an established pedigree.
- A betrothed, juvenile couple who are in love.
- The interruption by the deity of the wedding / betrothal process, impregnating the bride through his signature, principal element, namely, Zeus's thunderbolt of fire (κεραυνός) or Yahweh's sacred wind (πνεῦμα).
- The virginal conception and birth of the hero child; the surrogate father abstains from sexual relations until the womb is opened through the birth of the child, namely, the breaking of the "seal."

- Drama over the sexual fidelity of the bride and the legitimacy of the conception.
- A distrust of the woman's account of the child's conception, precipitating the need for the groom's divine dream, thus restoring confidence in the bride's story.
- A prophetic description of the child given in the groom's dream, establishing supreme expectation regarding the destiny of the child.
- A later association with magic, though perhaps applied differently.

Aside from Jesus, the birth narrative of no other individual in the ancient world shared so many striking commonalities with that of Alexander. It is no accident that these exposed resemblances also came to define and govern each respective narrative. This observation holds true to such an extent as to dissuade the reader from mistaking the signals as a mere topos. Instead, archetypal mimesis of Alexander accounts for Matthew's birth narrative. The story would have been quite well known, given Plutarch's presumption, Alexander's towering legacy over the Hellenistic East, and the resultant profusion of prior accounts. Indeed, by the time of Matthew's composition (ca. 80–90 C.E.), Alexander's fame still vastly exceeded that of the relatively unknown Galilean, belying any effort to construe imitation in the opposite direction. Plutarch himself prologues his biography in the preceding paragraph by spelling out his editorial method; he would compile and comment upon established accounts from Alexander's life, that is, those that helped to expose his heroic character and virtue. Various Roman authors later alluded to and epitomized now non-extant sources for the divine birth myth composed in the Hellenistic period (that is, before the Common Era), such as Satyrus's *Vita Philippi* (third century B.C.E.) and Pompeius Trogus's *Historiae Philippicae* (first century B.C.E). Drawing on the mythic birth account of one who was the single most famous figure of the eastern Mediterranean, Matthew's birth narrative, therefore, as *imitatio Alexandri*, casted Jesus as the *novus* Alexander, bearer of the Greek imperial legacy of the Hellenistic East. Whatever Jewish elements one may identify in Matthew's account often merely amount to mimetic coloring, that is, Judaic decals, as it were, subsuming Jewish messianism under the aforesaid, governing metanarrative. Matthew's myth served not merely as an adaptation of the Alexandrine tale, but as a transcendent, mimetic contestant within the Mediterranean marketplace of cultural production.

Though acknowledgment of Matthew's mimetic intent may require little further evidence, two additional points seem to render the case still more compelling. Noting the major contours of Alexander's career in relation to his deification, one observes three outstanding events. The study has already discussed the first of these, namely, Alexander's divine birth. The second event transpired after Alexander's pilgrimage to the Oracle of Ammon-Ra at Siwa. Here the oracle declared the conqueror to be the son of Ammon, the supreme Egyptian deity whom the Greeks equated with Zeus; thus, according to the prominent tale, Alexander received the appellation υἱὸς θεοῦ. The infamous προσκύνησις episode provided the third protuberant event defining the divine image of Alexander in the Hellenistic mind. The Persians customarily prostrated themselves before the king of the Persian court. By 327 B.C.E., once Alexander had conquered all of Persia and even some portion of India, Alexander received προσκύνησις from the Persians as their new, absolute monarch. When Alexander attempted to implement the policy with his own generals and officials, the Macedonians and Greeks rejected the custom, considering such obeisance an act of worship. Immediately following Matthew's birth narrative, the writer provides two additional cultural-geographic associations: the προσκύνησις of the magi and Jesus' journey to Egypt. While the narrative supplied no further content regarding the latter, these mimetic signals appear nonetheless to succeed in patterning Matthew's hero after Alexander's divine career as emperor and would have invoked an unmistakable Alexandrine association for the ancient reader.

Also resembling Matthew's *magi orientales*, Cicero in the first century B.C.E. provided the following legend, also available in Plutarch (*Alex.* 3.3):

> Qua nocte templum Ephesiae Dianae deflagravit, eadem constat ex Olympiade natum esse Alexandrum, atque ubi lucere coepisset, clamitasse magos pestem atque perniciem Asiae proxuma nocte natam.
>
> (*Div.* 1.23)

> On the same night when Diana's Temple at Ephesus was burned, it coincided that Alexander was born from Olympias, and when daylight had come, magi cried out that the prior night there had been born the plague and demise of Asia.

The story provided precedence for Matthew's account, offering an additional cue for the reader, casting the protagonist as Alexander's mimetic successor. Matthew's Parthian sorcerers, moreover, helped to expand the religio-cultural appeal of the praise-sung hero, thus reflecting the broadening program of Matthew's community in the Levant.[67]

Both Olympias and Alexander's hired propagandist historiographer Callisthenes assisted with the political mythologization of Alexander according to extant sources. Accounts indicate that Alexander sought throughout his career to model himself after Heracles and Dionysus (*Liber Pater*), both Hellenic demigods of ancient tradition. In the case of the divine birth narrative, Heracles provided the archetypal figure in Mediterranean antiquity. Hesiod's *Shield* (1.27–55) served as the *locus classicus* for the account, wherein Zeus impregnates Alcmene prior to her consummation with Amphitryon. Amphitryon subsequently also conceives with his bride, thus producing twins, one of whom being the demigod. The mimetic cues between the divine birth myth of Heracles and that of Alexander, despite the differences, were so apparent as to become commonly acknowledged both in antiquity and at present. Comparatively speaking, Matthew's mimetic cues vis-à-vis the

Alexander myth far exceed the former, affording all clarity and indeed seizing the ancient reader's anticipation regarding the child's political fortune.

As with the Macedonians of his homeland, the later Romans showed disdain and disapprobation for Alexander's accommodation of oriental, regnal customs, particularly in his own claim to divinity. The customs and cultures, however, of the exotic East ever increasingly required such embellishments as the proper decorum of their rulers. The keener Roman generals and emperors recognized and adapted to this necessity, though oftentimes in tension and conflict with Roman Republican *mos maiorum*.

Like Matthew, Suetonius applied Alexander's birth myth as a pattern for his *Divus Augustus*. According to Suetonius, the story circulated that Atia had been impregnated by Apollo in the form of a serpent, after having fallen asleep in Apollo's sacred temple in Rome. Suetonius's account, moreover, immediately includes two prophetic dreams given to Atia and to the child Octavian, regarding the divine destiny of the boy referred to henceforth as *Apollinis filius*. The entire account, of course, imitated that of Alexander and, therefore, promoted Augustus as divine king according to the Alexandrine tradition:

> In Asclepiadis Mendetis Theologumenon libris lego, Atiam, cum ad sollemne Apollinis sacrum media nocte venisset, posita in templo lectica, dum ceterae matronae dormirent, obdormisse; draconem repente irrepsisse ad eam pauloque post egreesum; illam expergefactam quasi a concubitu mariti purificasse se; et statim in corpora eius exstitisse maculam velut picti draconis nec potuisse umquam exigi, adeo ut mox publicis balineis perpetuo abstinuerit; Augustum natum nese decimo et ob hoc Apollinis filium existimatum. Eadem Atia, prius quam pareret, somniavit intestina sua ferri ad sidea explicarique per omnem terrarium et caeli ambitum. Somniavit et pater Octavius utero Atiae iubar solis exortum.
>
> (Suet., *Aug.* 94.4)

> I have read the following story in the books of Asclepias of Mendes entitled Theologumena. When Atia had come in the middle of the night to the solemn service of Apollo, she had her litter set down in the temple and fell asleep, while the rest of the matrons also slept. On a sudden a serpent glided up to her and shortly went away. When she awoke, she purified herself, as if after the embraces of her husband, and at once there appeared on her body a mark in colours like a serpent, and she could never get rid of it; so that presently she ceased ever to go to the public baths. In the tenth month after that, Augustus was born and was therefore regarded as the son of Apollo. Atia too, before she gave him birth, dreamed that her vitals were borne up to the stars and spread over the whole extent of the land and sea, while Octavius dreamed that the sun rose from Atia's womb.
>
> (Rofle)

Here again the mimetic cues are quite adequate, though few in comparison with Matthew's imitation of the Alexander myth. Notice that, as was nearly always the case in ancient Mediterranean mimesis, the author does not make explicit the story's antecedent. Classicist Diana Spencer comments:

> when talking about (potential) early Roman Alexanders, divine explanations and justifications for their power and success are usually offered, and the role of omens is clearly important. Authors attempting to come to terms with the destiny of men of power can offer the connexion with Alexander either as a sobering reference, or as a glorification of the new Roman version. Potentially divine ancestry is a plus, . . . but we should be aware that a strong cultural association between Alexander and these kinds of legends must have existed for authors to have dropped them without explanation into their narratives.[68]

With the rise of imperial propaganda after the death of Julius Caesar (44 B.C.E.), the Caesars became the objects of political mythologization in Roman literature. Similar to Matthew's treatment of Jesus, the later Roman historian Dio Cassius frames his biography of Augustus with a mythic *Einzelrahmen*, that is, a decorative narrational frame of divine embellishment. Charles Talbert comments:

> The mythology of the immortals also attaches itself to Augustus in historical and biographical writings of the empire. In Dio Cassius' "Roman History" the normal chain of social and political events in Rome's history is broken both at the birth and at the death of Augustus by the inclusion of the myth. In 45.1, in the narrative about his birth, we read of the belief that he was engendered by Apollo. The narrative of his death in 56.46 tells of Augustus' being declared immortal, with attending priests and sacred rites.[69]

According to Menander Rhetor and Libanius, such embellishments, namely, at the beginning and ending of a biographic narration, served as the prescribed encomiastic protocol in the honor of supernal figures.[70]

While other scholars have identified generic commonalities between early Christian renditions of Jesus' divine birth and the birth narratives of other legendary figures of the ancient world, such as one finds in Campbell's *Hero with a Thousand Faces* and Robert J. Miller's recent compilation, the present methodology has the promise of providing the much-needed subtext in Matthew's project.[71] Instead of being reduced to a mere nebulous Jungian archetype or a generic "divine birth" topos (behind the stories of Alexander, Augustus, and Matthew's Jesus), a pattern arising out of the general cultural currents of classical antiquity, one witnesses deliberate political strategies played out through mythographic propaganda and the politicized textualizations of these icons of Mediterranean antiquity. The application of such myths then became for the ancients a protocol signaling the tacit *exaltatio* of one who would rule the exotic East. Matthew thus orients his reader toward a political, albeit transcendent reading of his composition.

As the result of a long-standing Judaic bias in Gospels research, many of the principal commentators have failed to perceive the Greco-Roman antecedents and antetexts behind the literature. This observation becomes all the more startling when one considers that David Friedrich Strauß, New Testament critic *avant la lettre*, had settled the fundamental question as to the mythic underpinnings of Jesus' divine birth narratives nearly two centuries ago (as Justin had seventeen centuries prior to Strauß; *1 Apol.* 21). In 1835, in his *Das Leben Jesu kritisch bearbeitet*, Strauß wrote:

> Man hat also, um sich die Entstehung eines solchen Mythus zu erklären, an die Neigung der alten Welt gedacht, große Männer und Wohlthäter ihres Geschlechts als Göttersöhne darzustellen. Die Beispiele sind von den Theologen reichlich beigebracht. Namentlich aus der griechisch—römischen Mythologie und Geschichte hat man an Herkules und die Dioskuren erinnert, an Romulus und Alexander, vor Allen aber an Pythagoras und Plato.
>
> (174)

> Some have, therefore, pointed out the tendency in the ancient world to present great men and benefactors of their race as sons of gods, in order to clarify the emergence of such a myth. The theologians have given us plenty of examples. From Greco-Roman mythology and history in particular, one is reminded of Heracles, the Dioscuri, Romulus, and Alexander, as well as, above all, Pythagoras and Plato.

Yet, for many, the antique Greek and Latin literary corpus has remained "pagan" and, as such, of marginal relevance, despite the observation that the Gospels systematically repudiated nearly every known separatist policy of early Judaism. Since these texts were composed in Greek and flourished in the Greek East, and since we know of no extant early Christian document composed in any Semitic language in the first centuries of the Common Era, the time is long past comfortably to broaden the research. In ancient Mediterranean cultures, mimesis was not merely the sincerest form of flattery; it was also the sincerest form of rivalry.

3.3 MIMICRY IN THE GOSPELS AS TRANSCENDENT RIVALRY

εἰ καὶ ἐγνώκαμεν κατὰ σάρκα Χριστόν, ἀλλὰ νῦν οὐκέτι γινώσκομεν.

Even if we once did acknowledged Christ as a flesh and blood person, yet we now do so no longer.

2 Corinthians 5.16

A Social History of Earliest Christian Traditions

Before addressing the considerable challenges and contributions of postcolonial theory with respect to the Gospels, some prior considerations require attention. As previously discussed, this book approaches the New Testament narratives as windows, not into the historical world of early first-century Palestine, but into the sociological world of the communities that composed, read, and signified these texts in the late first and early second centuries (*der Sitz im Gemeinschaftsleben*). As Bultmann has reminded us, the content of these ancient booklets reflected and served that context, not that of a historical figure, Jesus.[72] For how long now, moreover, have biblical scholars sought to reconstruct a cohesive portrait of the historical Saul of Tarsus from the authentic Pauline *corpus*? These documents survive from a most nascent period of Christian origins due to their socially authorized performance as sacralized scripts of social formation and identification. That is to say, the predominant value of these earliest extant documents for the historian resides in their rich provision of data helpful toward reconstructing the disparate social topography of nascent Christian movements. Indeed, the appeal and social code inscribed in a given text arguably more reflected the diverse communities originally signifying and sacralizing these texts than any private proclivity of a supposed author.

Following the basic divisions of texts wherever the data may lead, one begins to paint with broad strokes a quite startling portrait of the radical diversity of early Christian societies. Aggregating the specific textual data, one witnesses distinct social movements, followings, or competing schools of nascent Christianity, often gathered under the names of originary figures or sundered by geographic region. As one develops an eye toward discerning the historical tension and dynamics between these social traditions, the "New Testament" begins to present itself as a hazardously trite namespace, feigning unity by the very glue that binds these diverse works. The theological interest, moreover, that has dominated the academic study of this anthology for centuries has popularized a misleading façade of earliest Christian solidarity and concertion. Under the surface, however, the tradition critic finds different stories, charged subtexts of struggle, rivalry, and subsumption arising from diverse, distinct socio-religious locations. When reading these texts, the social critic asks: (1) What was at stake socially in this expression or passage with regard to social space, identity, or formation? and (2) As a social script, what did this expression or passage *do* in the social theater of contending Christian movements or traditions? and, perhaps most important (3) How does such a social subtext *describe* a given social, ideological formation in the topography of earliest Christian societies? Collectively, the answers to these fundamental questions yield a working portrait of earliest Christianity fraught with social contestation.

When considering the Gospels in this way, one can hardly avoid touching upon the present turbulent debate over source criticism and the Synoptic

Problem, perhaps the most divisive topic facing modern scholarship. While the thesis of the present book succeeds despite which theory or sub-theory one may apply here, the two most dominant (and compelling) theories advanced prove particularly enlightening, that is, the Farrer theory and the Two-Document theory.[73] Nearly all Gospels scholars today find their way into one or the other of these two adjacent camps, both correctly endeavoring to derive the most comprehensive explanation for the textual dependencies evident between the Synoptic Gospels. That these decades-long debates persist may of itself prove informative regarding the inherently messy complexity of the relation between these ancient texts. Despite the divisiveness of the debate, the two leading theories have established two weighty conclusions: (1) Mark was the earliest Gospel, and (2) extensive, distinctly primitive material becomes first visible to us in Matthew, henceforth, for the sake of this study, to be referred to as Matthew's λόγια.[74] Whether Matthew's λόγια had previously circulated as one or more written documents, "Q" according to the dominant Two-Document theory, or these sayings and stories variously found their way into Matthew through oral circulation, as implied in the Farrer theory, one discerns in this content the survival of several distinct, primitive social and ideological markers.

Indeed, when applying a social-critical lens while scanning the earliest Christian writings, several distinct social entities manifest in relation to one another: the John the Baptist Movement (JBM), the Syro-Palestinian Sayings Movement (SSM or λόγια Movement), the Pauline Movement (PM), the Petrine School (PS), the Johannine School (JS), the Zealot Movement (ZM), Pharisaic Judaism (PJ), *et cetera*. With regard to the New Testament, one may scarcely overstate the explanatory power of this basic methodology, allowing for a simple schematization of most any chapter, passage, or verse as the relation of one or more of these social entities. The largest nascent Christian gulf or disparity, one that effected much of the New Testament *corpus*, appears to have resided between PM (the nascent urban Christian societies of Anatolia, Macedonia, and Greece) and SSM (λόγια Movement of Syrian Palestine). Burton L. Mack and the Society of Biblical Literature "Seminar on Ancient Myths and Modern Theories of Christian Origin" correctly observed that, when one compares these two earliest textual manifestations of Christian origins, one finds a vast disparity between the two bodies of material, whether geographically, ideologically, or in terms of their most basic conceptions of Jesus.[75] On the one hand, instead of Paul's χριστός, the λόγια applied two disparate "Son of Man" images as derived from classical Hebrew and early Jewish tradition: one, a lowly, mantic servant (Isaianic and Ezekielic), the other, an apocalyptic cosmic president (Danielic and Enochic).[76] The sage's frequent use of the "Son of Man" in the third person suggests that, as Bultmann and Collins have argued, this identification likely came at a later stage.[77] Accordingly, the apocalyptic "Son of Man," a figure more fully expressed in the *Similitudes of Enoch* (*1 En.* 53–57; 60–63; Cf. *4 Ezra*), became identified with Jesus in Mark, though refashioned in humbler terms so as to synthesize the apocalyptic themes with the more modest rendition of Jesus in the λόγια, that is, the cultivated memory of the historical Jesus as thaumaturgist, charismatic teacher, peasant, executed *provocateur, et cetera.*[78] Paul's missives, on the other hand, show nearly no interest in a circulation of such handed-down traditions related to Jesus. Aside from the resurrection / apotheosis of his Christ-figure, these dense didactic letters show no interest in Jesus' sayings, wonders, or healings. If such λόγια and stories were compelling or significant to Paul and his burgeoning society in Anatolia and Greece, it stands to reason that such traditions would routinely meet us through the Pauline letters by way of quotations and anecdotes. Such logic proves conclusive, and not mere *argumentum ex silentio*, given the extensive sample preserved as the most sacralized of Paul's writings, as well as the reasonable premise that any society that prioritized the teachings of the mundane Jesus would have required such authoritative appeal within their centralized didactic tradition.

Contrary to the Syrian λόγια Movement, the Greek-Anatolian Pauline Christ-cult held Jesus as a mystical celestial avatar, not a mundane itinerate Galilean teacher with disciples and a didactic following. We find evidence that the two traditions knew of one another and consciously disparaged the other. The λόγια Movement described Jesus as fully condemnatory toward an unnamed sizable body of people who exalted Jesus in title but disregarded his sayings (Mt 7.21–27; cf. Mt 25.11–12). Obversely, the Pauline Movement apparently celebrated Paul's brazen boasts of independence from the originary tradents of Jesus' sayings, that is, the mocked Syro-Palestinian "pillars" (Gal 1–2), revealing prevalent cynical attitudes toward the λόγια Movement. As a society, they had long decided not to comprehend Jesus in such mundane, human terms (2 Cor 5.16), but as a transcendent majestic icon, a mystical ascetic figurehead for a potent counter-cultural, philosophical Mediterranean movement sprung up in the urban centers of Anatolia, Macedonia, and Greece. The Christ of the Pauline Movement was a celestial (Platonized / protognosticized) avatar, perhaps only in the most distant fashion tethered to any flesh and blood, historical person. Paul's apparent lack of need to quote from his κύριος Ἰησοῦς Χριστός not only reflects a blatant lack of relevance for the historical person; this lack also—and this point proves all the more substantial—demonstrates that for the region of societies receiving and sacralizing his letters, such a historical person was equally irrelevant.

This chasm between the Jesusology of the λόγια Movement and transcendent Christology of the Pauline Movement provides the explanatory framework for the observed synthesis of these utterly disparate traditions as they became conflated in the Gospel traditions that sprang from and spread into regions previously evangelized by Paul and others promulgating the political, ahistorical Christ-Myth. The Gospel of Mark in part achieved these historicizing objectives through the at-times crude mimetic play on several of the most conspicuous Homeric tropes and themes. In the case of Mark's "Messianic Secret" (Wrede), the fabulation rendered the protagonist as a type of Odysseus, a supreme monarch, a son of a god, a Hellenistic savior whose true identity only became known by a select few. This theme loosely combined with the mimetic application of Telemachus to achieve the climactic themes seen in Mark's "Temple Incident," imitating the charged, climactic motifs present in the cleansing of the House of Odysseus at Ithaca. Dovetailing with this stratagem, Mark drew up a cast of close disciples whose foibles and fears mimicked those of Odysseus's legendary crew. In this way, Mark sufficiently discredited the chief tradents of the λόγια Movement—Indeed, Jesus' family fares all the worse in Mark—artfully making way for Mark's forceful ahistorical, Pauline-compatible embellishments. Mark thus applied fictive mimetic techniques (vis-à-vis Homer and 1–2 Kings) using Jesus as a literary vehicle for the negotiation and registration of a post-70 C.E. political and religious social location developing in the text's turbulent sociological, compositional contexts in urban Syria and Anatolia.[79]

Much like the lavish incongruities observed in the apocalyptic genre, the panoply of early Christian gospel texts appears more or less disinterested in conforming to any particular narrative of Christian origins and instead exhibits an all-but-whimsical freedom, an astonishing prose creativity in depiction and variance in the telling and ordering of scenes. Of the hundreds of Christian works that survive from the first three centuries of the Common Era, no reliable histories exist aside perhaps from fragments of the five books of Papias. Of these hundreds, setting aside the various epistles and apologies, thus focusing on the narratives, we find a single unifying feature: the early Christian narratives were all fictive in modality. Whether one considers the collection of early Christian gospels, the various apostolic *acta*, the assortment of apocalypses, or the burgeoning stock of hagiographa, until Eusebius's fourth-century *Historia Ecclesiastica*, itself a myth of Christian origins, though intended to be read as a history, one encounters nothing deserving of the genus "historiography"; one finds only legends, myths, folktales, and novelistic fictions. Albeit, considering the characteristic gravitas of these texts, one would be mistaken to dismiss them merely as works of aesthetic entertainment. As all of these works exclude the requisite signals distinguishing ancient works of historiography, that is, no visible weighing of sources, no apology for the all-too-common occurrence of the supernatural, no endeavor to distinguish such accounts and conventions from analogous fictive narratives in classical literature (including the frequent mimetic use of Homer, Euripides, and other canonized fictions of classical antiquity), no transparent sense of authorship (or even readership) or origin, the ecclesiastical distinction endeavored by Irenaeus of Lyons *et alii* to segregate and signify some such works as canonical, reliable histories appears wholly political and arbitrary.

The academy should, therefore, avoid the application of qualitative designations such as "apocryphal" or "heretical" when discussing the non-canonized, early Christian gospels. Other than their popular circulation and relatively early publication (70–120 C.E.), no apparent remarkable trait distinguished these four texts from the larger pool. Assessing the remaining gospels that circulated in the first few centuries, Hans-Josef Klauck has

written that "their *Sitz-im-Leben* is the wide current of early Christian literature antecedent to the process of the formation of a scriptural canon. There
was no such canon that could have provided a criterion for the authors
or for the evaluation of their writings."[80] One, therefore, is mistaken to
suppose a significant modal leap between these four texts (and Acts of the
Apostles) and the remainder of the "gospel" collection or the larger corpus
of early Christian narratives. The diversity of these texts, rather, reflects the
variety of (often competing) social contexts, literary functions, and measures
of prolific creative freedom characterizing the Christianities of this nascent
religion. From the most primitive periods of the religion, one observes tremendous diversity and corresponding literary imagination, despite the later
myth of unity created by centralized Roman ecclesiastical power and resultant endeavored reduction and control of a single Christian narrative of
origins.[81] Indeed, even as Tatian's late second-century composition of the
Diatessaron (an attempted harmonization of the four later to be canonized Gospels) demonstrates, the centralizing power of the so-called orthodox movement became increasingly uncomfortable with and incompatible
with the extensive plurality of tales of Christian origins. What was once
viewed as an exciting, free-spirited array of movements and corresponding mythopoeic narrations came to be viewed as a cacophony of heresy
and intolerable diversity. The "orthodox" movement signified and held as
sacred only those texts useful to the legitimation of that single trajectory of
Roman ecclesiastical power; the remaining early Christian texts were to be
marginalized, denigrated, or altogether banned. Over the course of three
centuries (50–350 C.E.), by increasing degrees, diversity came to be labelled
as deviance. The "orthodox" bishops certified their own sacred texts as
credible, while denigrating the sacred texts of other groups as heretical. The
same socio-political process came to define not only "heretical" literature,
but "heretical" doctrine, "heretical" teachers, and "heretical" communities.

Although the function of a story or saying may have determined or established various formal patterns in the primitive traditions that became Matthew's λόγια, with the composition of Mark and thereafter, one finds the
softening of these paratactic forms toward the more fluent narratives of Acts
and the *Gospel of Peter*. One can account for the intermediate stages in this
shift simply by presuming the likelihood that Mark loosely applied parataxis
as a formal economy, namely, that known in the λόγια tradition. One must
discern the function of each passage, therefore, from careful literary, cultural, and sociological critical analysis, as with all other ancient literary
works, and not predominantly from the segment's form, *contra* Bultmann.[82]

The Gospels as Counter-Imperial Tracts

While the recent upsurge in political readings of the New Testament has ben-
eficially alerted the discourse to the imperial language of these ancient documents, such as provided by Richard Horsley, John Dominic Crossan, and

various postcolonial theorists, such interpretations appear to overlook the ascetic, other-worldly disposition of the early Christian movement(s), often yielding reductionistic, specious conclusions. The four Gospels, as fabulous compositions, rendered ὁ χριστός as the transcendent king, not a mundane opponent of the political structures of the day.

Jesus' literary foes in his execution in the Gospel passion narratives commit this same transgression, namely, in seeking to frame the protagonist as a seditious rebel, a counter-imperial insurrectionist seeking to foment a political struggle or endeavoring to found a mundane, competing movement in opposition to Rome. The Gospel narratives, however, dramatically and potently articulate a subtext *tout àu contraire*. In each of the four Gospels, the narrative drives the reader through a disturbing sequence of injustice, confronting the reader with the singular question: If not a mundane revolutionary insurgent, then what? The tragedy of these texts obtained inasmuch as the ancient reader had succeeded in formulating and approximating the intended inference. The subtext failed inasmuch as the reader failed by conferring guilt upon the protagonist as one endeavoring a political revolt. For, in such a case, would not his penalty have seemed reasonable, if not fitting? Instead, in each of the four passion narratives, like a bewitching darkness, a madness descends upon all presiding over Jesus' execution; not one sane mind attends the calamity, thus resulting in a freakish, supremely tragic miscarriage of justice. The four texts each succeeded in painting this same unsettling undercurrent of unholy atrocity. Mark introduced the betrayer as "Judas," a name perhaps eponymous with "Judas the Galilean," famous for having led a most notorious rebellion (ca. 6 C.E.), or perhaps a thinly veiled metonym in a most general way symbolizing the *populi Iudaicus*. This constructed persona, a close student of Mark's protagonist, in an act recalling the visceral public sentiments of Brutus's betrayal of Caesar on the Senate floor, comes with men "armed with swords and clubs" to arrest Jesus (Mk 14.43). Matthew adds Jesus' response: "Have you come out with swords and clubs to capture me as though I were a bandit?" This term ληστής, often mistranslated as "thief" in the Gospels, functioned as a trope during and after the First Jewish War in reference to Jewish separatist insurgents, as for instance often applied by Josephus (*B.J.* 4.134–162; under Chapter 1, "Hellenistic Judaism and the Urban Greek East") and later even applied to Bar Kokhba (Eusebius, *Historia ecclesiastica* 4.6.2.). Indeed, the Gospels apply the term interchangeably with those guilty of στάσις καὶ φόνος ("sedition and murder") in reference to Barabbas (Cf. Lk 23.19 and Jn 18.40). These narratives intentionally juxtaposed Jesus and Barabbas in order to draw out the contrast and the scandal of Jesus' trial. In the Synoptic Gospels, the λησταί in the Temple Incident (Mk 11.15–18 *et al.*) and those on the crosses to Jesus' right and left (Mk 15.27 *et al.*) reemphasized the same disturbing contrast. Cultural sentiment regarding the culpability of the Jews in provoking the Jewish War apparently drove the topicality of these various themes of "sedition" in Mark, as becomes most manifest in Josephus. Having artfully proffered Jesus as a metonym for the later movement (ca. 70 C.E.), the Gospel of Mark sought to distance the protagonist from such culpability.

Repeatedly, when Pilate asked Jesus whether he was a "king," Jesus turned the question around. "That's what you say." In none of the Gospels does either Herod or Pilate find any fault with Jesus. Pilate's wife, moreover, in Matthew warns the prefect of Jesus' innocence because of a dream she had had (27.19). Only the Gospel of John had Jesus actually admit to being a king (18.36), but even this text served to distance Jesus from any charge of sedition. "My kingdom is not of this world, otherwise my people would fight."[83] In all four Gospels, moreover, the epithet "King of the Jews" always becomes applied to Jesus by his accusers and executioners (Cf. Jn 19.12–16). Jesus' mockery as "king" in the toil of his voluntary execution invoked the ascetic themes of Heracles's labors and tragic death, the archetypal king. 4 Maccabees drew the same connection between transcendent royalty and ascetic certitude in the face of grueling martyrdom ("O reason, more royal than kings and freer than the free"; 4 Macc 14.2).[84] The "tyranny" being conquered through the spectacle of martyrdom in the Gospels, unlike with the Seleucid king Antiochus IV, however, became the institutional authority of Palestinian Judaism(s). The βασιλεύς of the Gospels consistently avoids mundane power or a clash with mundane authorities, except inasmuch as he was depicted as self-determined to die as a spectacle at their hands (e.g., Mk 8.31–38; Lk 9.51; as well as the Temple Incident), echoing the philosophical ascesis and certitude of the misunderstood Socrates (even misunderstood by his own disciples up to the point of his death) and his willful archetypal martyrdom.[85] In the Gospels, the narratives present Jesus' accusers as a foil—they are always wrong about him—in order to provoke the reader to find the more sophisticated, alternate interpretation, namely, the veiled meaning and self-understanding of the rendered Jesus. These texts brought to visceral attention within the ancient reader the swelling question of culpability behind Jesus' dramatized death. His blood was to be upon the hands of the Jewish sectarian authorities in Jerusalem, not upon Caesar's government.[86]

The only criticism of Roman political power in the Gospels, either latent or explicit, seems to be evident in a tacit lack of commitment to justice over and against pacifying unrest and accusations against Jesus at his trial. Jesus' interests function in his unrelenting priority for the transcendent. While some may attempt to detect a criticism of Rome's "legions" in the "drowning of the swine" episode, demons, not soldiers, comprise such legions. The Gospel of Matthew, as an early interpretation of and expansion of Mark, appears oblivious to such a pejorative political reading of Mark, namely, one implying that Roman legions are demonic; the Matthean Jesus likewise applied the term to angels.[87] All of the centurions in the Gospels, moreover, consistently become favorably disposed to Jesus. Not only do they find nothing offensive about him, they each remarkably comprehend and admire him. Would not one expect the injunction, "leave your life of Roman tyranny, lay down your sword, and follow me," were the Gospels endeavoring to picture "conversion" in fundamentally political terms? Neither Hardy, Wilken, nor Martin has displayed any evidence that the Roman government comprehended the early Christians as seeking to foment sedition against the state, if by "sedition" one means any effort to organize insurrection or revolt.[88] The New Testament works were often subversive, but never seditious, in their endeavor to transcend the political structures of their day.

The application of postcolonial theory, moreover, breaks down inasmuch as early Christian kerygma remained universal in its appeal, not merely drawing in converts from among the disenfranchised provinces, but from Italy, including the political aristocracy and soon even members of the Senate and Caesar himself.[89] "Conversion," for the early Christians, was first counter-cultural, religious, and philosophical in nature, not political.[90] Despite ongoing subversive political friction, the essence of early Christianity as a proliferating ascetic, martyrological movement had in view a socio-cultural revolution, not a political overthrow. The Gospel narratives asserted the transcendent preeminence of Jesus in relation to all spheres of authority: family, vocation, self-preservation, as well as social, religious, and political powers. The call to discipleship conversion fundamentally transacted in the commission of an act prioritizing the divine, transcendent order to the mundane. "Kingdom" themes in the four Gospels operated invariably within this governing paradigm. One must not, therefore, mistakenly reduce the movement's alterity to that of a "colonized vs. oppressor" template, as has become something of an alluring preoccupation in recent biblical studies. The transcendent, ascetic disposition of the earliest Christian societies behind the Gospel narratives governed the function of the mimicry variously witnessed. These counter-cultural texts effectively applied such themes as their primary philosophical transaction with the classical order. The descriptor proposed in this study "transcendent *rivalitas*" fundamentally realigns the discourse with the broader classical phenomenon taken up by the earlier Christians, namely, an ascetic critique of mundane civilization, thus transvaluing the codes and structures of antiquity, turning them on their head.

Earliest Christian writings depicted Jesus as imitating, embodying, and emulating a large array of figures from classical Hebrew, classical Greek, and classical Roman traditions. While, for instance, one may recognize that the renditions of Jesus in the New Testament intentionally rivaled the ancient renditions of Moses, Elijah, and David by their imitation, one would err to adduce these as instances of implied enmity. Mimesis of Homer's Odysseus, whether with Jesus in the Gospels or with Virgil's Aeneas, meant to rival and eclipse the former, but never to supplant. Congruent with the many varieties of *imitatio, aemulatio,* and *rivalitas* in the Gospels, imperial imitation in the Gospels did not serve to threaten or to unseat Caesar; such imitation served to promote the transcendent significance of the founder, comparing with and rivaling fidelity to the chief classical institutions of power. For this reason, the apostolic missive could formally decree (1 Pet 2.17): τὸν βασιλέα τιμᾶτε. Homi Bhabha's notion of mimicry as a menacing mode of resistance to domination, therefore, a methodological model that works quite well in the contexts of nineteenth- and twentieth-century British imperial India, cannot transpose suitably into nascent Christian contexts, inasmuch as early Christian contestation arose as a philosophical dynamic of ascetic duality, that is, as transcendent *rivalitas*. Aggressive Oedipal readings of these early Christian etiologies with respect to their mimetic predecessors, to apply the perspicacity of Harold Bloom's *The Anxiety of Influence* (1973), intensified as a matter of shifting significance, resulting from escalating, shifting requirements in use in the second and third centuries (as set forth in Chapter 1).

NOTES

1. Jacques Derrida, *Points de suspension* (Paris: Galilée, 1992), 213.
2. For a complete story of this historic project, see Carl Sagan *et al.*, *Murmurs of Earth: The Voyager Interstellar Record* (New York: Random House, 1978).
3. Roland G. Barthes, *Elements of Semiology* (trans. Annette Lavers and Colin Smith; London: Jonathan Cape, 1967), 89ff.
4. James Harkness, translator's introduction to *This Is not a Pipe with Illustrations and Letters by René Magritte*, by Michel Foucault (Berkeley: University of California Press, 1983), 5.
5. James C. Scott, *Domination and the Arts of Resistance: Hidden Transcripts* (New Haven: Yale University Press, 1990), 183–84.
6. Or, should one find theories of Matthean priority persuasive (e.g., the Neo-Griesbachian theory proposed by William R. Farmer, Michael D. Goulder, and most recently by Mark Goodacre), these themes nevertheless prove inchoate to the Gospel tradition, in this case via Matthew.
7. Roland Barthes, "The Death of the Author," in *Image, Music, Text* (trans. Stephen Heath; New York: Hill and Wang, 1977), 142–48.
8. This observation strengthens when considering the malleability of paratactic "sayings" collections (*Gospel of Thomas*, the *Logoi* of Jesus, etc.) and the cobbled, episodic narrative form inherent to the Gospel tradition. Such a conclusion, namely, describing a socio-religious tradition behind each Gospel text, follows from the *Traditionsgeschichte* methodology made famous by R. Bultmann. Rudolf Bultmann, *Das Evangelium des Johannes* (KEK; Göttingen: Vandenhoeck & Ruprecht, 1941); Rudolf Bultmann, *Die Geschichte der synoptischen Tradition* (FRLANT 29; Göttingen: Vandenhoeck & Ruprecht, 1921).
9. Roland Barthes, "The Death of the Author," 146.
10. "Literary Theory" blog by John Weatherford [http://literarytheory.wordpress.com], entered March 29, 2007.
11. Barthes applies the French term *scriptor*. "Composer," however, more closely approximates his methodological conception, from the Latin *componere*, one who "puts items together."
12. In turn, and altogether in reverse order to standing methods, a robust linguistic, social, and cultural comprehension of a given text may then supply some bare contours and defining strokes toward a useful sketch or profile of a particular composer. Thus, while the commentary by Adela Yarbro Collins has, for instance, suggested a possible comparison between Roman apotheosis and Jesus' missing body in the Gospel of Mark, the proposition unduly hesitates

over the question of authorial awareness and intent. Not only does such a question hinder and ultimately impede the analysis, it is both unanswerable as a requisite consideration and indeed irrelevant from the standpoint of textual, linguistic performance. One ought first instead to ask, how would such a narrative originally have been read in the primary urban centers of the Hellenistic (or better, Hellenizing) East? Adela Yarbro Collins, *Mark: A Commentary* (Hermeneia; Minneapolis: Fortress Press, 2007), 782–94.

13. Ferdinand de Saussure, *Cours de Linguistique générale* (Paris: Éditions Payot & Rivages, 1916), 33.

14. Ibid. On the same page, Saussure first postulated "Semiology" as a distinct field of study. "On peut donc concevoir *une science qui étudie la vie des signes au sein de la vie sociale ;* elle formerait une partie de la psychologie sociale, et par conséquent de la psychologie générale ; nous la nommerons *sémiologie* (du grec sëmeîon,. « signe »)."

15. Michel Foucault, *Les mots et les choses* (Paris: Gallimard, 1966), 32.

16. Michel Foucault, *The Order of Things* (trans. Alan Sheridan; New York: Vintage Books, 1994), 17.

17. The fourth-century Prudentius provides one typical example of the early Christian use of *paganus* in the *praefatio* of his *Libri contra Symmachum* (1.1–10).

18. Umberto Eco, *The Limits of Interpretation* (Indianapolis: Indiana University Press, 1994).

19. Barthes, *Elements of Semiology*, 14.

20. Yuri M. Lotman, *Universe of the Mind: A Semiotic Theory of Culture* (trans. Ann Shukman; Indianapolis: Indiana University Press, 1990).

21. Gregory J. Riley has described this relationship between convention and innovation in earliest Christian literature and thought in his unassuming monograph. Gregory J. Riley, *The River of God: A New History of Christian Origins* (New York: HarperCollins, 2001).

22. In his 1835–36 *Leben Jesu,* Strauß argued that the New Testament Gospels were fundamentally mythological in character. Immediately after its publication, the Earl of Shaftesbury called the work "the most pestilential book ever vomited out of the jaws of hell." Strauß's publication was met with such rancorous opposition from the faith-based theological community that Strauß was unceremoniously dismissed from his faculty position at the University of Tübingen. David Friedrich Strauß, *Das Leben Jesu, kritisch bearbeitet* (2 vols; Tübingen: Osiander, 1835–1836); Heinrich Eberhard Gottlob Paulus, *Das Leben Jesu als Grundlage einer reinen Geschichte des Urchristentums* (2 vols; Heidelberg, 1928).

23. Cf. Daniel Merkur, *Psychoanalytic Approaches to Myth* (New York: Routledge, 2005).

24. Pierre Maquet, Carlyle Smith, and Robert Stickgold, eds., *Sleep and Brain Plasticity* (Oxford: Oxford University Press, 2003), 1.

25. Patrick McNamara, *An Evolutionary Psychology of Sleep and Dreams* (Westport, CT: Praeger Publishers, 2004).

26. Lacan saw the metonymy that strings together human narrative fundamentally as a function of desire. Unsatisfied desire, conjured by the story itself, drives the reader toward its conclusion with the hope of justice and resolution. See Jacques Lacan, "Le Stade du miroir comme formateur de la fonction du Je, telle qu'elle nous est révélée dans l'expérience psychanalytique" (1949) in *Écrits* (Paris: Seuil, 1966), 93–100; translated by Alan Sheridan as "The Mirror Stage, as Formative of the Function of the I as Revealed in Psychoanalytic Experience" in *Écrits: A Selection* (London: Tavistock, 1977), 1–7. Concerning death as a narrative conclusion, cf. Peter Brooks's helpful notion of *détour* in his analysis of Freud, namely, as a function of tension toward a "proper"

ending. Peter Brooks, "Freud's Masterplot," *Yale French Studies* 55/56 (1977): 280–300, esp. 291–92.

27. Alan Dundes, "The Hero Pattern and the Life of Jesus," in *In Quest of the Hero* (ed. Robert A. Segal; Princeton, NJ: Princeton University Press, 1990), 179–223.

28. Carl Gustav Jung, ed., *Man and His Symbols* (New York: Doubleday, 1964), 56–57.

29. With the modern rise of literalism in Christian biblical hermeneutics, regrettably, the suggested presence of myth, legend, fiction, and folklore in biblical narrative has come to be equated with "falsehood" or "lies," an intolerable proposal considered wholly incompatible with a modern Christian doctrine of divine inspiration. The Western Enlightenment has had the tacit effect of placing Christian thought on the defensive, out of which has arisen the bizarre stance that the Bible comprises a series of absolute propositional (even scientific and historical) truths that the faithful are to accept as infallible. All but the most liberal end of the Christian theological spectrum tragically have lost sight of the "truth" value to be found in fables, poems, folklore, and divine myth-making, arguably the most nourishing and inspiring modes and facets of quality literature.

30. Cf. Stephen Halliwell, *The Aesthetics of Mimesis: Ancient Texts and Modern Problems* (Princeton, NJ: Princeton University Press, 2002); Gunter Gebauer and Christoph Wulf, *Mimesis. Kultur—Kunst—Gesellschaft* (Reinbek: Rowohlt, 1992). Biblical studies scholars have all too often missed this key observation, instead mistakenly supposing Hellenism to have been merely a matter of passive influence or, at best, a secondary, resisted state of hybridity, with Judaism providing the dominant cultural, literary context(s) of the New Testament texts. This misstep has so grossly dislocated the linguistic and ideological position of earliest Christian literature, effectively bifurcating New Testament Studies from its parent field, Classical Studies, that, at the present, only a small minority of New Testament scholars has pursued proper training in the classical Greek and Latin literature.

31. This bare fact, namely, that political aristocrats predominantly tended to obtain divine status in classical culture, reveals the scandal of the story of the executed *parvenu* from Galilee having been embellished with divinity. At the heart of this scandal resided a recurring early Christian counter-cultural subtext menacing the classical social order, namely, the promulgation of the disruptive, often inverted order of the Kingdom of God.

32. Cf. Paul Veyne, *Did the Greeks Believe in Their Myths? An Essay on the Constitutive Imagination* (trans. Paula Wissing; Chicago: University of Chicago Press, 1988); John Creed, "Uses of Classical Mythology," in *The Theory of Myth, Six Studies* (ed. Adrian Cunningham; London: Sheed and Ward, 1973), 1–21.

33. Compare this same "Euhemeristic" phenomenon with regard to the Egyptian deities as given in Hecataeus of Abdera. Sources for Euhemerus's *Sacred History* survive only in fragmentary form in quotations of Diodorus Siculus, *Bibliotheca* 6 and Ennius's translation of Euhemerus, *Sacra historia*. See Marek Winiarczyk, *Euhemeros von Messene. Leben, Werk und Nachwirkung* (Munich and Leipzig: K. G. Saur, 2002); Truesdell S. Brown, "Euhemerus and the Historians," *HTR* 39 (1946): 259–74.

34. Concerning this latter set, see Christopher Jones, *New Heroes in Antiquity: From Achilles to Antinoos* (Cambridge, MA: Harvard University Press, 2010), 38–47, 68.

35. Anton Elter, *Donarum Pateras* (Bonn, 1905–7), 40.

36. Cf. Cicero, *Leg.* 2.19: Ritus familiae patrumque seruanto. Diuos et eos qui caelestes semper habiti sunt colunto et ollos quos endo caelo merita locauerint,

Herculem, Liberum, Aesculapium, Castorem, Pollucem, Quirinum, ast olla propter quae datur hominibus ascensus in caelum, Mentem Virtutem, Pietatem, Fidem, earumque laudum delubra sunto nec ulla uitiorum sacra sollemnia obeunto. Quintus Horatius Flaccus (Horace), another interior writer in the Augustan Age, provided the same short list. Horace, *Carm.* 3.3; cf. Porphyry, *Marc.* 7.

37. John Pollini, "Man or God: Divine Assimilation and Imitation in the Late Republic and Early Principate," in *Between Republic and Empire: Interpretations of Augustus and His Principate* (ed. Kurt A. Raaflaub and Mark Toher; Berkeley: University of California Press, 1990), 334–35.

38. Clifford Weber, "The Dionysus in Aeneas," *CP* 97 (2002): 322–43.

39. Simon Price, "From Noble Funerals to Divine Cult: The Consecration of Roman Emperors," in *Rituals of Royalty: Power and Ceremonial in Traditional Societies* (ed. David Cannadine and Simon Price; Cambridge: Cambridge University Press, 1987), 73–76. Nero, among others, famously engaged in *imitatio Herculis* (Cf. Suet., *Nero* 53).

40. Peter Green, "Introduction," in *Argonautika*, by Apollonios Rhodios (exp. ed.; Berkeley: University of California Press, 1997), 15.

41. Matthew Fox, *Roman Historical Myths: The Regal Period in Augustan Literature* (Oxford: Clarendon Press, 1996).

42. Cf. Walter Burkert, "Caesar und Romulus-Quirinus," *Historia* 11 (1962): 356–76; Kenneth Scott, "The Identification of Augustus with Romulus-Quirinus," *TAPA* 56 (1925): 82–105.

43. Simon Price, "From Noble Funerals to Divine Cult," 73–74.

44. Scipio had gone so far as to shave his facial hair, in imitation of Alexander, a trend that persisted among Roman rulers into the periods of the later Roman Empire.

45. For a more in-depth study of Roman *imitatio Alexandri*, see especially Diana Spencer, *The Roman Alexander: Reading a Cultural Myth* (Exeter: University of Exeter Press, 2002) and Angela Kühnen, *Die imitatio Alexandri in der römischen Politik (1. Jh. v. Chr.—3. Jh. n. Chr.)* (Münster: Rhema Verlag, 2008).

46. Deborah T. Steiner, *Images in Mind: Statues in Archaic and Classical Greek Literature and Thought* (Princeton: Princeton University Press, 2001), 5–6. Cf. Claudia Bohm, *Imitatio Alexandri im Hellenismus: Untersuchungen zum politischen Nachwirken Alexanders des Grossen in hoch-und späthellenistischen Monarchien* (München: Tuduv, 1989) and A.B. Bossworth, *The Legacy of Alexander: Politics, Warfare, and Propaganda under the Successors* (Oxford: Oxford University Press, 2002).

47. Diana Spencer, *The Roman Alexander*, 17–18.

48. Karl Galinsky, *Augustan Culture: An Interpretive Introduction* (Princeton, NJ: Princeton University Press, 1996), 167–69.

49. For further discussion regarding these and related primary references, see Mary Beard, John North, and Simon Price, *Religions of Rome* (2 vols.; Cambridge: Cambridge University Press, 1998), 1:147. Contra n. 93 in Beard, Appian apparently did not indicate that Hadrian had been responsible for the inscription, but rather suggested that the epigram had been written quite prior to his reign.

50. Ibid., 140–49. This observation roughly concurs with Beard, North, and Price, namely, that the classical Mediterranean world understood deification not in a hard, literal fashion, but as a tacit function of supreme social and cultural signification. Cf. K. Galinsky, *Augustan Culture*, 322.

51. Plutarch, for instance, began his rendition of Pompey, writing: ἐν ἀρχῇ δὲ καὶ τὴν ὄψιν ἔσχεν οὐ μετρίως συνδημαγωγοῦσαν καὶ προεντυγχάνουσαν αὐτοῦ τῆς φωνῆς, τὸ γὰρ ἐράσμιον ἀξιωματικὸν ἦν φιλανθρώπως, καὶ ἐν

τῷ νεαρῷ καὶ ἀνθοῦντι διέφαινεν εὐθὺς ἡ ἀκμὴ τὸ γεραρὸν καὶ τὸ βασιλικὸν τοῦ ἤθους, ἦν δέ τις καὶ ἀναστολὴ τῆς κόμης ἀτρέμα καὶ τῶν περὶ τὰ ὄμματα ῥυθμῶν ὑγρότης τοῦ προσώπου, ποιοῦσα μᾶλλον λεγομένην ἢ φαινομένην ὁμοιότητα πρὸς τὰς Ἀλεχάνδρου τοῦ βασιλέως εἰκόνας. "At the outset, too, he had a countenance which helped him in no small degree to win the favour of the people, and which pleaded for him before he spoke. For even his boyish loveliness had a gentle dignity about it, and in the prime and flower of his youthful beauty there was at once manifest the majesty and kingliness of his nature. His hair was inclined to lift itself slightly from his forehead, and this, with a graceful contour of face about the eyes, produced a resemblance, more talked about than actually apparent, to the portrait statues of King Alexander" (Plutarch, *Pomp.* 2.1, Perrin).

52. This skepticism regarding the fairness of Antony's treatment in the ancient writers has not always been fully shared. See, for example, Paul Zanker, *The Power of Images in the Age of Augustus* (trans. Alan Shapiro; Ann Arbor: University of Michigan Press, 1988), 57–65.

53. With specific regard to numismatic evidence, see John Pollini, "Man or God," 340–41.

54. Diana Spencer, *The Roman Alexander*, 193–94.

55. Richard Stoneman, "The Latin Alexander," in *Latin Fiction: The Latin Novel in Context* (ed. Heinz Hofmann; London: Routledge, 1999), 170.

56. With regard to this complex relationship that Augustus negotiates with the Greek East, see especially Glen W. Bowersock, *Augustus and the Greek World* (Oxford: Clarendon Press, 1965).

57. *Ep.* 2.1.156–7; "Captive Greece took its feral captor captive and invaded uncultivated Latium with her Arts."

58. Simon Price, "The Place of Religion: Rome in the Early Empire," in *The Augustan Empire, 43 B.C.—A.D. 69* (ed. Alan K. Bowman, Edward Champlin, and Andrew Lintott; vol. 10 of *CAH*; Cambridge: Cambridge University Press, 1996), 814–17.

59. Cf., concerning the appropriation of the role and title *pontifex maximus,* Glen W. Bowersock, "The Pontificate of Augustus," in *Between Republic and Empire: Interpretations of Augustus and His Principate* (ed. Kurt A. Raaflaub and Mark Toher; Berkeley: University of California Press, 1990), 380–94.

60. Regarding the liminality of Augustus, see Walter Eder, "Augustus and the Power Tradition," in *The Cambridge Companion to the Age of Augustus* (ed. Karl Galinsky; Cambridge: Cambridge University Press, 2005), 13–32. Due to the success of this towering, transitional figure, Augustus became the imperial archetypal monarch, a mythic figure to be repeatedly emulated by later rulers of the principate and dominate periods. Augustus himself had become a founder, not unlike his own Romulus.

61. Duncan Fishwick, *The Imperial Cult in the Latin West* (2 vols; Leiden: E. J. Brill, 1991), II, 1–96. Cf. Simon Price, "Gods and Emperors: The Greek Language of the Roman Imperial Cult," *Journal of Hellenic Studies* 104 (1984): 79–95.

62. Cf. Livy, *Perioche* 134; Ovid, *Fasti* 1.608–616; Flor., *Epit.* 2.34.66.

63. Karl Galinsky, *Augustan Culture,* 313. For a more detailed study of Augustus's mimetic propaganda with regard to the image of Romulus, see Kenneth Scott, "The Identification of Augustus with Romulus-Quirinus."

64. With regard to the Greco-Roman philosophical traditions, see especially Paul Zanker, *The Mask of Socrates: The Image of the Intellectual in Antiquity* (trans. Alan Shapiro; Berkeley: University of California Press, 1995). With regard to Zoroaster and the magian traditions of the classical and the early medieval Mediterranean world, see Jenny Rose, *The Image of Zoroaster: The Persian Mage through European Eyes* (New York: Bibliotheca Persica Press, 2000).

65. See Mt 1.1–25 specifically. For a similar mimetic study of the Lukan birth myth, see Dennis R. MacDonald, *Luke and Vergil: Imitations of Classical Greek Literature* (The New Testament and Classical Greek Literature; Lanham, MD: Rowman and Littlefield, 2014). For a broader study, one more comparative in methodology with respect to Alexander and Jesus, see also Ory Amitay, *From Alexander to Jesus* (Berkeley: University of California Press, 2010).

66. This shift, namely, from a "quest for the historical Jesus" to a "quest for the historical communities that produced the early Christian Gospels," becomes visible once one juxtaposes the works of those who constitute the "First Quest," namely, such works as those of Reimarus, Strauß, and Wrede, with that of Bultmann, particularly in his *History of the Synoptic Tradition* (1921; trans. J, Marsh; Oxford: Basil Blackwell, 1963). To this point, the shift has found its most mature and clear articulation in the work of Burton Mack. Burton L. Mack, *The Christian Myth: Origins, Logic, and Legacy* (New York: The Continuum International Publishing Group, 2003), 25–40.

67. Note the oriental, cosmopolitan metaphysical range reflected (and tacitly legitimated) in Matthew's M material: Parthian sorcery, astrology, and oneiromancy (with both Joseph and Pilot's wife).

68. Diana Spencer, *The Roman Alexander*, 180.

69. Charles H. Talbert, *What Is a Gospel? The Genre of the Canonical Gospels* (Philadelphia: Fortress Press, 1977), 32.

70. Menander Rhetor, *On Epideictic Speeches* 370–71; Libanius, *Progymnasmata* Encomium 1. For a more thorough treatment of these protocols, see Donald Russell, "The Panegyrists and Their Teachers," in *The Propaganda of Power: The Role of Panegyric in Late Antiquity* (ed. Mary Whitby; Leiden: Brill, 1998), 17–50.

71. Robert J. Miller, *Divine Birth: The Births of Jesus and Other Sons of God* (Santa Rosa, CA: Polebridge Press, 2003).

72. As one of several examples of this central idea in Rudolf Bultmann, see his *Die Geschichte der synoptischen Tradition* (Forschungen zur Religion und Literatur des Alten und Neuen Testaments 29; Göttingen: Vandenhoeck & Ruprecht, 1921; trans. J Marsh; Oxford: Basil Blackwell, 1963), 8; for the English translation, see *The History of the Synoptic Tradition*, 11.

73. The Farrer theory holds that Mark wrote first, Matthew used Mark, and Luke used Mark and Matthew. Mark Goodacre provides the most up-to-date case for this position. Mark Goodacre, *The Case against Q: Studies in Markan Priority and the Synoptic Problem* (Harrisburg, PA: Trinity Press International, 2002). Still far and away the majority hypothesis, the four-source, with varying degrees of complexity, incorporates a hypothetical source document Q. Delbert Burkett provides perhaps the most recent comprehensive case for the Q hypothesis. Delbert Burkett, *Rethinking the Gospel Sources, Vol. 2: The Unity and Plurality of Q* (Society of Biblical Literature Early Christianity and Its Literature 1; Atlanta: Society of Biblical Literature, 2009).

74. This primitive material also includes content visible in Mark via Matthean doublets, perhaps one of the strongest arguments in favor of the existence of a textual Q.

75. Burton L. Mack, *Mark and Christian Origins: A Myth of Innocence* (Philadelphia: Fortress Press, 1988), 1–24.

76. The λόγια Mt 11.2–19 (Q 7.18–35) transforms the Baptizer's heralded, eschatological ὁ ἐρχόμενος into Isaiah's foretold Servant (intertexts: Isa 26.19 [dead], Isa 29.18–19 [deaf, blind, poor], Isa 61.1 [message to the poor and blind]). The "Son of Man" in the early Synoptic tradition often takes on more mundane, earthly connotations, images paradoxical to the mighty apocalyptic

Judge of humanity given in Daniel 7 and the *Similitudes of Enoch* (*1 En.* 53–57; 60–63; Cf. *4 Ezra*). This radical tension, from a *Traditionsgeschichte* perspective, points toward a contrived effort to reconcile two previously disparate constructs, namely, the remembered Jesus and the "Coming One" proclaimed by the Baptizer. As a basic introduction to the *Similitudes* and early Christian thought, see George W. E. Nickelsburg, *1 Enoch 2: A Commentary of the Book of 1 Enoch Chapters 37–82* (Hermeneia; Minneapolis: Fortress Press, 2011); Cf. Gabriele Boccaccini, ed., *Enoch and the Messiah Son of Man: Revisiting the Book of Parables* (Grand Rapids: Eerdmans, 2007).

77. Rudolf Bultmann, *The Theology of the New Testament* (trans. Kendrick Grobel; 2 vols; New York: Charles Scribner's Sons, 1954; German orig., 1951), 1:30–31; Adela Yarbro Collins, "The Origin of the Designation of Jesus as 'Son of Man,'" *HTR* 80 (1987): 391–407. Cf. Simon J. Joseph, *The Non-Violent Messiah: Jesus, Q, and the Enochic Tradition* (Minneapolis: Fortress Press, 2014). This enticing observation may suggest a plausible degree of similarity and continuity between the historical proclamation of the Baptizer and that of Jesus, his cousin according to Luke, with the latter historically having born (rather than fulfilled) the legacy of the former.

78. The basic proclamation of Jesus in the earliest stratum of Q was essentially identical with the message of the Baptizer: "Repent, for the Son of Man is coming to exact judgment upon the earth." "Son of Man" for both figures is ὁ ἐρχόμενος, the ultimate apocalyptic judge, just as presented in the *Similitudes of Enoch*. Q 7.18–35, therefore, presented the accretion of a later stratum, that is, the earliest point at which Jesus himself became identified with the "Son of Man" figure. Mark took up this same task, namely, that of associating the more modest bare aspects of the Jesus story as here described. The single most dramatic turning point in the Markan narrative occured over this very redefinition, namely, at the end of Mk 8. Καὶ ἤρξατο διδάσκειν αὐτοὺς ὅτι δεῖ τὸν υἱὸν τοῦ ἀνθρώπου πολλὰ παθεῖν (Mk 8.31a).

The term "myth" above refers to the commonly held mental sketch of the man that circulated at the time and does not imply that no historical person "Jesus" had existed as founder of an original movement. The escalation in embellishment in the Gospel traditions, and not merely its accretion, serves to disprove the Jesus Myth theory. From this trajectory, one is able to derive a more modest, human figure behind the earliest stratum. The recent Jesus Myth movement in academia, however, contributes substantively to the understanding of these early Christian renditions of Jesus in that, for the most part, the texts did present a mythologized founder and emblem for the ancient movement(s). This shift away from the faith-based presumption of postulating historical accuracy in the Gospel portrayals of Jesus realigns the discussion with the conventional literary and cultural patterns of classical antiquity, precisely where that discussion belongs, and frees the discourse from the delusive a priori impact of socially governed systems of "belief" that have all too often derailed the modern discourse. One must remain mindful that these texts have served as the sacred bedrock of Western myth and, as such, have presented a most formidable resistance to conclusive academic inquiry.

79. Our modern regard for Homer's epics as high literature should not delude us into overlooking their universal familiarity and appeal throughout popular Hellenistic society. For a more extensive proposal of Mark's mimetic use of Homer, see Dennis R. MacDonald, *The Homeric Epics and the Gospel of Mark* (New Haven: Yale University Press, 2000).

80. Hans-Josef Klauck, *Apocryphal Gospels, An Introduction* (trans. Brian McNeil; New York: T & T Clark, 2003; German orig., 2002), 2. The conclusion that the qualification "canonical" as a means of dividing the larger corpus

of early Christian gospels was a later, arbitrary political imposition comports with the works by Helmut Koester, Ron Cameron, and Elaine Pagels and seems only to receive considerable objection from the faith-based community. Helmut Koester, *Ancient Christian Gospels, Their History and Development* (Harrisburg, PA: Trinity Press, 1990), 1–48; Ron Cameron, *The Other Gospels, Non-Canonical Gospel Texts* (Philadelphia: Westminster Press, 1982); Elaine Pagels, *The Gnostic Gospels* (New York: Random House, 1979).

81. These conclusions cohere with general thesis of Walter Bauer, that of Gregory J. Riley, and the common findings of the quite recent SBL Seminar on Christian Origins. Walter Bauer, *Orthodoxy and Hersesy in Earliest Christianity* (trans. a team from the Philadelphia Seminar of Christian Origins; ed. Robert A. Kraft and Gerhard Krodel; Mifflintown, PA: Sigler Press, 1971); Gregory J. Riley, *One Jesus, Many Christs: How Jesus Inspired not One True Christianity, but Many* (Chicago: University of Chicago Press, 1997); Ron Cameron and Merrill P. Miller, eds., *Redescribing Christian Origins* (SBLSS 28; Leiden: Brill, 2004).

82. These adjustments to Bultmann generally concur with the critical directives outlined by Burton Mack in more recent years. For example, Mack concludes that "we need to start over with the quest for Christian origins. And the place to start is with the observation that the New Testament texts are not only inadequate for a Jesus quest, they are data for an entirely different phenomenon. They are not the mistaken and embellished memories of the historical person, but the myths of origin imagined by early Christians seriously engaged in their social experiments. They are data for early Christian mythmaking. The questions appropriate to these texts should be about the many Christian groups and movements in evidence, their particular social circumstances and histories, and the various social reasons they had for imagining a teacher in so many different ways. To read these texts only in the interest of the quest to know the historical Jesus has been to misread them, to misuse them. They simply do not contain the secrets of the historical Jesus for which scholars have been searching. Early Christians were not interested in the *historical* Jesus. They were interested in something else. So the question is whether that something else can be identified." Mack then correctly proceeds to describe these subtexts of early Christian mythmaking as primarily concerned with social struggle, legitimacy, and identity negotiation. Mack is precisely correct in this assessment. Burton L. Mack, *The Christian Myth: Origins, Logic, and Legacy,* 40.

83. John's depiction, through the metonymic image of the founder, repudiated the interpretation of the Christian cult as a political force. See particularly Jn 18.29–38.

84. The monograph by Jan Willem van Henten and Friedrich Avemarie surveys appropriations of these classical literary themes within both the Hellenistic Jewish and the early Christian traditions. Jan Willem van Henten and Friedrich Avemarie, *Martyrdom and Noble Death: Selected Texts from Greco-Roman, Jewish and Christian Antiquity* (London: Routledge, 2002).

85. The "cup" of which he was determined to drink (Mk 10:38; Mt 20:22) invoked the well-known dialogue given by Socrates to his disciples as he faced his imminent death by drinking his poisonous cup of hemlock. While such a tale may seem distant and obscure to modern eyes, the story of the death of Socrates occupied a central place within even a most basic, popular notion of "philosophy" in the classical world.

86. The Apostle Peter's speech on Pentecost in Acts of the Apostles (Acts 3) addressed this injustice and the matter of culpability, seemingly unaware of any theological significance of the execution of his master. Indeed, vicarious "death for sins" was altogether absent as an idea throughout Luke-Acts.

Martyrdom in the narratives performed as an inculpatory spectacle, that is, the scandalous death of the innocent.

87. "Do you think that I cannot appeal to my Father and he will at once send me more than twelve legions of angels"; Matt 26.53.

88. Ernst George Hardy, *Christianity and the Roman Government* (London: George Allen & Unwin, Ltd., 1952); Robert Louis Wilken, *The Christians as the Romans Saw Them* (New Haven: Yale University Press, 1984); and Dale B. Martin, *Inventing Superstition: From the Hippocratics to the Christians* (Cambridge, MA: Harvard University Press, 2004).

89. Ramsay MacMullen, *Christianizing the Roman Empire, A.D. 100–400* (New Haven: Yale University Press, 1984). The conversion of Roman political figures implies a sufficient degree of compatibility between the religion and the Roman state, somewhat analogous to the conversion of various such persons to Stoicism in the Late Republic and thereafter. Cf. Michele Renee Salzman, *The Making of a Christian Aristocracy: Social and Religious Change in the Western Roman Empire* (Cambridge, MA: Harvard University Press, 2002).

90. Cf. Arthur Darby Nock, *Conversion: The Old and the New in Religion from Alexander the Great to Augustine of Hippo* (Oxford: Clarendon Press, 1933), 99–253.

BIBLIOGRAPHY

Amitay, Ory. *From Alexander to Jesus*. Berkeley: University of California Press, 2010.

Anderson, Andrew Runni. "Heracles and His Successors: A Study of a Heroic Ideal and the Recurrence of a Heroic Type." *Harvard Studies in Classical Philology* 39 (1928): 7–58.

Barthes, Roland. *Elements of Semiology*. Translated by Annette Lavers and Colin Smith. London: Jonathan Cape, 1967.

———. "The Death of the Author." Pages 142–48 in *Image, Music, Text*. Translated by Stephen Heath. New York: Hill and Wang, 1977.

Bauer, Walter. *Rechtgläubigkeit und Ketzerei im ältesten Christentum*. Tübingen: Mohr, 1934.

———. *Orthodoxy and Heresy in Earliest Christianity*. Translated by a team from the Philadelphia Seminar of Christian Origins. Edited by Robert A. Kraft and Gerhard Krodel. Mifflintown, PA: Sigler Press, 1971.

Beard, Mary, John North, and Simon Price. *Religions of Rome*. 2 vols. Cambridge: Cambridge University Press, 1998.

Boccaccini, Gabriele, ed. *Enoch and the Messiah Son of Man: Revisiting the Book of Parables*. Grand Rapids: Eerdmans, 2007.

Bohm, Claudia. *Imitatio Alexandri im Hellenismus: Untersuchungen zum politischen Nachwirken Alexanders des Grossen in hoch-und späthellenistischen Monarchien*. München: Tuduv, 1989.

Bossworth, A. B. *The Legacy of Alexander: Politics, Warfare, and Propaganda under the Successors*. Oxford: Oxford University Press, 2002.

Bowersock, Glen W. *Augustus and the Greek World*. Oxford: Clarendon Press, 1965.

———. "The Pontificate of Augustus." Pages 380–94 in *Between Republic and Empire: Interpretations of Augustus and His Principate*. Edited by Kurt A. Raaflaub and Mark Toher. Berkeley: University of California Press, 1990.

Brooks, Peter. "Freud's Masterplot: Questions of Narrative." *Yale French Studies* 55/56 (1977): 280–300.

Brown, Truesdell S. "Euhemerus and the Historians." *Harvard Theological Review* 39 (1946): 259–74.

Bultmann, Rudolf. *Die Geschichte der synoptischen Tradition*. Forschungen zur Religion und Literatur des Alten und Neuen Testaments 29. Göttingen: Vandenhoeck & Ruprecht, 1921.

———. *Das Evangelium des Johannes*. Kritisch-exegetischer Kommentar über das Neue Testament. Göttingen: Vandenhoeck & Ruprecht, 1941.

———. *The Theology of the New Testament*. Translated by Kendrick Grobel. 2 vols. New York: Charles Scribner's Sons, 1954. (German orig., 1951).

Burkert, Walter. "Caesar und Romulus-Quirinus." *Historia* 11 (1962): 356–76.

———. *Greek Religion*. Cambridge, MA: Harvard University Press, 1985.

Burkett, Delbert. *Rethinking the Gospel Sources, Vol. 2: The Unity and Plurality of Q*. Society of Biblical Literature Early Christianity and Its Literature 1. Atlanta: Society of Biblical Literature, 2009.

Cameron, Ron. *The Other Gospels, Non-Canonical Gospel Texts*. Philadelphia: Westminster Press, 1982.

Cameron, Ron and Merrill P. Miller, eds. *Redescribing Christian Origins*. Society of Biblical Literature Symposium Series 28. Leiden: Brill, 2004.

Collins, Adela Yarbro. "The Origin of the Designation of Jesus as 'Son of Man.'" *Harvard Theological Review* 80 (1987): 391–407.

———. *Mark: A Commentary*. Hermeneia. Minneapolis: Fortress Press, 2007.

Creed, John. "Uses of Classical Mythology." Pages 1–21 in *The Theory of Myth, Six Studies*. Edited by Adrian Cunningham. London: Sheed and Ward, 1973.

Derrida, Jacques. *Points de suspension*. Paris: Galilée, 1992.

Descartes, René. *Discours de la méthode pour bien conduire sa raison, et chercher la vérité dans les sciences*. Paris: Théodore Girard, 1668.

Dundes, Alan. "The Hero Pattern and the Life of Jesus." Pages 179–223 in *In Quest of the Hero* Edited by Robert A. Segal. Princeton, NJ: Princeton University Press, 1990.

Eco, Umberto. *The Limits of Interpretation*. Bloomington and Indianapolis: Midland Books, 1994.

Eder, Walter. "Augustus and the Power Tradition." Translated by Karl Galinsky. Pages 13–32 in *The Cambridge Companion to the Age of Augustus*. Edited by Karl Galinsky. Cambridge: Cambridge University Press, 2005.

Elter, Anton. *Donarum Pateras*. Bonn, 1905–7.

Evans, Jane DeRose. *The Art of Persuasion: Political Propaganda from Aeneas to Brutus*. Ann Arbor: University of Michigan Press, 1992.

Fishwick, Duncan. *The Imperial Cult in the Latin West*. 2 vols. Leiden: E. J. Brill, 1991.

Foucault, Michel. *Les mots et les choses*. Paris: Gallimard, 1966.

———. *The Order of Things*. Translated by Alan Sheridan. New York: Vintage Books, 1994.

Fox, Matthew. *Roman Historical Myths: The Regal Period in Augustan Literature*. Oxford: Clarendon Press, 1996.

Galinsky, Karl. *Augustan Culture: An Interpretive Introduction*. Princeton, NJ: Princeton University Press, 1996.

Gebauer, Gunter and Christoph Wulf. *Mimesis. Kultur—Kunst—Gesellschaft*. Reinbek: Rowohlt, 1992.

Goodacre, Mark. *The Case against Q: Studies in Markan Priority and the Synoptic Problem*. Harrisburg, PA: Trinity International Press, 2002.

Green, Peter. "Introduction." Pages 1–41 in *Argonautika*. By Apollonios Rhodios. Exp. ed. Berkeley: University of California Press, 1997.

Halliwell, Stephen. *The Aesthetics of Mimesis: Ancient Texts and Modern Problems*. Princeton, NJ: Princeton University Press, 2002.

Hardy, Ernst George. *Christianity and the Roman Government*. London: George Allen & Unwin, Ltd., 1952.

Harkness, James. Translator's introduction. Pages 1–12 in *This Is not a Pipe with Illustrations and Letters by René Magritte*. By Michel Foucault. Berkeley: University of California Press, 1983.

Henten, Jan Willem van and Friedrich Avemarie. *Martyrdom and Noble Death: Selected Texts from Greco-Roman, Jewish and Christian Antiquity.* London: Routledge, 2002.

Joseph, Simon J. *The Non-Violent Messiah: Jesus, Q, and the Enochic Tradition.* Minneapolis: Fortress Press, 2014.

Jung, Carl Gustav, ed. *Man and His Symbols.* New York: Doubleday, 1964.

Klauck, Hans-Josef. *Apocryphal Gospels, An Introduction.* Translated by Brian McNeil. New York: T & T Clark, 2003. (German orig., 2002).

Koester, Helmut. *Ancient Christian Gospels, Their History and Development.* Harrisburg, PA: Trinity Press, 1990.

Kühnen, Angela. *Die imitatio Alexandri in der römischen Politik (1. Jh. v. Chr.—3. Jh. n. Chr.).* Münster: Rhema Verlag, 2008.

Kümmel, Werner Georg. *Introduction to the New Testament.* Translated by Howard Clark Kee. Nashville: Abingdon Press, 1975.

Lacan, Jacques. "Le Stade du miroir comme formateur de la fonction du Je, telle qu'elle nous est révélée dans l'expérience psychanalytique" (1949). Pages 93–100 in *Écrits*. Paris: Seuil, 1966.

———. "The Mirror Stage, as Formative of the Function of the I as Revealed in Psychoanalytic Experience." Pages 1–7 in *Écrits: A Selection.* Translated by Alan Sheridan. London: Tavistock, 1977.

Lotman, Yuri M. *Universe of the Mind: A Semiotic Theory of Culture.* Translated by Ann Shukman. Indianapolis: Indiana University Press, 1990.

MacDonald, Dennis R. *The Homeric Epics and the Gospel of Mark.* New Haven: Yale University Press, 2000.

———. *Luke and Vergil: Imitations of Classical Greek Literature.* The New Testament and Classical Greek Literature. Lanham, MD: Rowman and Littlefield, 2014.

Mack, Burton L. *Mark and Christian Origins: A Myth of Innocence.* Philadelphia: Fortress Press, 1988.

———. *The Christian Myth: Origins, Logic, and Legacy.* New York: The Continuum International Publishing Group, 2003.

MacMullen, Ramsay. *Christianizing the Roman Empire, A.D. 100–400.* New Haven: Yale University Press, 1984.

Maquet, Pierre, Carlyle Smith, and Robert Stickgold, eds. *Sleep and Brain Plasticity.* Oxford: Oxford University Press, 2003.

Martin, Dale B. *Inventing Superstition: From the Hippocrats to the Christians.* Cambridge, MA: Harvard University Press, 2004.

McNamara, Patrick. *An Evolutionary Psychology of Sleep and Dreams.* Westport, CT: Praeger Publishers, 2004.

Merkur, Daniel. *Psychoanalytic Approaches to Myth.* New York: Routledge, 2005.

Miller, Robert J. *Divine Birth: The Births of Jesus and Other Sons of God.* Santa Rosa, CA: Polebridge Press, 2003.

Nickelsburg, George W. E. *1 Enoch 2: A Commentary of the Book of 1 Enoch Chapters 37–82.* Hermeneia. Minneapolis: Fortress Press, 2011.

Nock, Arthur Darby. *Conversion: The Old and the New in Religion from Alexander the Great to Augustine of Hippo.* Oxford: Clarendon Press, 1933.

———. "Notes on Ruler-cult, I-IV." *Journal of Hellenic Studies* 48 (1929): 21–43.

Pagels, Elaine. *The Gnostic Gospels.* New York: Random House, 1979.

Paulus, Heinrich Eberhard Gottlob. *Das Leben Jesu als Grundlage einer reinen Geschichte des Urchristentums.* 2 vols. Heidelberg: C. F. Winter, 1928.

Pollini, John. "Man or God: Divine Assimilation and Imitation in the Late Republic and Early Principate." Pages 334–63 in *Between Republic and Empire:*

Interpretations of Augustus and His Principate. Edited by Kurt A. Raaflaub and Mark Toher. Berkeley: University of California Press, 1990.

Price, Simon. "From Noble Funerals to Divine Cult: The Consecration of Roman Emperors." Pages 56–105 in *Rituals of Royalty: Power and Ceremonial in Traditional Societies.* Edited by David Cannadine and Simon Price. Cambridge: Cambridge University Press, 1987.

———. "The Place of Religion: Rome in the Early Empire." Pages 812–47 in *The Augustan Empire, 43 B.C.—A.D. 69.* Edited by Alan K. Bowman, Edward Champlin, and Andrew Lintott. Vol. 10 of *The Cambridge Ancient History.* Cambridge: Cambridge University Press, 1996.

Raglan, Lord. *The Hero: A Study in Tradition, Myth, and Drama.* London: Methuen, 1936.

Riley, Gregory J. *One Jesus, Many Christs: How Jesus Inspired not One True Christianity, but Many.* Chicago: University of Chicago Press, 1997.

———. *The River of God: A New History of Christian Origins.* New York: HarperCollins, 2001.

Rose, Jenny. *The Image of Zoroaster: The Persian Mage through European Eyes.* New York: Bibliotheca Persica Press, 2000.

Russell, Donald. "The Panegyrists and Their Teachers." Pages 17–50 in *The Propaganda of Power: The Role of Panegyric in Late Antiquity.* Edited by Mary Whitby. Leiden: Brill, 1998.

Sagan, Carl et al. *Murmurs of Earth: The Voyager Interstellar Record.* New York: Random House, 1978.

Salzman, Michele Renee. *The Making of a Christian Aristocracy: Social and Religious Change in the Western Roman Empire.* Cambridge, MA: Harvard University Press, 2002.

Saussure, Ferdinand de. *Cours de Linguistique générale.* Paris: Éditions Payot & Rivages, 1916.

Scott, James C. *Domination and the Arts of Resistance: Hidden Transcripts.* New Haven: Yale University Press, 1990.

Scott, Kenneth. "The Identification of Augustus with Romulus-Quirinus." *Transactions of the American Philological Association* 56 (1925): 82–105.

Spencer, Diana. *The Roman Alexander: Reading a Cultural Myth.* Exeter: University of Exeter Press, 2002.

Stoneman, Richard. "The Latin Alexander." Pages 167–86 in *Latin Fiction: The Latin Novel in Context.* Edited by Heinz Hofmann. London: Routledge, 1999.

Strauß, David Friedrich. *Das Leben Jesu, kritisch bearbeitet.* 2 vols. Tübingen: Osiander, 1835–1836.

Streeter, Burnett Hillman. *The Four Gospels: A Study of Origins.* Rev. ed. London: Macmillan, 1930. (Orig., 1924).

Sumi, Geoffrey S. "Impersonating the Dead: Mimes at Roman Funerals." *American Journal of Philology* 123 (2002): 559–85.

Talbert, Charles H. *What Is a Gospel? The Genre of the Canonical Gospels.* Philadelphia: Fortress Press, 1977.

Weber, Clifford. "The Dionysus in Aeneas." *Classical Philology* 97 (2002): 322–43.

Wilken, Robert Louis. *The Christians as the Romans Saw Them.* New Haven: Yale University Press, 1984.

Winiarczyk, Marek. *Euhemeros von Messene. Leben, Werk und Nachwirkung.* Munich and Leipzig: K. G. Saur, 2002.

Zanker, Paul. *The Power of Images in the Age of Augustus.* Translated by Alan Shapiro. Ann Arbor: University of Michigan Press, 1988.

———. *The Mask of Socrates: The Image of the Intellectual in Antiquity.* Translated by Alan Shapiro. Berkeley: University of California Press, 1995.

4   Translation Fables and the Gospels

> It would seem that mythological worlds have been built up, only to be shattered again, and that new worlds were built from the fragments.
>
> [Franz Boas, 1898][1]

Considering the occidental-oriental heterogeneity of the crossroads cultures of urban Anatolia and Syria during Roman governance, regions formerly held by the Achaemenid, the Seleucid, and the Parthian empires, the philologist of antique Greek narrative properly anticipates such a provenience to yield a cultural-linguistic bricolage. This cradle of nascent Christian traditions, according to visible evidence and the broad assessment of scholars, provided the linguistic-literary milieu of the four etiological Christian narratives, that is, the New Testament Gospels.[2] Without determined indication to the contrary, the reader, therefore, must identify the *langue* of these episodic tales as fundamentally that of the northern littoral regions of the Hellenistic Levant, indeed despite the Jewish Palestinian setting of these narratives and appropriated Jewish content. To compose in Greek implied Hellenism, that is, the conscious and deliberate art of drawing on and adapting Hellenic cultural-literary convention. All such compositions spoke to and from Hellenic cultural codes and the canons of Greek literature. The demonstration and degree of this structural valence displayed the qualification of such compositions within high and middle Hellenistic cultures well into the Roman period. The Hellenizing *bricoleur* of the Romano-Greek East, along with the rising influence of a robust Latin literary tradition from the West, relied upon this rich storehouse of Greek literary and cultural conventions through the innovative strategies of resemblance, interplay, and mimesis.

Such literature subserved social and cultural identity negotiation in provincial Anatolia and Syria, typically in relation to the cultural dominion of the classical Hellenic *oeuvre* and the Greek *way*, as well as, to a lesser degree, emergent Romanism. Within the instability and currents of social and cultural upheaval and displacement one observes the agency and performance of such literature, as cultural anthropologist Victor W. Turner wrote:

The social world is a world in becoming, not a world in being (except insofar as "being" is a description of the static, atemporal models men have in their heads), and for this reason studies of social structure *as such* are irrelevant. They are erroneous in basic premise because there is no such thing as "static action." That is why I am a little chary of the terms "community" or "society," too, though I do use them, for they are often thought of as static concepts. Such a view violates the actual flux and changefulness of the human social scene.[3]

Rather than a memento or *souvenir* dispensed from this socio-cultural turbulence and flux, the text itself comes as a center-stage participant; indeed, the text survived as a vehicle of flux precisely due to its persistent, dynamic agency in redrawing and forging new spaces of socio-cultural identity over and against the *status quo*, a *status quo* that was itself but a cultural illusion. Tim Whitmarsh writes:

Cultural identity is not innate, but constructed and vied for in social space. In Stuart Hall's terms, it is "not an essence but a *positioning*" . . . Identity is never self-evident, but it can be experienced or constructed as such. Paradigms of identity-construction may be more or less unified in some cultures than in others. It is important to be precise on this point, because I am categorically not stating that harmonious socio-political conditions lead axiomatically to a sense of security amongst the people in relation to patterns of identity. Notwithstanding that it is empirically untrue, this is also a flawed means of describing historical change: there is a danger of imposing a seductively trite historiographical narrative that describes movement from order to fragmentation. . . . No society is "stable," in the sense of being free from tensions and currents that make the future an object of struggle. "Continuity" is only visible in retrospect: as such, it is a historiographical fiction rather than a necessarily accurate characterization of contemporary experience in the society in question.[4]

For those who produce and signify a text, what is at stake in the composed depiction is not the past, but the future. The renegade emerging Christian movement(s) of the northern provinces of the Levant struggled, perhaps as much as any other movement in cultural-history, to stake out their identity in relation to the unstable tensions of upheaval at work in the latter first century and early second. The creolized pastiche of charged images and rhetoric packaged and delivered in the Gospels found its meaning, traction, and purposefulness there, in that freighted context.

The hybridic cultures of ancient Levantine urban society alert the careful reader to the expected structural complexities in language in the Gospels; such complexities combined with a prevalent heterogeneity of genre, fashionable and present in most writings of that period.[5] Consequently, as one may perhaps anticipate, determination of the genre of the New Testament Gospels has proven quite problematic. The four documents simply defy any tidy literary category, whether one speaks of the document as a whole or of the generic qualities of episodes, themes, or conventions contained within each text. Adding yet another dimension to the heterogeneity of Hellenism and Orientalism in the Gospels came the compositional art of weaving traditional forms and modes together with fresh and novel expression.[6] The second of the four composers, undoubtedly qualifying himself as a skilled γραμματεύς and, as such, standardizing the written Gospel tradition, articulated this principle: πᾶς γραμματεὺς μαθητευθεὶς τῇ βασιλείᾳ τῶν οὐρανῶν ὅμοιός ἐστιν ἀνθρώπῳ οἰκοδεσπότῃ, ὅστις ἐκβάλλει ἐκ τοῦ θησαυροῦ αὐτοῦ καινὰ καὶ παλαιά (Matt. 13.52; "Every writer who has been taught the kingdom of heaven is like a householder who from his treasury exhibits items both new and antique"). Following Barthes, however, even the new elements (τὰ καινά) of any composition, from a semiotic standpoint, represent recognizable forms mixed and reconstituted in fresh ways that coalesce into distinct, inventive products. Upon closer examination, such a process accounts for all literary innovation and novelty, a most general phenomenon that often illudes the reader that a genuine leap of originality has arisen.[7] This compositional process, as much as in any other counter-cultural movement through the ages, characterized the creative Muse or Spirit behind the New Testament Gospels. Complex, beautiful, dangerous, these laconic narratives teased, flipped, and ultimately transformed the cultural space of Roman antiquity, bursting Hellenistc Judaism at its seams. The "new wine" of the Gospels found a proper wineskin, the whole of the classical Mediterranean world.

Further grasp of the radical heterogeneity in the Gospels arises from fundamental socio-religious and source-critical intricacies, as has been touched upon in Chapter 3. While the λόγια tradition appears to have originally served the needs of and arisen from an apocalyptic Hellenistic Jewish sect of Syria Phoenice and perhaps northern Syria, Mark and the remaining content sources of the Gospels at several points transgressed the outskirts of sectarian Judaism, perhaps here better termed Judaic Hellenism. Despite the Palestinian Jewish setting, occasional sprinkled Semitisms, and rhetorical inculpatory critiques of Palestinian Judaisms, the fundamental cultural-linguistic constitution of the Gospels often adapted the broader cultural and literary structures and conventions of the Hellenistic, Roman-governed Levant. Such a daring measure of hybridity tests the limits of those apt to confine the Gospels to familiar "in-house" varieties of Hellenistic Judaism. Fierce bi-directional appropriation and adaptation distinguished these texts, with potent forms drawn from early Jewish and Persian tradition as well as from Hellenistic and Roman culture.[8]

The myths of Roman origins, moreover, established the scaffolding for the empire's new transcendent rival, Christianity, as this book in part endeavors to demonstrate. Much of early Christian social structure, nomenclature, and rhetoric mimicked the empire by providing its transformed, counter-cultured alternative. As Emma Dench has vividly illustrated, with the rise of the imperial period came the creative rewriting of Latin etiology, the forging of myths of the plurality of Roman roots. The legendary rape (*raptio;* "stealing") of the Sabine women and the Latin asylum policies provided by the founder of Rome, divine Romulus, served as fabulous justification for the de-centering of Latinality under Caesar and the Julio-Claudian dynasty. Caesar became both famous and infamous for his admission of senators and citizens from the dregs of society and from foreign lands, that is, those outside Italy.[9] Augustus likewise extended citizenship to numerous groups in his far-flung, expanding empire, not to mention his radical expansion of senatorial seats, often granted to men outside Roman aristocracy as well as to favored foreigners. Claudius became notorious, according to Seneca, for his liberal application of this policy of granting citizenship (*Apol 3*): *Constituerat enim omnes Graecos, Gallos, Hispanos, Britannos togatos videre* ("He decided indeed to see the whole world in a toga, Greeks, Gauls, Spaniards, and Britons"). The provision of foreign asylum and clemency, as a strategy of imperial expansion and the requisite appropriation and reconstitution of power, became the hallmark of the Roman *princeps*. The Gospels mimicked these precise strategies even in their most primitive content, visible behind Matthew's redacted λόγια:[10]

πολλοὶ ἀπό ἀνατολῶν καὶ δυσμῶν ἥξουσιν καὶ ἀνακλιθήσονται μετὰ Αβραὰμ καὶ Ἰσαὰκ καὶ Ἰακὼβ ἐν τῇ βασιλείᾳ τῶν οὐρανῶν, οἱ δὲ υἱοὶ τῆς βασιλείας ἐκβληθήσονται εἰς τὸ σκότος τὸ ἐξώτερον· ἐκεῖ ἔσται ὁ κλαυθμὸς καὶ ὁ βρυγμὸς τῶν ὀδόντων.

(Mt 8.11–12)

Many will come from the East and from the West and will recline with Abraham, Isaac, and Jacob in heaven's kingdom, but you will be exiled to the furthest darkness, where there will be crying and the grinding of teeth.

This mimetic subtext continued throughout the four New Testament Gospels, finding its fullest articulation in the foundation narratives of Luke-Acts.[11] Elementary to this book, one considers the broadening Levantine appeal of the Gospels, executed through the invoked range of cultural codes, conventions, and semiotic structures, both occidental and oriental, and quite often not indigenous to Judaism or to the classical Hebrew tradition.

Awareness of the heterogeneity and cosmopolitan valences of the Gospel narratives establishes the basis of this, the fourth chapter of the book, and ironically allows for a more refined inquiry of examination:

- Given the multiplicity of themes, conventions, and traditions at work within these four documents, does any or all of these works apply the translation fable to their aretological portrayal of the movement's sacred founding sage, Jesus? Is the presence of such signals sufficient in any or each of these texts to direct the ancient reader to signify the respective final episode in this fashion?

- What other or contrary signals may have complicated these earliest readings?
- Besides Justin's apologies, did other early Christian works indicate the early Christian reception of New Testament "resurrection" narratives?

The thesis concludes with the endeavor to answer these principal questions. While the study does not propose a comprehensive philological treatment of each "resurrection narrative" in the four Gospels, the inquiry does aim carefully to address the above-indicated questions, focusing to assess the matter raised by Justin's confession (Chapter 1), namely, the cultural and anthropological congruity of these narratives within the standing forms of Mediterranean antiquity.

4.1 THE "RESURRECTION" POLYSEME IN THE GOSPELS

To what extent do the New Testament Gospels direct their ancient readers to comprehend the so-called resurrection narratives as "translation narratives"? What clear linguistic signals appear in these closing episodes? Complicating the matter, readings of the English New Testament have come to place no distinction between polysemic applications of "resurrection" in describing three quite different phenomena, each to be taken in turn.

The Renovation of Creation and the End of Hades

Prompting an interpretation from an early Jewish linguistic domain, the Gospels themselves parse the Palestinian Jewish social cast through various responses to notions of general eschatological resurrection (ἀνάστασις). Comprehensive surveys of early Jewish resurrection belief have demonstrated that these delineations indeed did serve the negotiation of socio-sectarian identity, particularly as forged within and vis-à-vis the crucible of the Maccabean revolt in the first and second centuries B.C.E.[12] Early Judaism emerged from within this fiery, protracted struggle between East and West, that is, between the Hellenistic empires (Seleucid, Ptolemaic, and Roman) and the Persian empires (Achaemenid and Parthian), as each vied for military, political, and cultural dominion over Palestine. Whereas שְׁאוֹל(She'ol; "the grave") had begun to take on connotations synonymous with the Greek Hades—Indeed, the Septuagint translates the term as such—in the classical Hebrew writings, that is, prior to the emergence of early Jewish apocalypticism, one finds inadequate evidence of myths of an eschatological resurrection of the dead.[13] Within the early Jewish apocalyptic works (e.g., Daniel,

1 Enoch, 2 Baruch, 4 Ezra, et al.), Pharisaic Judaism, and early Christian writings, notions of a "day of resurrection" and an awaited eschatological renewal of creation emerged. The evidence indicates that this trend had its genetic origin in early Persian theology, namely, in dominant Zoroastrian eschatology of the Achaemenid period and its continued prevalence into Parthian culture. As John J. Collins proposes, corporate resurrection of the dead and *creatura renovata* (cosmic renewal) invoked themes of the Orient, namely, as systemic to Persian eschatology:

> Neither the Egyptians nor the Greeks conceived of an end of history that might be the occasion of a general resurrection. Such an idea was, however, an integral part of Persian eschatology and can be documented already in Hellenistic times. There is surely some influence from these sources on the early Jewish apocalypses. (The overtones of astral immortality in Dan. 12 provide a case in point). But the ideas of immortality that we find in these texts can not be categorized as simple borrowings. They adapt motifs from the surrounding cultures, but they re-configure them in a distinctive way. Immortality in these apocalypses is primarily life with the heavenly host, the holy ones known from Near Eastern mythology since the second millennium B.C.E. The notion of a fiery hell is more novel, but here again the novelty is achieved by *bricolage*.[14]

Like culturally disparate traditional themes, motifs, and cadences, mixed together to create a *nouveau* piece of music—indeed, the cultural success of most music relies upon this art—the apocalypticists played upon stereotypic oriental elements, conjuring and celebrating a sentimentality of orientalism as a theme or tacit mood of resistance in the face of occidental power. In this way, namely, by identification with the broader defiant cultural force in the East, early Jewish texts delineated their own cultural contestation and space in relation to Seleucid and Roman cultural encroachment. The heroes in the Book of Daniel exhibit in their modes of resistance, not their Jewishness per se, ironically, but the superiority of their (stereotypical) Persianness! In the superiority of their oneiromancy, their visions, their eschatology, their authority over lions and fire, their dietary ascesis, these heroes trump the seers (*magi*) of the Persian court.[15]

The earliest expressions of hope of a physical resurrection of the dead in Jewish literature occurred in Daniel 12 and in 2 Maccabees 7, both texts idealizing and modeling a subtext of Jewish political resistance vis-à-vis the Seleucids in the second century B.C.E. through superior mastery of the oppressor's cultural capital.[16] The earliest known attestations in human civilization to the belief, the fourth-century B.C.E. works of Theopompus, of Chios and Eudemus of Rhodes, described the eschatological resurrection of the dead as a signature tenet of Persian (Zoroastrian) theology. Diogenes Laërtius quoted Theopompus's *Philippica*, stating: ὅς καὶ ἀναβιώσεσθαι κατὰ τοὺς Μάγους φησὶ τοὺς ἀνθρώπους καὶ ἀθανάτους ἔσεσθαι, καὶ τὰ ὄντα ταῖς αὐτῶν ἐπικλήσεσι διαμενεῖν ("He also said that, according to the magi, human beings will come back to life and will be immortal and that, by means of their incantations, the cosmos will persist").[17] On account of the basic contours of magian doctrine that Diogenes sketched, he wrote that some acknowledged Judaism to have had roots in ancient Magian religion (1.9). Plutarch, moreover, provided a second, even more elaborate witness to the treatment by Theopompus in his *De Iside et Osiride* (47), covering the dualistic and millenarian dynamics of classical Persian eschatology, several elements of which received overt adaptation in *2 Baruch*, *4 Ezra*, and perhaps most notably in the closing chapters of Revelation. In the final, utopian state, the supreme God of light (ὁ ἀγαθός θεός), Oromazes, destroys the principal evil demon (ὁ κακός δαίμων), Areimanius, and, presumably, once having raised its inhabitants to immortality, terminates Hades.[18]

Of the two basic sects of Palestinian Judaism present in the New Testament Gospels, namely, the Pharisees and Sadducees, only the Pharisees had freely adapted Persian doctrine (e.g., angels, demons, resurrection, apocalypticism, Son of Man / Saoshyant, etc.) and claimed opposition to Hellenism, an identifying disposition extending back to the rebellion movement of Judas Maccabeus; indeed, these orientalizing elements characterized and distinguished the sect as the popular trademark of Palestinian Judaism, an alternative to Hellenistic Judaism and the aristocratic, conciliatory Sadducean cast (cf. Acts 23.8).

In reading the New Testament, awareness of these roots from a *traditionsgeschichtlische* lens becomes especially informative regarding the language of the text insofar as discernment of genetic origins assists in filling in the *lacunae* regarding the (later recognizable) semiotic structures adapted, conflated, and applied in various early Jewish and early Christian writings, in this case, the New Testament. As Josephus demonstrated, even the alterity of Pharisaic "resistance" theology had undergone some Hellenization as it shifted its separatist strategies toward the confrontation of a new occidental force, namely, that of Rome.[19] These appropriated oriental elements in early Christian texts continued originally under a metanarrative of subversion vis-à-vis occidental cultural dominion, while, at the same time, appealing to a quite vogue orientalism variously witnessed throughout the Roman world. To wit, eschatological "resurrection of the dead" functioned fundamentally as a register for socio-cultural-religious identity and perhaps only secondarily as a peculiar element of belief. One may, in this sense, deem such early Jewish and early Christian credo as code for the exertion of socio-political association and dissociation.[20]

From earliest Christian textual evidence, that is, in Paul's missives, the theme of eschatological resurrection of the dead appears integral to the emerging movement (e.g., 1 Cor. 15.12–58 and 1 Thes. 4.16–17). Integrating his primitive λόγια, Matthew conveyed an eschatological day of resurrection and judgment, a day in which the Queen of the South and the Ninevites would one day rise up in judgment against Jesus' inattentive generation

(Mt 12.41–42). The altercation with the Sadducees in Mark 12 registered the fundamental position of the Synoptic communities.[21] The composition has rendered in episodic form, as typically characterizes the Gospels' storyboard, a dialectic encounter delineating a fresh, hybridic position on the signature Jewish sectarian and Mediterranean socio-ideological indices. At the eschaton, bodies are not raised in a common sense, but translated into new bodies, like those of the angels (εἰσιν ὡς ἄγγελοι ἐν τοῖς οὐρανοῖς).[22] This teaching comports with both the Pharisaic understanding as set forth by Josephus (*B.J.* 2.151–58), and the magian understanding as set forth by Plutarch (*De Iside et Osiride* 47), although these, by tacitly disqualifying the perishable body, may represent philosophical, Hellenistic adaptations of their respective traditions.

In similar fashion, the composer of Luke-Acts constructed the (dubious) story of Paul's confrontation with the chief Epicureans and Stoics in the ἀγορά and the Ἄρεος πάγος of Athens (Acts 17), the connotative capital of Hellenistic philosophical tradition, for the purpose of contesting and laying claim to socio-philosophical legitimation with respect to bodily resurrection, that is, on behalf of a second-century, rising early Christian movement. Paul's unsavory proposal ran aground with the fundamental, common philosophical tenets of classical antiquity, namely, the body–soul duality introduced by Plato *et alii* that subordinated the body as inferior and indeed a hindrance to philosophical ascesis and the ultimate liberation of the transcendent soul. As Dale Martin has elucidated, this pervasive, simplistic sketch of body–soul duality corresponded to a general conception of Hellenistic philosophy more so than the complexion of any particular school or thinker of the Hellenistic traditions.[23]

The inexorable Christianization of Platonism obtained fullest manifestation with the Marcion school and variously with early Christian Gnosticism. In these traditions, ἀνάστασις became a Christianized tag for the principal preoccupation of Middle and Neo-Platonism, namely, psychical liberation, a general ideal perhaps most famously detailed in Plato's *Phaedo* and *Timaeus*. As arguably their most identifying, common tenet, such traditions held personal resurrection to be essentially non-physical.[24] Set in structural tension with the Platonizing Thomasine school, the late first-century Johannine school found its eschatological *tertium quid*, a fresh soteriological space midway between the Markan / Matthean tradition and the Thomasine tradition. For the Johannine school, salvific πίστις had taken the place of salvific γνῶσις and encompassed the entire person, not just the immaterial.[25] To be reborn meant to be granted immortal life, both physical and psychical. The children of the Johannine θεός claimed to have realized an inner, pneumatic translation from death to life (John 1.12; 5.24), assuring them of their awaited somatic translation at the eschaton (John 6.25–71), as that prototyped by Jesus, the tradition's uniquely begotten demigod (John 1.18; 3.16; 6.62).[26]

As a negotiation of social identity in earliest Christian writing, the matter of philosophical dialectic regarding the postmortem state provided much of the subtext. This one observation proves vital to comprehending the nature and function of early Christian resurrection as an ideology and not as an argued event of history. The articulation of this subtext manifested in both fabulous narrative and theological treatise. The resurrection tale, as imaged within the former category, did not operate as a defensible historical event in early Christian literature, but as an etiological subject, symbol, or metonym of this negotiation. Jesus, as ὁ πρωτότοκος τῶν νεκρῶν (Rev 1.5; "the first-born of the dead"), served as the principal literary vehicle registering the inchoate movement within the standing Jewish and broadly Mediterranean socio-philosophical fray. In this sense, the so-called orthodox narratives rendering Jesus' resurrection as physical were just as creative and deliberate as the so-called unorthodox treatments that rendered his raised state as psychical or pneumatic. Each early Christian school narrativized their respective socio-ideological station, deploying Jesus as a mythic literary vehicle, a dynamic that accounts for the observed malleability in the resurrection tradition and the heterodox contestation of early Christian identity. The works of the apologists and proponents of early Christian κήρυγμα, such as Athenagoras's *De resurrectione mortuorum* and Tertullian's *De resurrectione carnis*, even when most vigorously addressing the subject of resurrection, did not attempt a case for the historicity of the resurrection of their founding figure. Instead, the early Christian records spent a seemingly limitless supply of argumentation, waging a philosophical campaign over the nature of raised bodies.[27]

Solitary Resuscitation

From the earliest stratum of the Gospel tradition, the notion of the thaumaturgic revival of a newly deceased body provided a common motif in all four New Testament Gospels. The primitive λόγια (Mt 11.2–6; Q 7.22), apparently seeking converts from and the legacy of the Baptizer's movement, described Jesus as one who was performing healings and raising the dead (νεκροὶ ἐγείρονται) in fulfillment of Isaianic motifs related to ὁ ἐρχόμενος ("the one who would come").[28] The Gospels portrayed this theme in three dramatic scenes:

- The raising of the widow's son at Nain (Luke 7.11–17)
- The raising of Jairus's daughter (Mark 5.21–43; Matt 9.18–26; Luke 8.40–56)
- The raising of Lazarus (John 11.1–46)

These resuscitation episodes have clear literary antecedents in Elijah's raising of the widow's son (1 Kings 17.17–24) and Elisha's raising of the Shunammite's son (2 Kings 4.18–37).[29] Note that, except in the language of the raising of Lazarus at John 11.23 (ἀναστήσεται ὁ ἀδελφός σου), a statement that connoted for the Johannine Martha images of eschatological resurrection, the Gospels do not apply ἀνάστασις (or cognates) to acts of solitary resuscitation. One instead consistently finds ἔγερσις.

In the broader compass of classical antiquity, numerous resuscitation accounts circulated, rendering these *miracula* within a commonly registered thaumatological motif of the Hellenistic Levant. Pliny the Elder, for example, passed along an impressive catalogue of such accounts in his *Naturalis Historia* (7.52), classifying only one of several such tales as exhibiting *fabulositas;* to the others, those passed on from Varro, he appears to have granted credence.[30] Without the presence of the theurgist, however, these accounts differed from the biblical resuscitation tales. Indeed, the Gospels offer no suggestion that Jesus needed to pray in order to perform these feats, unlike the petitions given by Elijah and Elisha. Of the two resuscitations in Acts, Peter prays for the raising of Tabitha (9.36–41), but Paul does not pray for the raising of Eutychus (20.7–12). On the cultural plain of classical antiquity, such theurgic tales of resuscitation drew upon a broader structural class, namely, that of the θεῖοι ἄνδρες, as Ludwig Bieler did extensively detail in the early last century.[31] Particularly provocative for this study, however, one notes the intersection between this cultural topos and the most prominent members of the "translation fable" Gallery. The ancients hailed Heracles, Empedocles, Asclepius, and Apollonius as divine persons, and each, within textualized episodic tales, famously exhibited the power to raise the dead.[32]

Most decisive in delineating the polysemic application of the English term "resurrection" regarding the Gospels with respect to this second category, one notes the principal distinction of the solitary resuscitation: Not one of these individuals rose to immortality. Their mortal, mundane bodies merely received an extension, invariably again to die.

The Postmortem Accounts of Jesus

Before positively exposing and identifying this third category of "resurrection" in the Gospels, one must be clear that the semiotic montage of postmortem accounts of Jesus in the four Gospel narratives did not structurally invoke either of the first two operative classifications. Neither pattern, whether eschatological resurrection or theurgic resuscitation, applies. Not one of the Gospels furnished adequate signals that the postmortem accounts were somehow to imply the eschaton, the apocalyptic establishment of mundane utopia. Matthew, developing and expanding Mark's abrupt "empty tomb" ending, perhaps offered a partial exception, though in a contrived, almost parenthetical claim, one that received no further testament in earliest Christian writing (27.52–53):

καὶ τὰ μνημεῖα ἀνεῴχθησαν καὶ πολλὰ σώματα τῶν κεκοιμημένων ἁγίων ἠγέρθησαν, καὶ ἐξελθόντες ἐκ τῶν μνημείων μετὰ τὴν ἔγερσιν αὐτοῦ εἰσῆλθον εἰς τὴν ἁγίαν πόλιν καὶ ἐνεφανίσθησαν πολλοῖς.

The tombs were opened and many bodies of the holy who had fallen asleep were raised, and, once having exited their tombs following his (Jesus') being raised, they entered the holy city and appeared to many.

Ulrich Luz seems quite fair in his assessment that this odd interposition, despite its corporate resurrection image, still drew more upon the translation fable tradition than upon early Jewish apocalyptic eschatology.[33] Note that the "many" do not at all approximate the grand, often universal scale described in general eschatological schemata, nor does the image suggest the dawn of a new era, a dispensation that brings resolution to a dilapidated world. Instead, as with the translation fable, only the iconic figures of the tradition (οἱ ἅγιοι) offer appearances (φαίνω), a Christianized transvaluation of the broader Mediterranean honorific tradition. The insertion, however awkward, Hellenized the text by allowing the premier patriarchs of the classical Hebrew tradition to join *post facta* the immortalized ranks of the most exalted of Greco-Roman lore, thus refurbishing the Hebrew tradition in keeping with ὁ Ἑλληνισμός.[34] As for the second category, solitary resuscitation, not one of the four Gospels in any way suggests that the protagonist's body rose only to die again. One also correctly excludes this possibility.

Only in the above-indicated Matthean text (27.52–53) did any of the four Gospel compositions associate Jesus' postmortem accounts with anything resembling a general eschatological event. Instead, proceeding by induction, rather than imposing the falsely supposed strictures of a single ancient term, namely ἀνάστασις, one observes that the dominant, most impressive features of Jesus' postmortem narratives in the Gospels happened also to have been the most fundamental signals of the broad Mediterranean translation fable convention. This book concludes with a survey of those features, their reception in early Christian thought, and a brief comment on present implications, both religious and humanistic.

4.2 TRANSLATION SIGNALS AND THE GOSPELS

The fourteenth chapter ("Probability and Induction") of Morris R. Cohen and Ernest Nagel's standard work, *An Introduction to Logic and the Scientific Method*, addressed the nature and challenges of applied analogical reasoning, that is, the validity of inference by resemblance. The treatment asserted that a set of known common traits, no matter how extensive, can only yield a probable, but not certain inference.[35] This assessment, however, only considered the sensory, scientific world of objects and empiricism, not the cultural, linguistic world of sign systems. In the latter realm, resemblance within the linguistic *langue* wholly governs the matter of valid inference. Accurate historical and literary studies, by their inductive inferential orientation, must operate within the realm of the probable, not the realm of the certain. In most cases, however, as quality analyses approximate a human, comprehensive familiarity with the semiotic domain of a text, particularly through the size and range of examples, this probability approaches and indeed achieves conventional certainty. The perspicuity of the translation fable in ancient Greek and Latin literature provides one of the clearest instances of a topos or stock pattern (sign) with a cluster of recurring traits (signifiers) and well-established, if at times tacit, implications (signifieds).

Belief bias has all too often perverted prior comparative studies between Jesus, the most sacralized figure of Western cultural history, and various images or patterns drawn from ancient society. The deluding will to believe (or to disbelieve) has characterized perhaps most treatments of the historicity of Jesus' resurrection, resulting in a malignant conflict of interest, that is, projects unduly driven by confirmation bias. Atheistic treatments have often suffered from what Samuel Sandmel termed "parallelomania," that is, whimsical, often contrived associations produced by those (and for those) who seem bent on dismissing such accounts as the mere banal product of ancient cultures.[36] The subtext of most faith-based studies has, on the other hand, tended to be that of isolating the resurrection accounts as *sui generis*. By quarantining the New Testament resurrection stories from ancient cultural analogues, the faith-driven presentation tendentiously has sought to allow for a different, non-mythic modality, thus rendering the tale as though historically plausible. The correct approach, however, does not reside in finding a middle-way between these two intellectually dishonest predilections, but first, with the utter dismissal of present interest and motivation, in ascertaining how such accounts referenced the semiotic registry of their cultural-linguistic province in antiquity.[37]

Common Traits

Peculiar to the translation fable, and never to early Jewish resurrection, three common traits present themselves and, not coincidently, have principally characterized the postmortem narratives in the Gospels, traits related to the conclusion of plot, the divine nature of the translated body, and the implied institution of *cultus*.

The Conclusion of Plot

Perhaps the most radical observation present in a semiotic evaluation of the translation fable resides in the fable's basal function with regard to plot. As Peter Brooks has explained, the tension between difference and resemblance drives both reader and story toward resolution:

> Transformation—a change in a predicate term common to beginning and end—represents a synthesis of difference and resemblance; it is, we might say, the same-but-different. Now "the same-but-different" is a common (and if inadequate, not altogether false) definition of metaphor.

If Aristotle affirmed that the master of metaphor must have an eye for resemblances, modern treatments of the subject have affirmed equally the importance of difference included within the operation of resemblance, the chief value of the metaphor residing in its "tension." Narrative operates as metaphor in its affirmation of resemblance, in that it brings into relation different actions, combines them through perceived similarities (Todorov's common predicate term), appropriates them to a common plot, which implies the rejection of merely contingent (or unassimilable) incident or action. The plotting of meaning cannot do without metaphor, for meaning in plot is the structure of action in closed and legible wholes. Metaphor is in this sense totalizing.[38]

The translation fable, through narrative emplotment, resolves the modal tension between the heroic and the tragic modalities of classical literature, with the heroic finding ultimate triumph. Not only for those translation fables with a pronounced theme of the tragic (e.g., a "heinous or ignoble injustice rectified by translation" and the "odious or dubious alternate account"; List 2.1), in a quite practical sense, translation fables functioned to undo tragic loss, reclaiming the hero in a modal reverie of heroic *exaltatio*. All endings in plot, as Brooks exposed, serve as eulogies casting their interpretive light of meaning upon the narrative that preceded.[39]

In the Gospels, as with the epitomic tragedy of the death of Heracles, this final reversal achieves supreme dramatic effect. The generic signals of the Passion narratives invariably operate under the directives of a metanarrative of philosophical ascesis, that is, the austerity of reason over base instinct as a ultimate social exhibition of (subversive) virtue. John's Gospel extends this scandalous theme of noble tragedy through *imitatio Socratis*, as John's protagonist "drinks his cup" of martyrdom with the stalwart resolve of a magisterial philosophical sage (Cf. Plato's *Crito* and *Phaedo*).[40] In the Gospels, the heroic demigod as benefactor expends his life in an ultimate trial of tragedy. The heroic is swallowed up by the tragic, thus suggesting Freud's claim that the pleasure principle does not necessarily occupy the highest level of human cognition.[41] The protagonist of the Gospels, through achievement of higher, rational self-government, overcame his passions, his most basic instinct of self-preservation, his id.

The New Testament Gospel paradigm of noble self-expenditure and consequent *exaltatio* found its predecession in the Pauline Christ cult:

τοῦτο φρονεῖτε ἐν ὑμῖν ὃ καὶ ἐν χριστῷ Ἰησοῦ, ὃς ἐν μορφῇ θεοῦ
ὑπάρχων οὐχ ἁρπαγμὸν ἡγήσατο τὸ εἶναι ἴσα θεῷ, ἀλλὰ ἑαυτὸν
ἐκένωσεν μορφὴν δούλου λαβών, ἐν ὁμοιώματι ἀνθρώπων γενόμενος·
καὶ σχήματι εὑρεθεὶς ὡς ἄνθρωπος ἐταπείνωσεν ἑαυτὸν γενόμενος
ὑπήκοος μέχρι θανάτου, θανάτου δὲ σταυροῦ. διὸ καὶ ὁ θεὸς αὐτὸν
ὑπερύψωσεν καὶ ἐχαρίσατο αὐτῷ τὸ ὄνομα τὸ ὑπὲρ πᾶν ὄνομα, ἵνα
ἐν τῷ ὀνόματι Ἰησοῦ πᾶν γόνυ κάμψῃ ἐπουρανίων καὶ ἐπιγείων καὶ

καταχθονίων καὶ πᾶσα γλῶσσα ἐξομολογήσηται ὅτι κύριος Ἰησοῦς
χριστός

(Phil 2.5–11)

This language would have sounded quite political in first-century Roman Macedonia, the language of royal *exaltatio* scandalously applied to an executed Palestinian peasant:[42]

> Have this mindset among you that was also in inaugurated[43] Jesus who, despite starting out in a god's semblance, did not regard being equal to a god as his prize, but emptied himself, taking a servant's form, being born in the manner of humans, and being found as a man in appearance, he did lower himself by become a subject to the point of death, a death on a cross. Consequently, God exalted him and granted him the name that is above every name, so that at Jesus' name every knee would bow, of those in the heavens, of those upon the earth, and of those of the netherworld, and every tongue would confess that inaugurated Jesus is ruler.

This early hymnic plot trajectory became the controlling template behind the Gospel storyboard of the four New Testament narratives. Notice that Paul nowhere includes the explicit notion of resurrection. "Resurrection" did not function as an essential structural element to the plot, but, as this book proposes, as nominal and ancillary to a metanarrative of *exaltatio*. The similitude spinning sage, on the one hand, a thaumaturgic divine king, on the other, an executed Jewish pariah *déclassé* of a politically volatile atmosphere portending its imminent demise (that is, the First Jewish War), became through the tapestry of early Christian fabulation a new metaphor for counter-cultural civil agency. The εὐαγγέλια presented an early Christian etiological subgenre of aretalogy, bestowing upon the founder the principal Hellenic honor of κλέος ἄφθιτον, thus promulgating the movement in the late first and early second centuries.[44]

The founding icon's socio-political mobility, as figured through his mythic metamorphosis, functioned as a pattern for a central early Christian ideology of socio-political transcendence. Emma Dench illuminates how the observed rise in popularity of myths and legends of metamorphosis into the imperial Roman period corresponded to exceptional patterns of such mobility.[45] The metamorphosis tale functioned as a metaphor, a cultural myth or "belief" applied to allow the exceptional mechanics of individual ascendency, the translation fable providing its supreme manifestation. The jeered reception of the incognito king of Gospel portrayal mimetically drew upon the most famous of all ancient tales, that of the returning king of Ithaca, Odysseus, once having been divinely transformed into a doddering vagrant (*Od.* 13–22). The anatomy of Mark, the most primitive and formative of the four Gospel narratives, seems incomprehensible apart from the treasured works of Homer. Many of Mark's most dramatic, defining themes and episodes make little sense until read in mimetic overlay to Mark's grand antetext (e.g., the "Messianic Secret," the transfiguration, and the cleansing of the temple).[46] Concerning the Transfiguration episode of the Synoptic narratives (Mark 9; Matt 17; Luke 9), preferably named the "Metamorphosis" episode according to the Greek term applied by the narratives, the mendicant monarch revealed his divine form to his three closest subjects. Not for comparison, but for the effect of contrast, did the New Testament *fabulae* include Moses and Elijah, two early Jewish patriarchs who famously had been assumed to heaven in conclusion to their sacred careers.[47] Speaking on behalf of himself and his companions James and John, Peter proposed the erection of three cult shrines atop the mountain for the three glorified figures (ποιήσωμεν τρεῖς σκηνάς).[48] At this point, the narrator intervenes with the divine uranic voice, contrasting the *exaltatio* of Jesus as alone achieving the supreme rank of demigod: οὗτός ἐστιν ὁ υἱός μου ἀγαπητός. Notice the translation fable signals present: cloud envelopment and mountain top (List 2.1), themes also employed in the Ascension narratives (Matt 28.16–20; Acts 1.6–11).[49]

With respect to plot, one inherent point warrants full clarity: the conventions of early Jewish resurrection never functioned within the stock repertoire of narrative elements as a conclusion to plot. This trait, however, without exception, defined and characterized the translation fable. Concerning the matter of a story's coda or protocol of endings, one calls to mind the grammar of narrative elements developed by Soviet formalist Vladimir Yakovlevich Propp in his 1928 *Morfológija skázki* (first translated into English in 1968 as *Morphology of the Folktale*), in which Propp taxonomized the structural elements of the traditional Russian fairytale, identifying the recurrence of stock components variously instanced and recombined. Following this basic methodological paradigm, one properly comprehends the translation fable as a customary syntagmatic feature of the narratives of iconified figures of classical antiquity, bringing formulaic closure to the stories of such lives. The New Testament Gospels each conclude their fabulous βίος of Jesus, applying this same stylized protocol.

The Body of a God

Often, if not in every instance, the most striking episodic themes of Jesus' postmortem accounts in the Gospels function as semiotic exhibitions of his distinct theosomatic properties. As established in Chapter 2, the ontological signals of translation precisely equal those that demonstrate that the corruptible body had become divine, superhuman, immortal. Several New Testament critics have mischaracterized translation as fundamentally spatial, rather than somatic, and, as such, have mistakenly perceived *ascensus* as the essential manifestation of translation.[50] The Gallery of translation fables in Chapter 2 demonstrates that, from the standpoint of literary convention, Hellenistic and Roman linguistic culture utilized a variety of optional subthemes (List 2.1) to convey the presence of the translation fable as a class of narrative ending. Of these, disappearance, appearance, metamorphosis, and ascension functioned as demonstrations of the deification of the hero, that is, the transcendence of the limitations of the mortal body; these were the signature abilities of the immortal gods, just as Arthur Pease, Jean-Pierre Vernant, and the present study have exposed.

Consequently, the most primitive account, Mark, provided in one powerful, singular gesture, namely, a missing body, an unmistakable semiotic conclusion to the narrative: Jesus could vanish; his body had been translated.[51] Following Mark, the three subsequent Gospels featured this same subtheme (Matt. 28.1–10; John 20.3–9; Luke 24.1–11). Unlike the suspense of John's portrait of the present, raised Lazarus emerging from his tomb, the Gospels instead spotlight the body's absence, its disappearance.[52] Chariton's Greek novel *Chaereas and Callirhoe* laid bare this structural linguistic sign in Callirhoe's empty tomb scene (*Chaer.* 3.3.1–7). Here, Chaereas arrives at his beloved Callirhoe's tomb at dawn, only to discover the tomb to be empty. With florid elaboration, Chaereas quite unpretentiously interprets the missing body of his recently interred bride to mean that she had been translated to become a goddess. As the Gallery of translation fables has shown, a vanished body in narrative typically implied translation. The legendary empty coffin account of King Numa (Plut, *Num.* 22.1–5), an account proposed without further explanation, provides one of a myriad of examples of missing bodies and implied postmortem translation tales that tacitly signaled the deification of the hero, that is, supreme cultural exaltation. The "missing body" subtheme arose as a form of archetypal mimesis with respect to the missing bones of Heracles, a tradition that found its most customary expression in the funerary *consecratio* of the Roman monarchs, symbolically enacted through the public cremation of the wax *imago* of the deceased emperor.

The bodies of the Hellenistic and Roman gods could materialize and vanish at will. The "missing body" theme simply resided under a larger trait or demonstration of the translated σῶμα, namely, disappearance. Luke's Jesus exhibits this ability by vanishing in front of his two disciples at the village of Emmaus (Luke 24.28–35). Heavenly ascension, also a distinctive Lukan feature (Luke 24.50–53; Acts 1.6–11), provided the grandest expression of this ability, optionally festooning the ancient translation fable.[53] The postmortem deified body of Jesus in the Gospels, moreover, could materialize at will, anywhere, even behind barred doors (John 20.19–23). The postmortem appearance tradition, following the apotheosis eyewitness tradition (discussed below), antedated the Gospels (1 Cor 15.3–9) where the tradition later became narrativized. The selective "Damascus road" appearance in Acts (9.3–9)—Indeed, Paul saw him, but none of his traveling companions could—provides a topic of particularly incisive study. When the *Odyssey* poetized Athena's metamorphosis of divine Odysseus (δῖος Ὀδυσσεύς) before Telemachus, the epic notes that Telemachus, unlike his father, could not see the goddess standing before them. The implied narrator then sets out the gloss: οὐ γάρ πως πάντεσσι θεοὶ φαίνονται ἐναργεῖς (*Od.* 16.161; "for the gods do not visibly appear to all").

One also notes the distinctive presence of the theme of metamorphosis in the Gospels, also a classic "translation fable" signal (List 2.1). This theme obtains expressions ranging from Paul's blinding light on the Damascus road (Acts 9.3–9)[54] to tales of his having transformed himself to be unrecognizable, such as his incognito appearance to Mary Magdalene (John 20.11–18) and to his two devotees on the Emmaus road (Luke 24.13–27).[55] Further displays of Jesus' postmortem ability to metamorphosize recur with regularity as a leitmotif in early Christian narrative, as for instance seen in the *Acts of Peter*, the *Acts of John*, and the *Infancy Gospel*.[56]

The prospect of postmortem accounts of the brutally executed Jesus left the ancient Hellenistic and Roman reader with two possible interpretations, the first and most clearly indicated option being that of bodily translation, with the second possibility being visitation by a *revenant* having returned from Hades, an immaterial phantom.[57] Ancient Greek and Latin literature enjoyed a rich tradition of tales of apparition.[58] After Mark, the subsequent three Gospels appear quite concerned, as evidenced by their demonstrations of Jesus' palpable, functional *corpus*, that the reader not make any mistake on this distinction (Cf. Matt 28.1–10; John 20.11–18; 20.24–29; 21.9–14; Luke 24.36–40). The Lukan narrative became most explicit on this point:[59]

ταῦτα δὲ αὐτῶν λαλούντων αὐτὸς ἔστη ἐν μέσῳ αὐτῶν. πτοηθέντες δὲ καὶ ἔμφοβοι γενόμενοι ἐδόκουν πνεῦμα θεωρεῖν. καὶ εἶπεν αὐτοῖς· τί τεταραγμένοι ἐστὲ καὶ διὰ τί διαλογισμοὶ ἀναβαίνουσιν ἐν τῇ καρδίᾳ ὑμῶν; ἴδετε τὰς χεῖράς μου καὶ τοὺς πόδας μου ὅτι ἐγώ εἰμι αὐτός· ψηλαφήσατέ με καὶ ἴδετε, ὅτι πνεῦμα σάρκα καὶ ὀστέα οὐκ ἔχει καθὼς ἐμὲ θεωρεῖτε ἔχοντα. ἔτι δὲ ἀπιστούντων αὐτῶν ἀπὸ τῆς χαρᾶς καὶ θαυμαζόντων εἶπεν αὐτοῖς· ἔχετέ τι βρώσιμον ἐνθάδε οἱ δὲ ἐπέδωκαν αὐτῷ ἰχθύος ὀπτοῦ μέρος· καὶ λαβὼν ἐνώπιον αὐτῶν ἔφαγεν.

(24.36–40)

After they spoke these things, he himself stood in their midst. They became dismayed and frightened, thinking that they saw a spirit. He said to them, "Why have you become troubled and why do questions arise in your hearts? Look at my hands and feet that it is I myself. Handle me and see; for, a spirit does not have flesh and bones like you see that I have." While they were still in disbelief from joy and amazement, he said to them, "Do you have anything here to eat?" So, they gave him a piece of broiled fish, and he took it and ate it in front of them.

Contrary to the inferences of many, namely, that those episodes rendering the physicality of Jesus' postmortem state functioned to convince the reader of the credibility of such a tale, one observes that those renditions tended instead to elicit worship of him as divine in the narrative (e.g., Matt 28.9 and John 20.28), thus implying a mode of iconic exaltation, not realism.[60] If he was not a *revenant*, according to the ancient mind, then he must have been a deity. No form of resurrection in early Jewish tradition called for worship or *cultus* toward the one raised. Translation alone called for the worship of one who had been mortal, then made immortal.[61]

Implied Institution of Cultus

In each case, the translation fable implied *cultus*, that is, the institution of veneration, worship, and petition to the divinized figure. In relation to empire, this meant analogues between the early Christian Christ and the imperial cult, a matter now drawn into the foreground of early Christian studies.[62] Perhaps most important to note here, the translation fable, and never early Jewish resurrection, essentially entailed deification and *cultus*, just as the postmortem accounts in the Gospels tacitly indicated (e.g., Matt 28.9 and John 20.28). Having identified and handled Jesus' immortal, divine *corpus*, Thomas salutes his monarch with the formulaic address reserved for Domitian himself: ὁ κύριός μου καὶ θεός μου (*Dominus et deus noster;* Suetonius, *Dom.* 13.2). As this study has demonstrated, the translation fable signified cultural deification, the customary ritualization of divine homage toward the sacralized figure.

Narrative Analysis

Evolving the Russian Formalist principles of Viktor Shklovsky and Vladimir Propp, Tzvetan Todorov has achieved what perhaps all great philosophy and literary theory has endeavored; he has articulated for readers what they already know: *Le récit se constitue dans la tension de deux catégories formelles, la différence et la ressemblance.*[63] The gallery of translation fables compiled in this study has, as a sample, demonstrated that the broad constellation of instances diversely exhibit both essential qualities: sufficient semiosis and striking variance. Even in variance, however, the literary critic of course finds but secondary resemblances. Consequently, as Aristotle exposed so many ages ago in his *Poetics*, the mastery of literary production and literary consumption obtains in the human discernment of resemblance (μίμησις), that is, in the analogical endeavor to signify. As the very engine of narrative signification, the cognition of *la différence et la ressemblance* not surprisingly governs at each point the correct assessment of the presence, function, and meaning of the translation fable in the New Testament Gospels, with each individual narrative variously applying the fable to achieve a distinctive, triumphal effect.

Mark

To modern eyes, this first of the four Gospel narratives terminates in a most curt, enigmatic manner: an empty tomb being fled in trembling and astonishment by Jesus' female disciples Mary Magdalene, Mary the mother of

James, and Salome (the same three whom Mark placed courageously attending the crucifixion; 15.40). William Wrede properly included this episode, namely, Mark 16.1–8, with the content he termed *das Messiasgeheimnis* (the "messianic secret"), that is, those portions in Mark suggesting or accounting for an allegedly explicable delay in revealing Jesus' exalted identity until a period after his death.[64] οὐδενι οὐδὲν εἶπαν· ἐφοβοῦντο γάρ ("They did not say anything to anyone, for they were afraid."; 16.8). These segments stand out as Mark's most flagrant embellishments and often relate to Jesus' glorified stature as the narrative's divine, messianic king. By this one semiotic gesture, namely, Mark's empty tomb, the narrative concludes with a vindicating confirmation of the centurion's *interpretatio Romana* of Jesus at his death: ἀληθῶς οὗτος ὁ ἄνθρωπος υἱός θεοῦ ἦν ("Certainly this man was a god's son."; 15.39). As an early, well-attested textual variant, this same anarthrous designation υἱός θεοῦ augmented the very title of the text in the opening line (1.1), producing an *inclusio* with Mark's dramatic, abrupt ending. Mark deliberately and expressly functioned as an honorific tribute elevating the founder of the movement to the rank of demigod. The Gospel of Mark textualized this deification, articulating the subtext from beginning to end, culminating in the protagonist's vanished body. This textual variant, therefore, despite likely having been a scribal accretion—indeed, the matter may prove all the more revealing because of this early interpretive choice of title—disclosed a central purpose of the composition and the closing import of Mark's translation fable. The abruptness of the ending thus did, contrary to the assessments of so many modern readers, supply a profound resolution to Mark's provocative narrative.[65]

The unveiling of the protagonist's concealed divine identity epitomized the cultural-linguistic hybridity of Mark as a composition. Midway through the story, this theme, as well as the narrative's principal characters, ascends to a summit with the Metamorphosis (Transfiguration) episode of Mark 9. The narrative previews Jesus' final exaltation, placing him alongside the translated Moses and the translated Elijah, privately revealing their glorified status to Jesus' three closest acolytes Peter, James, and John. Here also, in keeping with *das Messiasgeheimnis* (the "messianic secret"), Jesus bids his disciples not to speak a word of his revealed, glorified identity until after he had "risen from the dead" (9.9), thus making more explicit the implied relation between these two narrated vignettes on the Markan storyboard. The Metamorphosis in Mark 9 established the governing dramatic tension in the narrative, chiefly between Jesus' concealed identity as divine king and the profanity of his mistreatment and execution. This theme drew heavily upon Homer's masterplot in the *Odyssey*, namely, in the energetic tension between King Odysseus's concealed majestic, god-like identity—He returns to his kingdom disguised by the powers of the goddess Athena as a beggar—and the tragic impudence of Penelope's array of suitors discovered upon his return to Ithaca. Markan hybridity, however, delved all the more deeply into Hellenism by driving a contrast between Jesus and the glorified patriarchs of early Judaism, namely, in asserting the divinity of Jesus as υἱὸς θεοῦ, a Judaic demigod to be uniquely exalted to the stature of *cultus* (9.5–8). The use of "resurrection" language with regard to his bodily disappearance (*translatio*) in the final scene further articulated such hybridity.

Considering the evidenced transvaluative antetextual relationship that Matthew's λόγια displayed with respect to Deuteronomy, as best explicated in the recent work of Dennis R. MacDonald in recent "Q" scholarship, scholars have speculated that the tradition already included some mention of Jesus' missing corpse, echoing that narrated concerning Moses (Deut 34.1–8).[66] With Mark, however, the story instead took shape in mimetic relation to the translation legends of divine, archetypal Romulus. Both the vanished body (proceeding from Heraclean tradition) and the affrighted flight from the scene more than suggested the invocation of this archetypal tale. The annual Festival of Romulus on the nones of Quintilis (July 7) and the related *Poplifugia* (July 5) reenacted this flight in cities throughout the empire, namely, the people fleeing in dismay when Romulus vanished during his *lustratio* on Campus Martius in Rome (Dionysius of Halicarnassus, *Ant. rom.* 2.56.5; Plutarch, *Rom.* 27.7).[67] Lest there remain any question as to this implicit mimetic connection at Mark's conclusion, note that the interpretive reception of Mark's translation fable, as *imitatio Romuli*, became the more graphic and exhaustive in Matthew, achieving fullest expression in Luke-Acts, as the study now proceeds to elucidate.[68]

Matthew

Scholars appear to agree concerning the originality of Matthew's framing *inclusio*, unlike the Gospel's conflated Markan content with that of a primitive λόγια tradition (understood by many as "Q"). This distinctly Matthean frame embroidered the composition with honorary flourish, exalting the divinity of Matthew's protagonist, the creative exploration of a principal theme bequeathed by the Gospel of Mark. Both the birth narrative and the translation narrative of Matthew indicated the προσκύνησις of the divine king, the messianic demigod (Matt 2.2 and 28.9 respectively). In the latter episode, a σεισμός μέγας provided a prodigy, in narrated form, signifying the translation of a truly great figure (28.2). Typical of Matthean redaction, the narrative dropped off the Markan detail of Salome's presence, including only the two Marys as witnesses of the vanished body. The women, having felt the divine quake at the tomb, observe the descent of a powerful heavenly messenger come to remove away the massive encasing stone at the sepulcher. Unlike the *Gospel of Peter*, however, no Christ emerges from the tomb; the chamber is vacant.[69] The body is absent, but it had not been physically removed, unlike the dubious alternative account (List 2.1) circulated by the Jewish authorities and the Roman guards (28.11–15).[70] Jesus' bodily disappearance in Matthew from the heavily guarded, sealed tomb dramatically clarified and augmented the Markan missing body ending. Only a deified *corpus* could have managed such an escape. The descent of Matthew's mighty angel to open the sealed chamber and reveal its vacancy provided the dramatic semiotic climax of the Gospel's narrative. It was first the body's absence, not a reanimated presence, that would have seized the attention of the ancient, Hellenized reader. Matthew's spectacular *angelus ex machina* served most dramatically to ostend the translated status of the legend's hero.

Matthew elsewhere did provide a somewhat disparate interpretation of Jesus' return from the dead, describing the tale as a κατάβασις tacitly comparable to the heroic descents and returns of other divine figures: Odysseus, Heracles, Pythagoras, Zalmoxis, Orpheus, and Aeneas (12.40; ἔσται ὁ υἱὸς τοῦ ἀνθρώπου ἐν τῇ καρδίᾳ τῆς γῆς τρεῖς ἡμέρας καὶ νύκτας).[71] While the invocation of these themes did not cohere at a narrative level with the notion of translation per se, at a subtextual level, these two topoi served quite similar ends; through the rendition of analogical imagery, they signaled potent honorific themes of Hellenistic eminence, decorating the founder of Matthew's late first-century Christian movement. The postmortem treatments of Jesus in Matthew and the subsequent Gospels did not serve to produce a coherent, credible account of a raised Jesus, but to clarify beyond ambivalence the precise semiology of *exaltatio* implied via these varied available conventions of narrated embellishment.

In Matthew, the empty tomb and the physical postmortem appearances evoked not amazement and wonder, but worship (28.9, 17), the appropriate response to Jesus' implied deification as crafted in the account. The theme of the divinized king achieved its consummation in the Great Commission, the scene that ultimately concludes Matthew (28.16–20). Of the translated figures arrayed in this study, Romulus alone became known for his great commission, passed through his trusted patrician Julius Proculus (as rendered in Livy's *Ab Urbe Condita Libri* nearly a century prior to Matthew):[72]

> Abi. Nuntia Romanis caelestes ita velle ut mea Roma caput orbis terrarum sit; proinde rem militarem colant, sciantque et ita posteris tradant nullas opes humanas armis Romanis resistere posse.
>
> (1.16.7)

> Go. Announce to the Romans that the heavens decree that Rome be capital of the world. Therefore, let them cultivate the art of war and know and thus teach their children that no human power can resist Roman military might.

Given such recurrent mimetic signals in the Gospels, beginning with Mark and culminating in Luke-Acts, Matthew's conclusion operated as a straightforward, albeit transvalued instance of *imitatio Romuli*, thus riffing on the inchoate Markan theme (see above). Like the gods, moreover, only a divinized Jesus could promise his perpetual invisible presence and aid to his acolytes (28.20).

John

When read chronologically as the third of the four New Testament Gospels, John's empty tomb and postmortem appearance narratives creatively developed and varied from those of Mark and Matthew. This time, Mary Magdalene alone arrives at the tomb at dawn, not to witness the spectacle of the mighty angel opening a sealed sepulcher, but later only to see that the stone had been rolled away thus to presume the body to have been stolen (20.1–2). In this rendering, Peter and the beloved disciple first witness the body wrappings and vanished body. This semiotic image, according to the narrative, evoked the πίστις of John, quite absent from any prediction of the event or a predetermination of its significance (20.8–9); the missing body alone sufficed. What, in that instant, had the beloved disciple come to believe?

Having interpolated the narrative's two leading disciples into the episode, the story then continues the variation on the legend of Mary Magdalene and her divine visitation by Jesus. Beyond the "missing body" motif, the narrative here supplies the next three signals that Jesus' empty tomb be comprehended as a translation and not merely as a mundane revival. The translated Jesus meets Mary outside the tomb, but appears unrecognizable in form to her, his most devout female disciple. As with the Matthean account, moreover, once she realizes the translated presence of her master, Mary physically clings to Jesus (20.17a).[73] The physicality of the raised Jesus assures the reader that he is not to be conceived as a mere *revenant*. The narrative then, in gratuitous semiotic redundancy, removes any doubt as to the proper inference. Jesus announces his departure, namely, that he is to ascend to heaven (20.17b). In Mediterranean antiquity, neither the ghosts of Hades nor revived corpses ascend to immortal, heavenly existence. The implied narrator politely and dramatically excluded these two inferences.

The Gospel of John's next σημεῖον that the protagonist had achieved translated deification and not mere revivification arose in the next scene, his appearance to his disciples within a bolted chamber (20.19–23). This episode combined with the one that followed, the famous "Doubting Thomas" scene (20.24–29), culminating in the purpose statement of the entire text (20.30–31). Jesus invites the incredulous Thomas to touch his wounds, that is, to identify that he was indeed the one executed and that his raised body is capable of physicality. His executed master had been translated and, as such, has become deserving of the highest imperial address: ὁ κύριός μου καὶ ὁ θεός μου, that universally applied to Domitian at the time of John's composition (*Dominus et deus noster;* Suetonius, *Dom.* 13.2).[74]

What was at stake in the Johannine Gospel? First, in continuity with the prior Gospels, Mark and Matthew, the text endeavored further to reconcile the two most primitive, disparate traditions, namely, the mundane reminiscence of Jesus as an historical figure as, for instance, cultivated within the λόγια Movement, and the exalted Christ figure of the Pauline tradition. Like the two prior Gospels, John essays to synthesize these two contrary primitive traditions. As John's purpose statement exposes, conversion in the Johannine "pistic" community meant the assertion of the fusion of these two fundamental socio-religious traditions, namely, that one might have believed that Jesus, the mundane figure of Palestine, was the Christ, the honorific demigod of Christian *cultus* (20.31). The sociological potency of the Gospel of John operated in the empowerment and enfranchisement of early Christians to exalt, to mythologize, and to apotheosize the figurehead of their movement, Jesus, a peasant sage of Galilee. These narrativizing acts of applying and of affirming his translated stature, according to the cultural-linguistic conventions of the day, unreservedly fulfilled John's stated purpose. The Palestinian peasant sage was to be the divine heavenly emperor, transcendent savior of humankind.

For the early Thomasine school, however, Jesus was none of that; he was a revealer of awakening gnosis (*Gos. Thom.* 5 and 28) and the docetic (immaterial) "twin" of Thomas, Apostle to the Orient (*Acts Thom.*).[75] This episode in John, therefore, employed Thomas as a metonym for a rivaling Thomasine tradition, redrawing this originary figure and rehabilitating him under Johannine ideology. As Riley, DeConick, and Pagels have begun to expose, the crafted characterizations of the Johannine storyboard often addressed pressing and substantial issues related to the respective legacies of the apostolic figures as these in turn related to the socio-ideological disposition of the Johannine community. The thematic reconciliation of various originary figures in the Gospel of John, Thomas included, correlated not with mere hostility or conflict, but also with the sequestration of contrary traditions under a singular, fully legitimated school, that of the beloved disciple.[76] Accordingly, one may come to perceive the "pistic" themes in the Johannine tradition as a grand endeavor to synthesize the disparate gnostic and synoptic branches of nascent Christian tradition. Indeed, the discernment of any substantial distinction between γνῶσις and πίστις, upon critical examination, appears quite elusive, as both fundamentally entailed, as soteriological, the assertion or indulgence of otherwise unwarranted inferences about the governing framework of mundane reality.

The postmortem appearance in the fishing episode that follows (21.1–23) continued this same theme of synthesis and reconciliation, this time with respect to an unfaithful Peter, perhaps suggesting a redeemed Petrine tradition. The correction of Peter, moreover, appears to be something of a recurring motif in the New Testament traditions (e.g., Gal. 2.11 and Mark 8.33), perhaps reflective of the turbulent liminality of the Petrine following vis-à-vis the northern, "Christologizing" movement of the mid-first century. Besides a possible mimetic tie to Pythagoras (i.e., the one hundred and fifty-three caught fish), the fishing episode provided an additional translation signal of bodily metamorphosis (List 2.1). The narrative depicts the disciples as unable readily to recognize their translated master speaking to them from the Galilean shore (21.4).

Luke-Acts

The postmortem episodes in Luke-Acts begin with a variation on Mark's single abrupt episode at Mark 16.1–8. The Lukan rendition (24.1–11) populated the scene with Mary Magdalene, Mary the Mother of James, Joanna, and other women who were first to visit the tomb at sunrise.[77] As with Mark and John, the stone was mysteriously rolled away from the entrance when the women arrive. Following the semiotic pattern of Mark and Matthew, the women peer into the sepulcher to discover that the body of their master was missing. Contrary to Mark, however, after speaking with the angels, the women returned and reported to the male apostles the news, this being met with incredulity.

Further embellishing the former three Gospel narratives, Luke-Acts added two particularly conspicuous translation signals: translated "road" encounters and translated ascensions, both prominent topoi of the translation tradition. As has been extensively elucidated in Chapter 2 (see "Julius Proculus and the 'Eyewitness' Tradition"), tales of road encounters of translated figures originated with the archetypal renditions of Romulus, with Aristeas of Proconessus having provided a secondary exemplum. This translation subtheme typically combined with a second, namely, a "Commission" given by the translated figure. While Paul's "Damascus Road" encounter quintessentially fit the Romulean mimetic structure (Acts 9.1–9; 22.6–11; 26.9–20), the "Emmaus Road" tale (Luke 24.13–35) provided a bit of a variation, one perhaps more in line with the famous legend given in Herodotus of the translated Aristeas having met a man on the road to Cyzicus, who then travels to the city of Aristeas's disappearance to report the encounter (Herodotus 4.13–16). Lest there remain any semiotic ambiguity with the reader of the Emmaus Road tale, the narrative supplied an additional linguistic cue: Jesus' translated form rendered him incognito to his two disciples. Jesus' body had the distinct, divine ability to metamorphosize, a signature subtheme of the translation convention as outlined in this study. This manifest theme crescendoed in the Gospel of Luke as Jesus allows the two disciples to see his recognizable form and then vanishes into thin air (Luke 24.30–31).

Once Cleopas and his companion speedily return to Jerusalem to report their encounter with the translated Jesus, they find the disciples all gathered together (Luke 24.36–49), a scene crafted after and conflating the two Johannine "Doubting Thomas" episodes (John 20.19–29), but without the spotlight on Thomas. With the Gospel of Luke having showcased Jesus' postmortem abilities of appearance, metamorphosis, and disappearance in the prior episode, Luke's account of the appearance to the gathered disciples effectively, and all the more forcefully when compared to John, removed any doubt about the physical capacities of Jesus' postmortem body. Jesus' visitation was not that of a mere phantom, but that of a translated demigod. Jesus not only could handle, prepare, and serve food, a theme seen elsewhere in his postmortem appearance narratives (John 21.9–14; Luke 24.30; *Gos. Heb.*

frag. 7); his translated body even could ingest broiled fish (Luke 24.36–43). These episodes functioned most fundamentally first to exclude two possible interpretations of the postmortem Jesus: (1) that he might have been merely revived from death, or (2) that he may have been a *revenant*, an apparition having returned from Hades. With these two possibilities having been dramatically removed from viable inference, only a third option yet remained in Hellenistic written culture: the Gospel narratives bestowed upon Jesus the honorific exaltation of divine translation, thus, through literary protocol, asserting for him a place among those most lionized in classical antique civilization. In truth, Luke-Acts followed in continuity with the prior three Gospels and, as such, illumed back upon those prior texts a full, second-century receptional *interpretatio* as translation narratives.

Duly having forsaken the myopia of Lohfink's *Die Himmelfahrt Jesu*, namely, the short-sightedness of reducing translation to mere ascension, the present book comprehends the Lukan exercise of the "ascension" convention as the culminating expression within the New Testament *corpus* (Luke 24.50–53; Acts 1.6–11). Not having fully descried the generic structure of the translation fable, Lohfink mistakenly surmised ascension in Luke-Acts to have been distinctly a matter of Lukan fabrication.[78] As this study has revealed, ascension merely served as an optional semiotic subtheme of the larger translation fable structure, the general convention already fully deployed in each of the four New Testament Gospels beginning with Mark's empty tomb. The postmortem accounts in Luke-Acts thus borrowed from and elaborated upon the episodes and themes available in the prior New Testament Gospels. Among these Gospels, moreover, Luke-Acts provided the most comprehensive display of mimetic signals with respect to the translation fable of Romulus, the archetypal figure of the apotheosis tradition of imperial Rome (Table 4.1).

As mentioned, the segment "Julius Proculus and the 'Eyewitness' Tradition" (Chapter 2) has analyzed the Romulean tradition of eyewitness testimony and various "road" encounter themes that arose during the Roman Principate with regard to translated emperors. Besides implementing these traditional patterns, the New Testament Gospels conspicuously arranged the mimetic signals of the Romulean tradition as variously deployed within Roman imperial propaganda.[79] The presence of these elements would have seemed quite reasonable, even anticipated within Jesus' translation fable. How could the etiological tales of the "King of Kings," the ruler who would usher in God's heavenly *imperium* upon inhabited earth, have decorated their supreme monarch with any less honor and embellishment than the Caesars did receive at their deaths? Table 4.1 (above) lists several of the most prominent echoes of the Romulean legends to be found in the New Testament.

Arnobius of Sicca's *Adversus nationes* (ca. 300 C.E.) provides a most candid window into the tropical, conventional character of Christ's translation in early Christian thought, with the postmortem ascension of Romulus shown as analogical, indeed, by precedence, archetypical to the tradition:[80]

Table 4.1 The Translation of Romulus and Jesus Compared

Mimetic Signal	References
Missing body	Dionysius of Halicarnassus, *Ant. rom.* 2.56.2–6; Plutarch, *Rom.* 27.3–5; Matt 28.11–14; Mark 16.6; Luke 24.3; John 20.2–10
Prodigies	Livy I.16.1; Ovid, *Metam.* 14.816–817; Dionysius of Halicarnassus, *Ant. rom.* 2.56.2–6; Plutarch, *Rom.* 27.6–7; Matt 27.51–54; Mark 15.38; Luke 23.45
Darkness over the land	Ovid, *Metam.* 14.816–822; Dionysius of Halicarnassus, *Ant. rom.* 2.56.2–6; Plutarch, *Rom.* 27.6–7; Matt 27.45; Mark 15.33; Luke 23.44
Mountaintop speech	Ovid, *Metam.* 14.820–824; Matt 28.18–20
Great commission	Livy 1.16.7; Ovid, *Metam.* 14.811, 815; Ovid, *Fasti* 2.475–511; Plutarch, *Rom.* 28.2; Dionysius of Halicarnassus, *Ant. rom.* 2.63.4; Matt 28.18–20
Ascension	Livy I.16.6; Ovid, *Metam.* 14.820–824; Dionysius of Halicarnassus, *Ant. rom.* 2.56.2–6; Plutarch, *Rom.* 27.7; Luke 24.51; Acts 1.9
Son of a god	Livy I.16.3 Mt 27.54; Dionysius of Halicarnassus, *Ant. rom.* 2.56.2; Mark 15.39; John 20.31
Meeting on the road	Ovid, *Fasti* 2.475–511; Dionysius of Halicarnassus, *Ant. rom.* 2.63.3–4; Luke 24.13–35; Acts 9.3–19
Eyewitness testimony	Cicero, *Rep* 2.10; Livy 1.16.1–8; Ovid, *Fasti* 2.475–511; Dionysius of Halicarnassus, *Ant. rom.* 2.63.3–4; Plutarch, *Rom.* 27–28; Luke 24.35; 1 Cor 15.3–11
Taken away in a cloud	Livy I.16.1; Dionysius of Halicarnassus, *Ant. rom.* 2.56.2–6; Acts 1.9
Dubious alternative accounts	Livy I.16.4–5; Plutarch, *Rom.* 27.5–6, 8; Dionysius of Halicarnassus, *Ant. rom.* 2.56.2–6, 2.63.3; Matt 28.11–14
Immortal / heavenly body	Livy I.16.8; Ovid, *Metam.* 14.818–828; Plutarch, *Rom.* 28.6–8; 1 Cor 15.35–50; 1 Pet 3.18
Outside the city	Livy I.16.1; Plutarch, *Rom.* 27.6; John 19.17
The people flee (*populifugia*)	Dionysius of Halicarnassus, *Ant. rom.* 2.56.5; Plutarch, *Rom.* 27.7; Matt (26.56), 28.8; Mark (14.50), 16.8
Deification	Livy I.16.3; Cicero, *Rep* 2.10.20b; Ovid, *Fasti* 2.475–511; Dionysius of Halicarnassus, *Ant. rom.* 2.56.5–6; Plutarch, *Rom.* 27.7, 28.3; Matt 27.54; Rom 1.4
Belief, homage, and rejoicing	Ovid, *Fasti* 2.475–511; Dionysius of Halicarnassus, *Ant. rom.* 2.63.3–4; Plutarch, *Rom.* 27.8; Matt 28.9, 17; Luke 24.41, 52; John 20.27
Bright and shining appearance	Plut. 28.1–2 Acts 9.3; Mt 17.2; Mk 9.3; Lk 9.29; Rev 1.16

(*Continued*)

Table 4.1   (Continued)

Mimetic Signal	References
Frightened	Plutarch, *Rom.* 28.1–2; Ovid, *Fasti* 2.475–511; Acts 9.3; Matt 17.2; Mark 9.3; Luke 9.29; Rev 1.16
All in sorrow over loss	Livy I.16.2; Ovid, *Fasti* 2.475–511; Plutarch, *Rom.* 28.2; Luke 24.18–24
Inspired message of apotheosis	Plutarch, *Rom.* 28.3; Acts 1.4–8, 2.1–4

Nonne ipsum Romulum patrem senatorum manibus dilaceratum centum et Quirinum esse Martium dicitis et sacerdotibus et pulvinaribus honoratis et in aedibus adoratis amplissimis et post haec omnia caelum ascendisse iuratis? Aut igitur ridendi et vos estis, qui homines gravissimis cruciatibus interemptos deos putatis et colitis, aut si certa est ratio cur id vobis faciendum putetis, et nobis permittite scire quibus istud causis rationibusque faciamus.

(1.41.5–6)

Father Romulus himself, who was torn in pieces by the hands of a hundred senators, do you not call Quirinus Martius, and do you not honor him with priests and with divine couches, and do you not venerate him in your most spacious temples; and in addition to all this, do you not confess that he has ascended into heaven? Either, therefore, you too are to be laughed at, who regard as gods men slain by the most heinous executions; or if there is sure ground for your thinking that you should do so, allow us too to feel assured for what causes and on what grounds we do this.

Note the presence of the subtheme (List 2.1) of the ignoble, tragic death of the hero. In Imperial Rome, even the betrayal and murder of an emperor would not deliver the final verdict concerning his honor. As with Julius Caesar, for instance, an emperor would receive *exaltatio* or *damnatio* posthumously and at the hands of the succeeding emperor, the senate, and the Roman citizenry. In some cases, such as in the case of Claudius, the public may through the weight of popular sentiment ultimately succeed in overruling the formal decision of the emperor and senate. At his ignoble death at the instigation of the senate, moreover, the public approbation and praise of Nero, particularly in the eastern provinces, gave rise to legends and tales of the *Nero redivivus*, the returning (translated), conquering potentate from the Orient come to vanquish and depose a corrupt Roman aristocracy.[81] Such counter-institutional enfranchisement appears precisely to have been the case with the early Christian deification of Jesus of Nazareth; despite the perceived ignobility and profanity of his execution, indeed perhaps due to such injustice, Jesus' followers awarded him the highest possible rank, even the rank of the glorified king and founder of the empire, divine Romulus.

The methodological incongruity between classicists and traditional New Testament scholars over the mimetic application of the etiological fables of Romulus found in Latin and Greek literature has posed perhaps the greatest irony. The former seem to meet little difficulty when identifying such mimesis in the works of the Roman imperial period even where a relative paucity of proper cues may exist.[82] The Gospels often have provided double and triple the number of signals as compared with the various other instances in Latin and Greek works, lest the reader entertain any doubt as to their intent. When this weight of evidence converges with the academy's growing awareness of the larger, political currents and subtexts variously articulated in the New Testament, recognition of these potent gestures of *imitatio* becomes all the more unavoidable; only the nuances and implications remain further to be expounded. Having not taken into consideration the matter of conventional adaptation, Arie W. Zwiep's analysis failed to comprehend this primary mimetic relation and implied trope, faltering under what the study terms a "monotheistic principle," that is, an *a priori* aversion toward "pagan" antecedents.[83] John E. Alsup's prior monograph, moreover, suffered from a similar ailment, namely, by not fully comprehending these ancient linguistic processes of mimesis and adaptation. Alsup thus mistakenly supposed that the secondary adaptive features of the Gospel postmortem appearance narratives, that is, those ancillary elements that derive from classical Hebrew and early Jewish theophanic tales, governed the primary semiotic operation of the Gospel texts.[84] At the most rudimentary level, the present monograph essays to correct these substantial methodological missteps. Those properly comprehending, yet prone to resist the present thesis then must answer: How might a Judaized, Christianized adaptation of the "translation fable," particularly one mimetically following that of Romulus, have appeared, if not more or less precisely as one finds crafted in the postmortem narratives of the New Testament Gospels?

4.3 CONCLUSION

Though one may suitably doubt if an historical man, Jesus of Nazareth, ever sought such personal honors as imperial *exaltatio*, he had, in his *Nachleben*, become the emblem of a potent, counter-cultural movement in the first and second centuries of the Common Era. As such, his mythic, iconic depictions in the New Testament Gospels served to subvert the cultural institutions of that world, both Jewish and Roman, through transvalued mimesis, metaphor, and hybridic alterity, thus promulgating a new alternative, though comprehensible paradigm for the structure of ancient society.

Lucian has provided a rather revealing window into the political program of the early Christians in his *de Morte Peregrini* (ca. 170 C.E.). Lucian satirized the spectacular suicide of the famous Christian philosopher then turned Cynic Peregrinus Proteus at the Olympic Games in 165 C.E. As a show of his philosophical ascesis, in resembling the death of Heracles and the ancient Indic, Brahmanic tradition, Proteus threw himself upon his massive pyre and was thus burned alive before his throng of spectators. Proteus had become famed for his anti-imperial rhetoric and for his prominence as a leading teacher and writer in the rising Christian movement. According to Lucian, the early Christians had bestowed upon Proteus the highest honors, next to Christ himself, calling him ὁ καινός Σωκράτης (the new Socrates). Later in his life, however, he had become a thoroughgoing Cynic, took residence in Athens, and, despite Lucian's apparent disdain for him, had achieved considerable renown as a philosophical sage and critic of Rome. Indeed, Aulus Gellius, upon meeting Proteus in Athens, described him as a venerable and steadfast man of tremendous wisdom (*Noct. att.* 12.11.1–6). After his death, one of his disciples swore that he had met the translated Proteus in white raiment walking along the Portico of the Seven Voices at the Olympic festival (Lucian, *Peregr.* 40). By this time, however, the political pungency of such a tale had likely subsided, besides the bare observation that Proteus had not been a part of the political establishment. Analogous to Jesus in the Gospels, his translation fable underscores the generic, honorific function of the tradition as set in contestation to Roman *imperium*. While likely abstracted from the overt political designs of the postmortem appearances of Jesus, namely, as these mimicked the Romulean legend, the Proteus tale allows a glance at a related incident, though refracted through the cultural permutations and evolution of second-century Athens and with a Cynic philosophical subtext. By tacit associations between the two figures, Lucian's cynical lens regarding Proteus and the crucified founder of the Christians exposes several of the implied structural underpinnings and conventions of the prior Gospel tales as read in the broad Hellenistic context, cultural and ideological structures that vividly comport with the findings of the present study.

The Apostle Paul, whose conceptions often became inchoate to the composition of the Gospels, contextualized the postmortem appearances of Jesus within a political, honorific framework in his first letter to Corinth (1 Cor 15).[85] The "eyewitness" tradition in the text signaled and certified Jesus' manifest destiny as supreme king. Paul had in view nothing short of the ultimate deposition of all imperial government (1 Cor 15.24–25). Even as Romulus had become founder of the greatest known dominion of world history, so the Christ (that is, ὁ Χρίστος, "the inaugurated one") would found the dominion of God upon the inhabited earth. By couching such counter-cultural, counter-imperial rhetoric within the realm of religious, supernatural fabulation, the early Christians had conceived a brilliant stratagem to subvert the perceived dominant social order. How could a man stand trial for claiming to have had a supernatural encounter while traveling upon the Damascus road? The Roman charge of *maiestas populi Romani minuta* ("belittling the majesty of the Roman nation") typically exempted religious and supernatural literature and storytelling. Early Jewish writers exploited such exemption during the Seleucid and Roman periods by publishing counter-imperial texts within the thinly cryptic apocalyptic genre. The apotheosis vision of Jesus in the Apocalypse of John (Rev 1.16) manifests one barefaced instance of the fusion of these two tactics in early Christian literature, with the Transfiguration account in the Synoptic Gospels providing a second. As *imitatio Romuli*, Paul's depicted Damascus road encounter of the translated Jesus given in Acts of the Apostles (9.1–9; 22.6–11; 26.9–20) served not only as his conversion tale, but as a later fulcrum for the framing of Pauline ideology, a Lukan design to coronate the preceding Gospel appearance tradition.[86]

Inasmuch as one recognizes the late antique cult of saints and traditions of postmortem apostolic veneration as early Christian transvalued survivals of the thematic phenomena of the cult of ἥρωες, an even more generic class that indeed encompassed the cult of demigods in classical antiquity, the observed continuity of this broader classification advances the present thesis regarding the adaptation of the translation fable as applied to Jesus. Justin Martyr, Origen, Celsus, Tertullian, Theophilus, and Arnobius each candidly classed the postmortem accounts of Jesus under the larger "translation fable" rubric.[87] Apart perhaps from the unsolicited, thus self-incriminating denial given in Ps.-Peter that such accounts were "cleverly devised tales" (2 Pet. 1.16–21), there appears not to have been a single attempt to controvert the semiotic classification of the "resurrection" narratives of the Gospels as falling under the "translation fable" linguistic structure.[88] Indeed, the overwhelming assemblage of semiotic and mimetic signals marshaled in these episodes, as this study has displayed, would have wholly delimited the ancient reader's range of warranted inference. The modal registry and general significance would have been altogether explicit and unmistakable to any participant of the cultural-linguist *langue* of the first and second-century Hellenistic Levant. Seen in this way, authorial intent and reader inference collapse into a single linguistic authority, a common grammar of classical Mediterranean culture. The Gallery of translation fables in Chapter 2 demonstrates the ubiquity, pliability, and adaptability of the convention in classical Mediterranean cultures. Even those traits that seem at first glance to distinguish the Gospel accounts, namely, death, a tomb, burial, eulogization, and consecration, find their extensive parallels within the translation tradition (as shown in Chapter 2). When, in the Gospels, one contrasts the extensive pageant of conventional signals of the "translation fable" protocol operative in Hellenistic and Roman literature with the absence of such conventional traits with regard to early Jewish "resurrection," one of necessity apprehends that the postmortem narratives of the New Testament Gospels applied the term "resurrection" in little more than a nominal sense; translation provided the true anatomy and subtext of these episodes.[89]

πίστις, therefore, regarding the "raised Christ" must have connoted something quite different for the earliest Christians, those who signified the four Gospels as sacred texts, than modern scholarship has typically inferred. Fidelity to the founding figure of the movement, of necessity, meant the elevation of his image through the established means, conventions, and protocols of Hellenistic and Roman culture: social and literary *exaltatio*. The innovation of the Gospel postmortem accounts did not reside in the employment of the translation fable convention per se, but in the scandal of the application of the embellishment to a controversial Jewish peasant, an indigent Cynic, otherwise marginal and obscure on the grand stage of classical antiquity. The credulity and zeal of early Christians hailed not the man himself, but the metonym that the literary figure came to embody and represent as the icon of a new paradigm, a new metaphor of classical order. Such fealty exalted and saluted this image of a counter-cultural ideology through the protocols of the ancient Hellenistic Roman world.

New Testament scholarship has long neglected the broader contextual domain of ancient Greek and Latin culture, instead fundamentally restricting itself to the tide pool of earliest Christian and early Jewish writings, rather than wading and venturing out into the sea of Hellenistic and Roman literature whence most of the linguistic conventions and cultural codes inscribed and contested in the New Testament derive. Even the similitude of the tide pool, however, fails by understating the circumstance inasmuch as earliest Christianity arose as a cross-current *within* the dominant centers of antique Mediterranean society, leveraging, upsetting, and frequently overturning the institutions of those presiding cultural structures. Indeed, the four Gospels survive as relics of that complex transaction precisely due to their success. Even the early Jewish strands of these traditions, once having met their complex appropriation within the Gospels, achieved a distinctly early Christian quality and found their traction, their cultural-linguistic purchase within these hubs of cosmopolitan urban culture. In the uptake of conventional early Jewish "resurrection," the variation on the translation fable in the Gospels, perhaps as much as any other element, epitomized this Hellenizing, Romanizing quotient.

4.4 IMPLICATIONS

> In diesem Dialektischen, wie es hier genommen wird, und damit in dem Fassen des Entgegengesetzten in seiner Einheit, oder des Positiven im Negativen, besteht das Spekulative.
>
> In this dialectic, as here understood, namely in the grasping of opposites into a unity or of the positive into a negative, does the speculative exist.
>
> [Hegel, 1812][90]

This book challenges the classic conception of what many regard as the most sacred narrative of Western civilization, namely, that the New Testament stories of Jesus' resurrection provided alleged histories variously achieving credibility among their earliest readers. The study instead has revealed the pronounced use of a stock cultural convention of divine translation, a distinct type of sacred legend commonly embellishing the biographic conclusions of the most celebrated, iconified figures of classical antiquity. The study has undertaken a methodologically luminous philological investigation of this translation fable in Hellenistic and Roman writing and has demonstrated that this same linguistic convention, thinly wrapped with hybridic cultural adaptation, principally governed the New Testament postmortem accounts of Jesus. As with the translation fable generally, and contrary to a presumption of many biblical scholars today, the early Christian works that reflected on these tales did not argue for their historicity. The earliest of these extant writings, for instance, Justin Martyr's *1 Apology* (ca. 150 C.E.), candidly confessed that the Gospel portrayals applied this ancient mythic convention to the founder of the Christian movement, indeed, that the Gospels presented "nothing new" in their crafting of the so-called resurrection accounts (*1 Apol.* 21).

In order to attain an adequate assessment of this claim, sufficient and conclusive where prior treatments seem to have fallen short, the investigation has sought to apply a formidable methodological repertoire, drawing analogical conclusions that stand upon fundamental linguistic and semiotic critical theory. The ancient Greek and Latin reader invariably recognized the translation fable by the presence of various tropic signals: metamorphosis, vanished / missing body, eponymous etiology, catasterism (becoming a star or comet in the night sky), post-translation speech, ascension, post-translation appearance, translation associated with a river or mountain, odious or dubious alternate accounts, being taken away by the winds or clouds, and so forth. What did it mean for ancient society to hail an individual as having been translated to divine stature? Seen through various lenses from the domain of cultural and literary studies, the general cultural significance of such a semiotic pattern draws into view a distinct protocol embroidering a vast panoply of ancient Mediterranean narratives. The shock of the Gospels must not then have been the presence of this standard literary trope, but the adaptation of such supreme cultural exaltation to an indigent Jewish peasant, an individual otherwise marginal and obscure on the grand stage of classical antiquity. The investigation shows that each of the four Gospels and Acts applied this convention with ever-redundant perspicuity, lest the reader entertain any doubt as to the proper inference.

This book stands out as the first truly coherent case that the earliest Christians comprehended the resurrection narratives of the New Testament as instances within a larger conventional rubric commonly recognized as fictive in modality. Most modern treatments have mistakenly assumed that these texts alleged to have provided a credible, albeit extraordinary account of an historic miracle, whether to defend the claim or to render the proposal the mere dubious indulgence of credulous early converts. The vast majority of works on the resurrection accounts of Jesus undertake the question from one of two polarized *loci*: (1) with a faith-based interest in honoring (defending) the most sacred tenet of Christianity; (2) with an atheistic interest to disprove the claims of orthodox Christian doctrine. Even those works that seem aptly rigorous in their academic appeal often find their way into orbit around one or the other of these two contemporary socio-religious centers. One considers Nicholas Wright's *The Resurrection of the Son of God* (Fortress, 2003) and Robert Price's *Jesus Is Dead* (American Atheist Press, 2007) as relatively recent examples of this polarity. The present book defies both of these tendentious affiliations, having strictly pursued its topic from a humanistic orientation, namely, through the methodological disciplines of the humanities, altogether deferring any interest in present implications as mere afterthought to the analysis.

In dialectical terms, upon the broad canvas of Western history, one may identify these two polarized *loci* as "thesis" and "antithesis." Having shown the error of both extreme positions, that is, that the resurrection of Jesus was neither proposed as an historical reality nor peddled as an early Christian hoax, this study has found the authentic synthesis (*tertium quid*): the early Christians exalted the founder of their movement through the standard literary protocols of their day, namely, through the fictive, narrative embellishment of divine translation. Acceptance of this understanding substantially reconciles the polarity of the discourse, yielding significant implications for these two until now disparate, mutually hostile groups.

Religious Implications

Truth is the prize of the daring, disciplined mind, not for those who indulge in unwarranted inferences about reality. Since the Enlightenment in the West, religious faith has become a culturally accepted sanctuary or asylum for all manner of irrationality. For some Christians readers of this book, those for whom truth stands as a superlative virtue and not merely a cipher for social credalism, the implications of the study may seem staggering. Indeed, one may scarcely overstate or enter hyperbole when describing the far-reaching religious ramifications of the aforesaid conclusions. Respecting the Christian tradition, moreover, a sincere, honest weighing of the present investigation requires a fearless, rational, unwavering commitment to the pursuit of truth, no matter where that may lead. For those other Christians for whom "faith" must mean the acceptance of particular propositions as true in the face of inadequate or contrary data, the present study will have been of little value. For them, such a book, once having assaulted the most sacred tenets of faith, has arisen in its ghastly offense as a village dragon to be slain. These are not the readers for whom this book is composed. For still other Christians, those likely residing at the more liberal end of the spectrum, this book perhaps threatens little. They, like sophisticated devotees of many of other religious traditions around the world, freely recognize (and value!) the mythological character inherent to their sacred texts.

This book has not sought to this point to advocate or to discourage any belief whatsoever. Indeed, any careful study of the sacred requires a suspension, a disinterest, a deferment of all consideration of implications as the business of mere afterthought. And so, the investigation draws to a close with a bit of speculation, attempting to shine a guiding light upon the path ahead. Herein lies the quandary: If the earliest Christians did not read the resurrection narratives as historical fact, but as fictive sacred legend, then on what basis should any other Christian hold such tales as credible?

Must Christians now abandon their religion in the face of such conclusions drawn in this book? In admitting that the swell of Christian ontological and historical claims, most principally that of the historicity of the resurrection of Jesus of Nazareth, has not ultimately withstood the critical gaze of the Enlightenment, must then Christians join Aesop's fox in crying "Sour grapes!" Perhaps by another means Christians may more deeply enjoy this fruit in a truer solidarity with humanity, having cleared away the brush, that is, their entanglement in *superstitio*. Every religion consists of three sacred components: myth, philosophy, and ritual. What role, according to this study, did the translation fable play in the nascent Christian religion? The framing embellishments of the Gospels, contrary to most present-day biblical theologies, served to exalt the content being framed, namely, the philosophy embodied in the iconic portrayal of the founder, Jesus. Set back upon that original footing, can a modern Christian philosophy compete in the marketplace of ideologies as it once did? What contributing role may such a humanistic Christianity play in a complex, pluralistic world beset by unprecedented challenges and the strain of demands further to civilize the species?

Humanistic Implications

In the West, many of the persistent fundamental conceptions of the Christian religion extend into the past, beyond the rationalism of the Enlightenment and the humanism of the Renaissance, into the Dark Ages. Indeed, the very roots of these myths and their radicalized, exclusive demands upon Western civilization apparently served to catalyze and to coalesce this near millennium of stagnation and intellectual depravity in the human plight. From this perspective, this book may appear to serve the eradication of this particular "weed" in the soils of the human civilization. In truth, however, these stories, namely, the New Testament Gospels, are humankind's stories, not merely the sacrosanct possession of a major religious tradition. As Augustine's fifth-century *De Civitate Dei contra Paganos* foreshadowed, Jesus' "Kingdom of God" functioned in a myriad of ways to shape the Western world, a master metaphor defining the very tenets and ideals of civilization. The monotheistic deity, as a hypostasis of this higher social consciousness, aided in the subjugation of the lower, mammalian human nature, an asceticizing partition in Western psychology that functioned to politicize the understood best and highest of human virtue. Despite the insufferable flaws and problems inherent in this historical path to civilize the West, one may appreciate Christianity as having been the West's primary tradent of many of humankind's highest virtues and most noble ideals.

One particular observation of this book deserves final attention as a matter of humanistic study. As this investigation has shown, the early Christian proclamation of the "resurrection of Jesus Christ" was no hoax, nor was this a mass delusion. Does not this bare observation dramatically reduce the offensiveness of the Christian religion from the standpoint of humanistic rationalism? From this newfound starting place, the religion itself may merit renewed humanistic interest as a scientific locus for comprehending and appreciating the human plight on the vast ambit of history. To know human nature most deeply, one must become a student of the sacred. As Descartes inspired, the heritage of Western thought is to question, not for the sake of petty disdain, but in order more fully to appreciate the human condition:

> Je ne fis autre chose que rouler çà et là dans le monde, tâchant d'y être spectateur plutôt qu'acteur en toutes les comédies qui s'y jouent; et faisant particulièrement réflexion, en chaque matière, sur ce qui la pouvait rendre suspecte, et nous donner occasion de nous méprendre, je déracinais cependant de mon esprit toutes les erreurs qui s'y étaient pu glisser auparavant. Non que j'imitasse pour cela les sceptiques, qui ne doutent que pour douter, et affectent d'être toujours irrésolus: car, au contraire, tout mon dessein ne tendait qu'à m'assurer, et à rejeter la terre mouvante et le sable, pour trouver le roc ou l'argile.[91]

> I did nothing but travel about the world, endeavoring to be a spectator rather than an actor in all of the dramas that are played out; and, particularly contemplating each matter concerning what might render it suspect or give cause for misunderstanding, I proceeded to eradicate from my mind all of the errors that had previously infiltrated into my thought. In doing this, I did not imitate the skeptics who doubt only for doubting's sake and pretend always to be undecided. On the contrary, my whole intention was to arrive at a certainty and to dig away the earth and sand until I reached the rock or clay beneath.

NOTES

1. Franz Boas, introduction to James Teit, "Traditions of the Thompson River Indians of British Columbia," *Memoires of the American Folklore Society*, vol. 4 (1898), 18.
2. While Richard Pervo indicates second-century Ephesus as the location of composition of the Luke-Acts volumes, François Bovon suggested the Roman province of Macedonia (northeastern Greece). The latter hypothesis can only strengthen the appeal to anticipate Hellenistic literary currents within this last of the four ancient works under consideration. Richard I. Pervo, *Acts: A Commentary* (Hermeneia; Minneapolis: Fortress Press, 2009), 5–7; François

Bovon, *Luke 1: A Commentary on the Gospel of Luke 1:1 to 9:50* (trans. Christine M. Thomas; Hermeneia; Minneapolis: Fortress Press, 2002), 8–10.

3. Victor W. Turner, *Dramas, Fields, and Metaphors: Symbolic Action in Human Society* (Ithaca, NY: Cornell University Press, 1974), 24.

4. Tim Whitmarsh, *Greek Literature and the Roman Empire: The Politics of Imitation* (Oxford: Oxford University Press: 2001), 295–96.

5. For further elaboration on this trend, see Richard F. Thomas, "Genre through Intertextuality: Theocritus to Virgil and Propertius," in *Greek Literature*, vol. 8, *Greek Literature in the Roman Period and in Late Antiquity* (ed. Gregory Nagy; New York: Routledge, 2001), 73–92; and Thomas G. Rosenmeyer, "Ancient Literary Genres: A Mirage?" *Yearbook of General and Comparative Literature* 34 (1985): 74–84.

6. As a quality parallel study, applying this principle to the Hellenistic poetic tradition, see Marco Fantuzzi and Richard Hunter, *Tradition and Innovation in Hellenistic Poetry* (Cambridge: Cambridge University Press, 2004). Cf. Gian Biagio Conte, *The Rhetoric of Imitation: Genre and Poetic Memory in Virgil and Other Latin Poets* (trans. Charles Segal; Ithaca, NY: Cornell University Press, 1986).

7. See under Chapter 3, Section 3.1, "Composers, Not Authors."

8. The Synoptic tradition as rooted in the Gospel of Mark positioned itself exterior to any urban Jewish milieu, despite the inclusion of the Synoptic Sayings Source (Q). The gloss, for instance, that one finds at Mark 7.3–4 ("For the Pharisees, and all the Jews, do not eat unless they wash their hands, observing the tradition of the elders, and when they come from the market place, they do not eat unless they purify themselves; and there are many other traditions which they observe, the washing of cups and pots and vessels of bronze.") belies any serious effort at locating a Markan community within any Jewish context. Such a statement would have been absurdly obvious, considering the fundamental ubiquitous practice of ritual purity throughout the Jewish Diaspora (cf. Adela Yarbro Collins, *Mark: A Commentary* [Hermeneia; Minneapolis: Fortress Press, 2007], 344–49). Even if one allows that basic Jewish pedagogy oftentimes practiced recitation of fundamental precepts, this passage in Mark served to ridicule and to repudiate, not to inculcate such codes. The additional gloss at 7.19 ("Thus he declared all foods clean"), however, underscores the ambivalent complexity of the Gospel of Mark; only those who understood themselves as bearers of the Judaic legacy will have required such emendation.

9. See especially Suet., *Iul.* 80. Concerning the appropriation of the conquered Gauls under Caesar, the song arose: *Gallos Caesar in triumphum ducit, idem in curiam; Galli bracas deposuerunt, latum clavum sumpserunt.* "In his triumph, Caesar led the Gauls. He led them into the senate too. The Gauls took off their trousers and put on senatorial tunics." See Dench's detailed treatment. Emma Dench, *Romulus' Asylum: Roman Identities from the Age of Alexander to the Age of Hadrian* (Oxford: Oxford University Press, 2005), 93–151.

10. Cf., the king's invited dinner guests (Mt 22.10; Q 14.23). Acknowledging the heightening significance of franchised Roman citizenship in the eastern provinces, the parable of the king's wedding guests quite likely registered as a topical parallel. Matthew's addition of the matter of the ἔνδυμα γάμου ("wedding garment") and the wearing of the *toga pura* as the distinguishing mark of Roman citizenship powerfully extended the mimetic parallel (cf. Virgil, *Aen.* 1.282; Suet., *Aug.* 40). See Hans-Rupprecht Goette, *Studien zu römischen Togadarstellungen* (Mainz: Philipp von Zabern, 1989), 10–19.

11. As with the present study, David Balch witnesses the Romulean analogue of multiethnicity as a subtext of Luke-Acts, understanding the work as a compendium of biographical foundation narratives rivaling the founding of Rome.

David L. Balch, "ΜΕΤΑΒΟΛΗ ΠΟΛΙΤΕΙΩΝ—Jesus as Founder of the Church in Luke-Acts: Form and Function," in *Contextualizing Acts: Lukan Narrative and Greco-Roman Discourse* (ed. Todd Penner and Caroline Vander Stichele; Atlanta: Society of Biblical Literature, 2003), 139–88.

12. Claudia Setzer, *Resurrection of the Body in Early Judaism and Early Christianity: Doctrine, Community, and Self-Definition* (Boston: Brill Academic, 2004); Casey Elledge, *Life after Death in Early Judaism: The Evidence of Josephus* (WUNT 2/208; Tübingen: Mohr Siebeck, 2006); George Nickelsburg, *Resurrection, Immortality, and Eternal Life in Intertestamental Judaism* (HTS 26; Cambridge, MA: Harvard University Press, 1972).

13. Cf. John J. Collins, *The Apocalyptic Imagination: An Introduction to Jewish Apocalyptic Literature* (Grand Rapids: Eerdmans, 1984), 23–25; Paul D. Hanson details some nascent elements of apocalyptic eschatology in the postexilic Hebrew prophets in Paul D. Hanson, *The Dawn of Apocalyptic: The Historical and Sociological Roots of Jewish Apocalyptic Eschatology* (Philadelphia: Fortress, 1975). Prior to the apocalyptic works, namely, with Daniel and *1 Enoch*, however, evidence of belief in an eschatological resurrection appears altogether absent. Isaiah 26 and Ezekiel 37, contrary to arguments for Hebrew roots, both apply resurrection imagery as mere metaphor, not as a systemic belief. These texts likely reveal, as Collins proposed, the looming cultural shadow of Persian thought. John. J. Collins, *Daniel* (Hermeneia; Minneapolis: Fortress Press, 1993), 396.

14. John J. Collins, "The Afterlife in Apocalyptic Literature," in *Judaism in Late Antiquity, Part 4: Death, Life-after-Death, Resurrection and the World-to-Come in Judaism of Late Antiquity* (ed. Jacob Neusner and Alan J. Avery-Peck; Leiden: Brill, 2000), 128. Cf. John J. Collins, "Apocalyptic Eschatology in the Ancient World," in *The Oxford Handbook of Eschatology* (ed. Jerry L. Walls; Oxford: Oxford University Press, 2008), 40–43.

15. The images invoked in Daniel and other early Jewish apocalyptic literature at points align well with the Avestan and Pahlavi literature. This, however, may be of little consequence. From the standpoint of orientalism, however, stereotypical magian belief and practice rather better inform the reading. In this sense, a genetic approach to "Zoroasterian influence" appears to mislead the investigation. The cultural critic and linguist, rather, seeks to understand how such images would have registered within the semiotic domain of the ancient, evaluating readership.

    Regarding evidence of these listed practices as stereotypical aspects of Persian cult, see Albert de Jong, *Traditions of the Magi: Zoroastrianism in Greek and Latin Literature* (Leiden: Brill, 1997). Porphyry, *Abst* 4.16, for instance, indicated that the highest-ranked magi of Persia did indeed abstain from eating meat. Regarding dreams, see Herodotus 1.107–108. Concerning the taming of lions, see Pliny, *Nat.* 6.35. Like Moses outcompeting Pharaoh's sorcerers in stereotypic Egyptian categories of magic, the heroes of Daniel best the metaphysical arts of their Persian captors.

16. With respect to 2 Maccabees 7 and its expansion, 4 Maccabees, the martyred brothers defeat the tyrant Antiochus through philosophical ascesis in their stalwart resistance to the point of gruesome martyrdom, that is, through the mastery of Hellenistic ideals. Regarding the Hellenistic underpinnings of ascesis, see John M. Dillon, "Rejecting the Body, Refining the Body: Some Remarks on the Development of Platonist Asceticism," in *Asceticism* (ed. Vincent L. Wimbush and Richard Valantasis; Oxford: Oxford University Press, 1995), 80–87.

17. See also the later Aeneas of Gaza as an additional witness to resurrection of the dead in Zoroastrian eschatology.

18. Cf. Nigidius Figulus (frag. 67) where he wrote that the magi taught that the earth would undergo a final ἐκπύρωσις (conflagration); concerning this, see also Dio Chrysostom, *Borysth*. Contrary to the standard Zoroastrian doctrine of bodily resurrection at the eschaton, Albert de Jong has argued that Plutarch's description presents a spiritual resurrection; this is due to the people having "no shadow" in the final condition. Plutarch describes Oromazes, however, as the god of light. The image may reiterate the destruction of darkness on the renovated earth. Many of these themes find analogues in John's apocalypse (Rev. 21.23–24; 22.5) and speak of the victory of light and incorruptibility. As found in Josephus's description of Pharisaic resurrection eschatology, however, Plutarch may provide an *interpretatio Graeca* of the tradition in suggesting superior "resurrection" bodies, bodies that do not need food and do not cast shadows. See Albert de Jong, "Shadow and Resurrection," *Bulletin of the Asia Institute*, N.S. 9 (1995): 215–24.

19. See especially Elledge, *Life after Death in Early Judaism*.

20. Claudia Setzer accurately describes this idea of a collective resurrection event at the end of the age as a place of alignment between Pharisaic and earliest Christian thought. Claudia Setzer, *Resurrection of the Body*, 53–70. This genetic trajectory of bodily resurrection into the Western tradition from Persian theology appears to have eluded the analysis of Onions who, in his classic work, traced the immortality of the soul, a Greek contribution particularly emphasized in the rise of Platonism and the later Gnostic movements. Richard Broxton Onions, *The Origins of European Thought about the Body, the Mind, the Soul, the World, Time, and Fate* (Cambridge: Cambridge University Press, 1951), 93–299.

21. Add to this Luke 14.14; Acts 4.1; 24.15–21.

22. M. David Litwa has provided a provocative study of Pauline soteriology, locating many of the roots of Pauline conception within the Hellenistic translation tradition, that is, metamorphosis as a rite of deification. M. David Litwa, *We Are Being Transformed: Deification in Paul's Soteriology* (Berlin: Walter de Gruyter GmbH & Co., 2012).

23. Body–Soul duality served as a generic commonality to the Hellenistic philosophical traditions, not just Middle and Neo-Platonism proper, but such diverse traditions as Cynicism, Stoicism, Neo-Pythagoreanism, and, as Martin exposes, even Epicureanism. Dale B. Martin, *The Corinthian Body* (New Haven: Yale University Press, 1995), 3–37.

24. See Kurt Rudolf, *Gnosis: The Nature and History of Gnosticism* (trans. Robert McLachlan Wilson; San Francisco: Harper & Row, 1983; German orig., 1977), 189–95; Birger A. Pearson, *Ancient Gnosticism: Traditions and Literature* (Minneapolis: Fortress Press, 2007), 15–18.

25. Although prior to the mid-twentieth-century discovery of the Nag Hammadi codices and the resultant scholarly illumination of early Christian Gnosticism, Rudolf Bultmann correctly drew comparison between Johannine πίστις and Gnostic γνῶσις. See R. Bultmann, *Das Evangelium des Johannes*. Kritisch-exegetischer Kommentar über das Neue Testament. Göttingen: Vandenhoeck & Ruprecht, 1941. The Pistics of the Johannine school (and Pauline school) actualized inner and eschatological salvation through the exertion of "belief," that is, otherwise unwarranted inference based upon inadequate empirical evidence. Although "knowledge" for the Gnostics typically meant esoteric or internal knowledge of the "true" self, Johannine soteriology shared striking analogues with the fundamental transcendental function of this special knowledge to transform the individual. *Nota bene*, this efficacious, salvific offer did not present itself in Q, Mark, or Matthew. R. Bultmann, "πιστεύω κτλ," *TDNT* 6.174–228.

26. Cf. Gregory J. Riley, *Resurrection Reconsidered: Thomas and John in Controversy* (Minneapolis: Fortress Press, 1995), 7–68.
27. Cf. Ps.-Justin, *De resurrectione;* the Coptic *Epistula ad Rheginum* (NHC I,4; "Treatise on the Resurrection"); Origen, *De resurrectione libri ii;* John Chrysostom, *De resurrectione mortuorum;* and Methodius of Olympus, *De resurrectione.*
28. Isa 26.19; 29.18–19; 35.5–6; 61.1. For a provocative comparison rooting this tradition (namely, the addition of "the dead are raised" to Isaiah's formula) within apocalyptic Judaism as revealed within the Qumran sectarian library, see James D. Tabor and Michael O. Wise, "4Q521 'On Resurrection' and the Synoptic Tradition: A Preliminary Study," in *Qumran Questions* (ed. James H. Charlesworth; Sheffield: Sheffield Academic Press, 1995), 151–63.
29. Cf. the man coming back to life after having been buried in Elisha's sacred tomb (2 Kings 13.21).
30. Since credible accounts of persons seemingly revived from death indeed arise even in the present day, one may perhaps speculate that Pliny *et alii* derived at least some stories of resuscitation from authentic occurrences.
31. Ludwig Bieler, *Theios Anêr: Das Bild des "Göttlichen Menschen" in Spätantike und Frühchristentum* (2 vols; Vienna: Höfels, 1935). See also Hans Dieter Betz, "Gottmensch II: Griechisch-römisch Antike u. Urchristentum," *RAC* 12 (1983): 234–312. Just as the Hellenistic hero tradition transformed into the cult of saints in late antiquity, this general tradition of the θεῖος ἀνήρ saw continuity, though much asceticized, in those whom Peter Brown has termed the "holy men" of late antiquity. Peter Brown, "The Rise and Function of the Holy Man in Late Antiquity," *JRS* 61 (1971): 80–101.
32. For a general reference, see Libanius, *Or.* 20.8. Concerning Heracles's resuscitation of Alcestis, wife of Admetus, see Euripides, *Alc.* 1136–63; Ps.-Apollodorus 1.9.15; Philostratus, *Vit. Apoll.* 4.45. Concerning Asclepius's resuscitation of Hippolytus (and many others), see Ovid, *Fasti* 6.743–62; Euripides, *Alc.* 122–29; Philodemus, *De pietate* 52; Ps.-Apollodorus 3.10.3; Virgil, *Aen.* 7.765–73; Sextus Empiricus, *Adversus mathematicos* 1.260–62. As to Empedocles's famous raising of the woman deceased for thirty-five days, see Diogenes Laërtius 8.2.60–62, 67. Regarding Apollonius of Tyana's halting of a funeral for a young girl and then resuscitating her, see Philostratus, *Vit. Apoll.* 4.45. As a further resource of theurgic wonder-working in antiquity, see Wendy Cotter, *Miracles in Greco-Roman Antiquity: A Sourcebook for the Study of New Testament Miracle Stories* (London: Routledge, 1999).
33. Ulrich Luz, *Matthew 21–28: A Commentary* (trans. James E. Crouch; Hermeneia; Minneapolis: Fortress, 2005), 567–69.
34. Josephus attempted something similar with his handling of the conclusion of his portrayal of Moses. See *Ant.* 4.315–31.
35. Argumentation theorists understand the scientific use of analogy as the commission of analogical fallacy, a type of inductive fallacy. Morris R. Cohen and Ernest Nagel, *An Introduction to Logic and the Scientific Method* (New York: Harcourt, Brace and Company, 1934), 286–88. Since language operates at a purely conventional level, however, Bayesian-like probability logic breaks down when discussing the mental and social sphere of signs and sign systems. Functional social confidence provides the foundation of all linguistic signs. In the human lexicon, no other standard exists.
36. Samuel Sandmel, "Parallelomania," *JBL* 81, no. 1 (1962): 1–13.
37. Here, perhaps more so than any other matter of sacred history, one finds that the tail has unduly wagged the academic dog.
38. Regarding this fundamental point shared by Jacques Lacan, Brooks agrees that "desire must be considered the very motor of narrative, its dynamic principle."

Peter Brooks, "Freud's Masterplot: Questions of Narrative," *Yale French Studies* 55/56 (1977): 280–81. Cf. Jacques Lacan, "Le Stade du miroir comme formateur de la fonction du Je," in *Écrits* (Paris: Seuil, 1966), 93–100 ("The Mirror Image as Formative of the Function of the I," in *Écrits: A Selection* [trans. Alan Sheridan; London, Tavistock, 1977], 1–7).

39. Peter Brooks, "Freud's Masterplot," 283–84. Regarding the translation sub-theme of the "dubious alternate account," compare Matt 28.11–15, Matthew's story of the stolen corpse.

40. Cf. the Hellenistic philosophical underpinnings of the martyrs of *4 Maccabees*.

41. Sigmund Freud, *Beyond the Pleasure Principle* (trans. James Strachey; London: Hogarth Press, 1973; German orig., 1920), 18:7–64.

42. I do not apply the term "Palestine" in any effort to invoke freighted connotations with the modern conflict in the region, but to reference ancient stereotypical, geo-cultural associates in the Hellenistic and Roman mind. This geographical label for the region continued in use from the time of Herodotus onward, e.g., Hdt. 1.105, 2.104; Ovid, *passim*; Josephus, *Ant.* 1.145; 8.260; Pliny, *NH* 5.66; Philo, *Prob.* 12; Arrian, *Anab.* 2.25, 4; Pausanias, 1.14.7; *etc.*

43. *LSJ*, s.v. χριστός: consecrated to kingly office.

44. Cf. Rom 10.9, a text that also conveys the language of *exaltatio*, perhaps suggesting a soft fideism in Pauline communities, that is rooted in Abrahamic modes of divine trust, not in historical assertion.

45. Emma Dench, *Romulus' Asylum*, 143–51.

46. The academic community of New Testament Studies has yet fully to recognize the central, canonical role that Homer played in Greek and Latin composition and the mimetic relationship that Mark invoked with Homer's epics. Indeed, several major themes in Mark often find their magnitude, even their intelligibility, only in their mimetic correspondence with the most conspicuous themes of Homer. If modern commentators were but half so familiar with the Homeric epics and antique compositional tendencies of Homerization as ancient Hellenistic readers, this tremendous oversight could not have arisen. Cf. Dennis R. MacDonald, *The Homeric Epics and the Gospel of Mark* (New Haven: Yale University Press, 2000).

47. Regarding the ascension of Moses, see Josephus, *Ant.* 4.315–31. Consider Roger David Aus, *The Death, Burial, and Resurrection of Jesus, and the Death, Burial, and Translation of Moses in Judaic Tradition* (Studies in Judaism; Lanham, MD: University Press of America, 2008). This characteristically tenuous comparison argues for a genetic traditional pattern governing the NT "resurrection" narratives, directly taken from the death and translation of Moses in early and Tannaitic Judaism. While the Transfiguration accounts clearly invoke an awareness of these assumed figures, the Gospel narratives involve them as much by contrast as by comparison. Jesus in the Gospels surpasses Elijah by *aemulatio*. Were one to merge the episodic, thaumaturgic style of the Elijah-Elisha cycle (1 Kings 17–19, 21; 2 Kings 1–4, 9, 13; cf. R. E. Brown) with a transvalued celebration of the dominant themes and motifs of the Homeric epics, the resulting narrative would achieve a remarkable generic proximity to the New Testament Gospels.

48. Cf. Romulus's cult shrine on the Quirinal in Rome, a tribute to his translation; Cicero, *Resp.* 2. 10.20b.

49. Notice also the theme of commission, recurring in Matthew and mimetically following that of Romulus (to be discussed).

50. Daniel A. Smith goes so far as to equate disappearance with assumption and appearance with resurrection, understanding these as genetically different themes converging in Jesus' postmortem accounts. Daniel A. Smith, *Revisiting the Empty Tomb: The Early History of Easter* (Minneapolis: Fortress Press, 2010). For an array of other commentators who have comprehended

translation as fundamentally a matter of assumption, see Elias J. Bickermann, "Das leere Grab," *ZNW* 23 (1924): 281–92; Neil Q. Hamilton, "Resurrection Tradition and the Composition of Mark," *JBL* 84 (1965): 415–21; Gerhard Lohfink, *Die Himmelfahrt Jesu: Untersuchungen zu den Himmelfahrts-und Erhöhungstexten bei Lukas* (SANT 26; Munich: Kösel, 1971). Adela Yarbro Collins also appears to lean in this direction when she presumes that Jesus' missing body in Mark must signal that Jesus has been "transformed, has left the world of human beings, and has transferred to the heavenly world." Adela Yarbro Collins, "Ancient Notions of Transferal and Apotheosis in Relation to the Empty Tomb Story in Mark," in *Metamorphoses: Resurrection, Body and Transformative Practices in Early Christianity* (ed. Turid Karlsen Seim and Jorunn Økland; Berlin: Walter de Gruyter, 2009), 41. John E. Alsup distinguished the appearance story as a *Gattung* derived from the theophanic, anthropomorphic appearance tradition of the Hebrew deity found in the classical Hebrew texts, ultimately not recognizing the linguistic signals present in the Gospel episodes and the all-but-exhaustive reliance upon Hellenistic convention. John E. Alsup, *The Post-Resurrection Appearance Stories of the Gospel-Tradition* (Calwer Theologische Monographien 5; Stuttgart: Calwer, 1975). Arie Zwiep's monograph, perhaps most contrary to the present study, favors the classical Hebrew "rapture" story over Hellenistic and Roman antecedents on account of what Zwiep calls his "monotheistic principle." One may view the present thesis as a necessary refutation of this proposal. Arie Zwiep, *The Ascension of the Messiah in Lukan Christology* (Leiden: Brill, 1997), 195.

Contrary to these critics and independently congruent with the present monograph, M. David Litwa applies a quite similar conception "corporeal immortalization" in his recent work to describe Jesus' transformed, postmortem body. Litwa's much more general study serves as a companion volume to this present book. Anent this point, Litwa's critique of Nicholas Thomas Wright proves particularly incisive: "In the end, Wright's highly apologetic attempt to establish the uniqueness of Jesus' resurrection fails because of a superficial comparison. In general, we might grant him that hellenized peoples may not have believed in a return of the dead to ordinary (mortal) human life—but this is not what Jesus' resurrection is! Jesus' resurrection much more resembles the stories of deified men immortalized after their deaths." M. David Litwa, *IESUS DEUS: The Early Christian Depiction of Jesus as a Mediterranean God* (Minneapolis: Fortress Press, 2014), 141–72.

51. Daniel A. Smith theorizes that Q 13.34–45 ("You will not see me again until you say, 'Blessed is the one who comes in the Lord's name'") implied Jesus' heavenly ascension. In light, however, of passages such as Q 11.31–32, that is, the Queen of the South and the Ninevites predicted to rise up in judgment against the Galilean cities, it seems reasonable to suppose that Q understood future judgment as a function of a day of resurrection. Rapture prior to death in the manner of Elijah seems excluded based upon Q's awareness of Jesus' crucifixion (Q 14.27). Daniel A. Smith, *The Post-Mortem Vindication of Jesus in the Sayings Gospel Q* (New York: T & T Clark, 2006). Dennis R. Mac-Donald, arguing from a perceived antetextual relationship to Deuteronomy throughout Q, on the other hand, speculates that Q may perhaps have concluded with a postmortem disappearance scene. Dennis R. MacDonald, *Two Shipwrecked Gospels: The Logoi of Jesus and Papias's Exposition of Logia about the Lord* (Society of Biblical Literature Early Christianity and Its Literature 8; Atlanta: Society of Biblical Literature, 2012), 406–9. For a more focused study of Mark's abrupt conclusion, see Richard C. Miller, "Mark's Empty Tomb and Other Translation Fables in Classical Antiquity," *JBL* 129, no. 4 (2010): 759–76.

52. The late second-century *Gospel of Peter* provided a more verbose, embellished rendering of the resurrection narratives of the Gospels, one that drops the "missing body" motif in favor of a dramatic tomb exit similar to that found in John 11 with the raising of Lazarus. See *Gos. Pet.* 34–42.

53. Cf. the ascension at the close of Mark's longer ending (16.19–20), a likely second-century accretion following Luke-Acts.

54. Cf. the glorified appearance of Jesus in John's Apocalypse; Rev 1.12–20.

55. As an intriguing *excursus*, one may consider early Christian baptism as a metaphor of the theme of "sacred river" translation. Paul seems to imply this metaphor in his discussion of vicarious resurrection realized through joint "baptism with Christ" (Rom. 6.1–4). Cf. Michael Peppard's political reading of the baptism of Jesus in the Gospels. Michael Peppard, "The Eagle and the Dove: Roman Imperial Sonship and the Baptism of Jesus (Mark 1.9–11)," *NTS* 56 (2010): 431–51; Michael Peppard, *The Son of God in the Roman World: Divine Sonship in Its Social and Political Context* (Oxford: Oxford University Press, 2011).

56. Cf. David Cartlidge, "Transfigurations of Metamorphosis Traditions in the Acts of John, Thomas, and Peter," *Semeia* 38 (1986): 53–66; Henri Charles Puech, in *Annuaire de l'École Practique des Hautes Études*, 1966/67, 128–36. Cf. Photius, *Bibliotheca* 114.

57. Virgil provided the requisite criterion for admission to Hades: the interment of one's bones (*Aen.* 6.428–34). The netherworld, therefore, did not admit as standard occupants those who had attained translation.

58. See Sarah Iles Johnston, *Restless Dead: Encounters between the Living and the Dead in Ancient Greece* (Berkeley: University of California Press, 1999); Daniel Ogden, *Magic, Witchcraft, and Ghosts in the Greek and Roman Worlds* (Oxford: Oxford University Press, 2002), 146–78.

59. Cf. Philostratus's tale of Apollonius's display of divine teleportation, as the sage sought to persuade Demetrius that he could be handled in order to reveal that he was not in fact a mere ghost. Philostratus, *Vit. Apoll.* 7.12. Hershbell concurs that this episode functioned as a demonstration of Apollonius's deification. Jackson P. Hershbell, "Philostratus's *Heroikos* and Early Christianity: Heroes, Saints, and Martyrs," in *Philostratus's Heroikos: Religion and Cultural Identity in the Third Century C.E.* (ed. Ellen Bradshaw Aitken and Jennifer K. Berenson MacLean; Leiden: Brill, 2004), 174. Luke's narrative compares with sentiments by Ignatius regarding the "flesh and bones" aspects of Jesus' raised body (Ign., *Smyrn.* 3).

60. This observation appears altogether contrary to the distinction proposed by Adela Yarbro Collins between "realistic" episodes and "theophanic" episodes among the postmortem appearance tales in the Gospels, with the touching and handling of Jesus residing in the former class. Adela Y. Collins, "Ancient Notions of Transferal," 47.

   Gregory J. Riley has persuasively accounted for the history of apostolic traditions behind John's story of the Doubting Thomas, proposing that the rendition articulated sectarian disagreement between the Johannine school and Thomas Christianity over the shedding of the mortal body. Following Platonic body–soul dualism and the consequent ideal of liberation from the human *corpus*, the Gospel of Thomas and early Christian gnostic texts presented Jesus' resurrection as psychical, not somatic. This interpretation of John's disabused Thomas, however, affords the same outcome as here discussed; Jesus is not a disembodied spirit, but a translated deity evoking sudden worship. Gregory J. Riley, *Resurrection Reconsidered: Thomas and John in Controversy* (Minneapolis: Fortress Press, 1995); Glenn Most takes a perspective similar to Riley's and also finds fruitful mimetic possibilities with Dionysus's treatment of the doubting Pentheus; cf. Glenn W. Most, *Doubting Thomas* (Cambridge, MA: Harvard University Press, 2005), 52.

61. Lack of this subtle though critical distinction between the somatic palpability of the translated hero and the essential immateriality of the revenant, according to this research, appears to have eluded the intriguing study of Glen W. Bowersock in his *Fiction as History: Nero to Julian*, where he classifies the ἀναβίωσις of the great Trojan War hero Protesilaus with the nominal "resurrection" tales of Jesus of the New Testament Gospels. Glen W. Bowersock, *Fiction as History: Nero to Julian* (Berkeley: University of California, 1994), 111–13. The otherwise quality edited volume by Aitken and MacLean also appears to have followed Bowersock in this confusion. Protesilaus better demonstrates a manifestation of the Hellenistic cult of heroes inasmuch as Protesilaus's remains had been entombed as a site of veneration and his temporary visitations from Hades never exhibited traits of a palpable, divine body in literature. Indeed, the tales of Protesilaus survive as illustrious instances of the heroic *revenant* and, as such, find more fitting analogues with the early Christian cult of saints. Cf. Herodotus 9.116–20; Hyginus, *Fab.* 103; 104; Philostratus, *Heroikos*. Ellen Bradshaw Aitken and Jennifer K. Berenson MacLean, eds., *Philostratus's Heroikos: Religion and Cultural Identity in the Third Century C.E.* (Leiden: Brill, 2004); see also Jennifer K. Berenson MacLean and Ellen Bradshaw Aitken, trans. *Flavius Philostratus: Heroikos* (Society of Biblical Literature Writings from the Greco-Roman World 1; Atlanta Society of Biblical Literature, 2001), liii–liv.

62. See, as one of many examples, Allen Brent, *The Imperial Cult and the Development of Church Order Concepts and Images of Authority in Paganism and Early Christianity before the Age of Cyprian* (Leiden: Brill, 1999). J. H. W. G. Liebeschuetz has provided a concise sketch of the emperor cult during the period. J. H. W. G. Liebeschuetz, "Religion," in *The High Empire, A.D. 70–192* (ed. Alan K. Bowman, Peter Garnsey, and Dominic Rathbone; vol. 11 of *CAH*; Cambridge: Cambridge University Press, 2000), 985–90.

63. "A story is formed in the tension between two formal categories: difference and resemblance." Tzvetan Todorov, "Les Transformations narratives," in *Poétique de la prose* (Paris: Seuil, 1971), 132.

64. William Wrede, *The Messianic Secret* (trans. J. C. G. Grieg; Cambridge: J. Clarke, 1971; German orig., 1901).

65. Such awkward, abrupt endings had become quite fashionable in Greek and Latin literature (e.g., endings to the *Iliad*, the *Odyssey*, and the *Aeneid*) as Stephanie West has revealed. Considering the semiotic force of Mark's concluding episode, as this monograph endeavors to expose, the Gospel of Mark superbly qualifies within West's literary pattern. Stephanie West, "Terminal Problems," in *Hesperos: Studies in Ancient Greek Poetry Presented to M. L. West on His Seventieth Birthday* (ed. P. F. Finglass, C. Collard, and N. J. Richardson; Oxford: Oxford University Press, 2007), 3–21. Adela Yarbro Collins sets forth a variety of commentators who have proposed numerous creative theories regarding a supposed lost ending to the narrative. In line with this study, Collins concludes that Mark's abrupt ending indeed was intentional and original, despite the later accretions of the shorter and longer endings. See Adela Yarbro Collins, *Mark: A Commentary*, 797–99.

66. MacDonald, *Two Shipwrecked Gospels*, 406–9. Cf., Daniel A. Smith, *The Post-Mortem Vindication of Jesus in the Sayings Gospel Q.*

67. Regarding this specific theme of fright, see also Plutarch, *Rom.* 28.1–2 and Ovid, *Fasti* 2.475–511, themes that recur in the New Testament translated appearance tradition: Acts 9.3, Matt 17.2, Mark 9.3, Luke 9.29, and Rev 1.16.

68. Losing sight of the text in a quest to uncover an ever-elusive author, rather than comprehending Mark as a free-standing semiotic entity, Adela Yarbro Collins appears needlessly speculative in her appraisal of Mark's ending: "The author of Mark was probably aware of the idea that some Roman emperors had ascended to heaven and become gods. He may also have known that their deifications were modeled on that of Romulus." Adela Yarbro Collins, *Mark*, 793. Bickermann and Hamilton, as has been noted, failed to see the traditional continuity that the translation fable maintained throughout the succeeding Gospels. Hamilton proceeded so far as to name Mark's empty tomb an "antiresurrection" narrative. Elias J. Bickermann, "Das leere Grab"; Neil Q. Hamilton, "Resurrection Tradition and Mark," specifically page 420. This most brief translation fable that one finds at Mark's abrupt ending exposes the traditional roots of the convention later applied in the remaining three Gospels and Mark's later appended shorter and longer endings, that is, in the appearance tradition. *Contra* John Alsup's monograph, the translation fable served as the inchoate, generic semiotic structure variously to be elaborated in the epilogues of the Gospel tradition subsequent to Mark's abrupt ending at 16.8. *Ergo*, the *Gattung* of the appearance tradition did not chiefly arise out of the "anthropomorphic appearances of YHWH" in the classical Hebrew texts, but as a subtheme of the translation fable as set forth and analyzed in this study. John E. Alsup, *The Post-Resurrection Appearance Stories of the Gospel-Tradition* (Calwer Theologische Monographien 5. Stuttgart: Calwer, 1975). Appreciating the qualities and contributions of these valuable studies, the aforesaid critical adjustments endeavor to clarify and to advance the topic.

69. Concerning Matt 28.1–8, Luz observes: "Not long after Matthew the author of the *Gospel of Peter* already depicts the resurrection of Jesus itself for the first time, even if 'from the outside,' from the perspective of the soldiers. Two angels approach the tomb; the stone rolls away by itself; they leave the tomb accompanied by a third figure; their heads reach the sky, and the cross follows them (9.36–10.40). It is amazing how little this direct description of the resurrection of Jesus was copied in the ancient church. It is also amazing that well into the Middle Ages the opinion was scarcely ever maintained in the interpretation that the angel rolled the stone from the tomb in order to set Jesus free. Instead, this miracle happened because of the guards and because of the women: because of the guards so they would be frightened and because of the women so that they could look into the tomb. Instead, Christ was raised out of a sealed tomb; how it happened remains a mystery." Ulrich Luz, *Matthew 21–28*, 599. The present study proposes that the Gospel of Matthew conveyed not a theme of "mystery" (Luz), but a clear semiotic sign, that of bodily translation, according to the ancient cultural-linguistic conventions outlined in this study, and in continuity with the rousing semiosis of Mark's empty tomb episode.

70. Matthew's creative editing of Mark appears as an effort to contradict stories that purportedly circulated even in the eighties that some of Jesus' devotees had taken his corpse. This provides the most reasonable explanation for the unaccounted disappearance of his remains, that is, with regard to the executed historical Jesus. Even into the second century, evidence suggests that such stories still circulated. Cf. Justin Martyr, *Dial.* 32.3–6, 106–108; *Gos. Pet.* 8; Origen, *Cels.* 1.51.

71. Concerning this topos, see the note under Pythagoras in the Gallery of Chapter 2. Zalmoxis provides a particularly intriguing study worthy of *excursus*. Cf. Yulia Ustinova, *Caves and the Ancient Greek Mind: Descending Underground in the Search for Truth* (Oxford: Oxford University Press, 2009), 100–104; Mircea Eliade, *Zalmoxis: The Vanishing God* (trans. W. R. Trask; Chicago: University of Chicago Press, 1972).

72. Wendy Cotter's prior essay generally concurs with the present proposal, namely, that the Romulean legends resided behind Matthew's epilogue, though perhaps not, in her case, described precisely in terms of archetypal mimesis and the broader translation fable convention. Wendy Cotter, "Greco-Roman Apotheosis Traditions and the Resurrection Appearances in Matthew," in *The Gospel of Matthew in Current Study: Studies in Memory of William G. Thompson, S.J.* (ed. David E. Aune; Grand Rapids: Eerdmans, 2001), 127–53.

73. Indeed, his request that Mary not cling to him makes no sense unless she was already in the act or apart from an imminent likelihood of her intent to do so. In either case, one correctly discerns the underlying subtext, namely, to indicate the palpability of Jesus' raised body.

74. As Justin elucidated, the deification of Jesus in John also had precedence in, for example, the λόγος myths of Hellenistic Hermes (*1 Ap.* 21.1). According to Acts of the Apostles, Paul received the same mythic interpretation as divine spokesman in Lystra (14.11–12). The Stoics, moreover, became known for such syncretic images of Hermes as demiurge of τὰ πάντα. Such a proposed thesis, while perhaps beyond of the scope of this study, could provide an otherwise lacking coherence between the λόγος Christology of John's prologue and the seemingly disparate themes visible in the remainder of John's narrative. Cf. Garth Fowden, *The Egyptian Hermes: A Historical Approach to the Late Pagan Mind* (Cambridge: Cambridge University Press, 1986), 24–25.

75. Although the latter (and most likely both) of these texts, that is, *Gospel of Thomas* and *Acts of Thomas*, postdate the Gospel of John, the primitive tenets of the Thomasine tradition appear to have been well established by the turn of the first century C.E.

76. The mistaken remark at John 11.16 ("Let's go too, that we may die with him.") at the proposed journey into hostile territory to revive Lazarus underscores this tradition-critical subtext. For the enlightened, the Thomasine school conceived of death as the final salvific event, the soul's ultimate liberation from the mundane *corpus*. Within such a framework, the bodily resuscitation of Lazarus gainsaid the fundamental structural body–soul duality of early Gnostic philosophy. One should not infer, therefore, from the disciple's death-wish an attitude of pessimism or sarcasm. Rather, the metanarrative of the text sought to disparage Thomasine theology as grossly misguided and in need of chastening, at least on these fundamental points. The restitution of Thomas at the end of John thus suggested or reflected the potential, albeit dramatic, redeemability of the Thomasine tradition in the sentiment of the adjacent Johannine school, reimagining and redrawing the etiology of the tradition. The very tension between these two socio-religious bodies underscores their similarities as much as their differences, with evidenced frustration that naturally impelled (even evangelized?) a hopeful reconciliation. Although an intertextual relationship may not seem likely between John and *Gospel of Thomas*, yet, as became common with all four New Testament Gospels, the Gospel of John's governing subtexts often involve the Johannine community's identity negotiation and struggle vis-à-vis relative traditions, schools, and socio-political entities, often constructing its chief characters as metonyms or literary vehicles for their later respective movements. In this general and grand sense, the present study concurs with those of Riley, DeConick, and Pagels. Gregory J. Riley, *Resurrection Reconsidered* (1995); April D. DeConick, *Voices of the Mystics: Early Christian Discourse in the Gospels of John and Thomas and Other Ancient Christian Literature* (JSNTSup 157; Sheffield: Sheffield Academic Press, 2001); Elaine Pagels, *Beyond Belief: The Secret*

Gospel of Thomas (New York: Random House, 2003). While Christopher W. Skinner's recent monograph rightfully cautions against perceiving John's characterization of Thomas as altogether unique in the narrative or worse as the story's singular villain—Indeed, one would be immoderate to reduce John to a single, "anti-Thomasine" subtext—the presence of such narrative artifice on the Johannine storyboard arguably appears throughout the story, for example, in relation to Peter, Nicodemus, Nathanael, *et alii*. The Pauline school and the Christologizing narratives of Syria and Anatolia, that is, the Gospels, shared a common challenge to explain their radical disparity in relation to the originary figures and movement(s) in Palestine (e.g., Gal. 1–2). Mark achieves this with the Messianic Secret and often by portraying the apostles as imbeciles. Matthew, having drawn in the early Sayings tradition Q, paints the disciples in a far more positive fashion, seeking a mutually respectful synthesis of the two primary socio-religious movements (i.e., the Palestinian Jesus movement and the Pauline Christ cult). *Contra* Skinner, the Gospel of John's often uncomplimentary portrayal of various primitive figures, in this sense, roughly follows a Markan subtextual strategy. Their reconciliation, moreover, exhibits the creative expression of John's metanarrative of sectarian reconciliation in a ca. 100 C.E. Syrian socio-religious context, seeking to unite the disparate legacies of these primitive Christian traditions by painting a common, originary "orthodox" (i.e., Johannine) ideology. Cf. Christopher W. Skinner, *John and Thomas: Gospels in Conflict?: Johannine Characterization and the Thomas Question* (Princeton Theological Monograph Series 115; Eugene, OR: Wipf and Stock, 2009).

As an aside, the proximity of the Johannine and Thomasine societies suggests a regional struggle and, therefore, a social and geographical proximity between these two communities.

77. The Gospel of Luke's inclusion of "other women" comports with a Lukan attempt to compose the most comprehensive (conflative) treatment based on his sources, which included the prior three New Testament Gospels, and at points suggests an effort to reconcile evident variances between those prior narratives, even if the composition selectively excludes other segments. Syntagmatic conflation at the level of sentence and verse, according to text-critical principle, suggests that Luke wrote last, dependent upon the other Gospels.

78. Gerhard Lohfink, *Die Himmelfahrt Jesu*, 240.

79. Romulus's famous ruminal fig tree at the Colosseum in Rome provides a promising study worthy of separate treatment as a comparison with Jesus' withered fig tree in Jerusalem, as rendered in the Synoptic tradition (e.g., Mark 11.12–14). Cf. Pliny, *Nat.* 77; Tacitus, *Ann.* 13.58.

80. Cf. Justin Martyr, *1 Apol.* 21; Tertullian, *Apol.* 21.20–23; *Nat.* 1.10.29–33; *Marc.* 4.7.3; Minucius Felix, *Oct.* 21.9–10; Origen, *Cels.* 2.55–56; 3.22–31; and Theophilus, *Autol.* 1.13; 2.27. Such texts demonstrate the continued awareness and admission of the conventional nature of Jesus' "resurrection" under the broader heading "translation fable," particularly in relation to Romulus and the apotheosis tradition of Rome.

81. See Edward Champlin's chapter "The Once and Future King" in Edward Champlin, *Nero* (Cambridge, MA: Harvard University Press, 2003), 1–35.

82. Cf. Walter Burkert, "Caesar und Romulus-Quirinus"; and Jean Gagé, "Le temoignage de Julius Proculus."

83. Arie Zwiep, *The Ascension of the Messiah in Lukan Christology*, 195.

84. John E. Alsup, *The Post-Resurrection Appearance Stories of the Gospel-Tradition*.

85. In the chapter, Paul presupposed the reader's awareness of earliest Christian "eyewitness" accounts to Jesus' postmortem appearances. That is to say, one

should not see Paul as the innovator of such stories; he merely joins a running list of prior Christians by whom such stories had already emerged. Paul employed the myth and its fusion with the standing, Judaic notion of a corporal "Day of Resurrection," a tradition of altogether different origin, in order to embark on a short, philosophical treatise on the nature of "raised" bodies. Note also the expressed δόξα of the opening line of Paul's missive to the Christians of Galatia (1.1), honorific language of *exaltatio* elevating Jesus to demigod stature.

Additionally, one may observe several strained, faith-motivated efforts to argue for an extremely early beginning to this tradition, based upon Paul's travel accounts in Gal. 1–2. With the prevalence of apotheosis myth-making in royal *consecratio*, arguments based upon the earliness of the tradition, however speculative, prove to be of no consequence to the proposals of this book. Indeed, many if not most translated figures received the embellishment either immediately or soon after their respective deaths. Notwithstanding, the very subtext of Gal. 1–2 belies any serious arguments for an allegedly harmonized "orthodoxy" or "orthopraxy" between Paul and Christian leadership in Judea (e.g., Peter, James, and John). These two chapters articulated as their central rhetorical point the brazen independence of Paul and his disregard for any and all traditional authority. His "trekking" about repeatedly (Gal. 2.2) to Judea to interact with the so-called pillars did not serve as any form of validation for Paul and his ideology. To the contrary, he sought to learn if his interactions with these primitive Judeo-Christian schools were worthy of his time at all. In the end, it would appear, both parties agreed to remain separate, under some palliation of mutual hostility.

86. Ovid, *Fasti* 2.475–511; Dionysius of Halicarnassus, *Ant. rom.* 2.63.3–4.
87. Justin Martyr, *1 Apol.* 21; Tertullian, *Apol.* 21.20–23; *Nat.* 1.10.29–33; *Marc.* 4.7.3; Minucius Felix, *Oct.* 21.9–10; Origen, *Cels.* 2.55–56; 3.22–31; and Theophilus, *Autol.* 1.13; 2.27; Arnobius, *Adv. nationes* 1.41.5–6.
88. Given this observation, were the earliest Christians to have meant something other than "translation" by their raised king, they would have needed to have been quite emphatic that their stories did not suggest such interpretation. One finds no evidence of such an effort, let alone the amount of attention needed to achieve such a distinction.
89. The recent book of Dag Øistein Endsjø has characterized "resurrection" as a long-standing convention in Hellenic culture. The study is to be commended for identifying the correct analogue in ancient thought, namely, in the protocols of classical Greek immortalization. The present book seeks to nuance this argument significantly by contending that the designation "resurrection" came to be superimposed over the classical tradition in the New Testament as a nominal Judaic variant or adaptation. Altogether contrary this study and that of Endjø, Nicholas Wright, in his tendentious apologetic volume, would have his Christian readers conclude that Jesus' postmortem accounts possessed no Greek or Roman antecedents whatsoever. The present study endeavors to disabuse the academy of such a misconception, recognizing the hybridic, adaptive constitution of the Gospel resurrection narratives as translation narratives. Dag Øistein Endsjø, *Greek Resurrection Beliefs and the Success of Christianity* (New York: Palgrave Macmillan, 2009); Nicholas Thomas Wright, *The Resurrection of the Son of God* (Minneapolis: Fortress Press, 2003).
90. G. W. F. Hegel, *Wissenschaft der Logik, Erster Band. Die Objektiv Logik* (Nürnberg: Johann Leonhard Schrag, 1812), 40–41.
91. René Descartes, *Discours de la méthode pour bien conduire sa raison, et chercher la vérité dans les sciences* (Paris: Théodore Girard, 1668), 29–30.

BIBLIOGRAPHY

Aitken, Ellen Bradshaw and Jennifer K. Berenson MacLean, eds. *Philostratus's Heroikos: Religion and Cultural Identity in the Third Century C.E.* Leiden: Brill, 2004.

Alsup, John E. *The Post-Resurrection Appearance Stories of the Gospel-Tradition.* Calwer Theologische Monographien 5. Stuttgart: Calwer, 1975.

Aus, Roger David. *The Death, Burial, and Resurrection of Jesus, and the Death, Burial, and Translation of Moses in Judaic Tradition.* Studies in Judaism. Lanham, MD: University Press of America, 2008.

Balch, David L. "*METABOLH POLITEIWN*—Jesus as Founder of the Church in Luke-Acts: Form and Function." Pages 139–88 in *Contextualizing Acts: Lukan Narrative and Greco-Roman Discourse.* Edited by Todd Penner and Caroline Vander Stichele. Atlanta: Society of Biblical Literature, 2003.

Betz, Hans Dieter. "Gottmensch II: Griechisch-römisch Antike u. Urchristentum." *Reallexikon für Antike und Christentum* 12 (1983): 234–312.

Bickermann, Elias J. "Das leere Grab." *Zeitschrift für die neutestamentliche Wissenschaft und die Kinde der älteren Kirche* 23 (1924): 281–92.

Bieler, Ludwig. *Theios Anêr: Das Bild des "Göttlichen Menschen" in Spätantike und Frühchristentum.* 2 vols. Vienna: Höfels, 1935.

Bovon, François. *Luke 1: A Commentary on the Gospel of Luke 1:1 to 9:50.* Translated by Christine M. Thomas. Hermeneia. Minneapolis: Fortress Press, 2002.

Brent, Allen. *The Imperial Cult and the Development of Church Order Concepts and Images of Authority in Paganism and Early Christianity before the Age of Cyprian.* Leiden: Brill, 1999.

Brooks, Peter. "Freud's Masterplot: Questions of Narrative." *Yale French Studies* 55/56 (1977): 280–300.

Brown, Peter. "The Rise and Function of the Holy Man in Late Antiquity." *Journal of Roman Studies* 61 (1971): 80–101.

Burkert, Walter. "Caesar und Romulus-Quirinus." *Historia* 11 (1962): 356–76.

Cartlidge, David. "Transfigurations of Metamorphosis Traditions in the Acts of John, Thomas, and Peter." *Semeia* 38 (1986): 53–66.

Champlin, Edward. *Nero.* Cambridge, MA: Harvard University Press, 2003.

Cohen, Morris R. and Ernest Nagel. *An Introduction to Logic and the Scientific Method.* New York: Harcourt, Brace and Company, 1934.

Collins, Adela Yarbro. *Mark: A Commentary.* Hermeneia. Minneapolis: Fortress Press, 2007.

———. "Ancient Notions of Transferal and Apotheosis in Relation to the Empty Tomb Story in Mark." Pages 41–57 in *Metamorphoses: Resurrection, Body and Transformative Practices in Early Christianity.* Edited by Turid Karlsen Seim and Jorunn Økland; Berlin: Walter de Gruyter, 2009.

Collins, John J. *The Apocalyptic Imagination: An Introduction to Jewish Apocalyptic Literature.* Grand Rapids: Eerdmans, 1984.

———. *Daniel.* Hermeneia. Minneapolis: Fortress Press, 1993.

———. "The Afterlife in Apocalyptic Literature." Pages 119–39 in *Judaism in Late Antiquity, Part 4: Death, Life-after-Death, Resurrection and the World-to-Come in Judaism of Late Antiquity.* Edited by Jacob Neusner and Alan J. Avery-Peck. Leiden: Brill, 2000.

Conte, Gian Biagio. *The Rhetoric of Imitation: Genre and Poetic Memory in Virgil and Other Latin Poets.* Translated by Charles Segal. Ithaca, NY: Cornell University Press, 1986.

Cotter, Wendy. *Miracles in Greco-Roman Antiquity: A Sourcebook for the Study of New Testament Miracle Stories.* London: Routledge, 1999.

———. "Greco-Roman Apotheosis Traditions and the Resurrection Appearances in Matthew." Pages 127–53 in *The Gospel of Matthew in Current Study: Studies in*

Memory of William G. Thompson, S.J. Edited by David E. Aune. Grand Rapids: Eerdmans, 2001.

Crossley, James G. "Paul, Mark, and the Question of Influence." Pages 10–29 in *Paul and the Gospels: Christologies, Conflicts and Convergences*. Edited by Michael F. Bird and Joel Willitts. London: T & T Clark, 2011.

DeConick, April D. *Voices of the Mystics: Early Christian Discourse in the Gospels of John and Thomas and Other Ancient Christian Literature*. Journal for the Study of the New Testament: Supplement Series 157. Sheffield: Sheffield Academic Press, 2001.

Dench, Emma. *Romulus' Asylum: Roman Identities from the Age of Alexander to the Age of Hadrian*. Oxford: Oxford University Press, 2005.

Descartes, René. *Discours de la méthode pour bien conduire sa raison, et chercher la vérité dans les sciences*. Paris: Théodore Girard, 1668.

Dillon, John M. "Rejecting the Body, Refining the Body: Some Remarks on the Development of Platonist Asceticism." Pages 80–87 in *Asceticism*. Edited by Vincent L. Wimbush and Richard Valantasis. Oxford: Oxford University Press, 1995.

Eliade, Mircea. *Zalmoxis: The Vanishing God*. Translated by W. R. Trask. Chicago: University of Chicago Press, 1972.

Elledge, Casey. *Life after Death in Early Judaism: The Evidence of Josephus*. Wissenschaftliche Untersuchungen zum Neuen Testament 2/208. Tübingen: Mohr Siebeck, 2006.

Endsjø, Dag Øistein. *Greek Resurrection Beliefs and the Success of Christianity*. New York: Palgrave Macmillan, 2009.

Fantuzzi, Marco and Richard Hunter. *Tradition and Innovation in Hellenistic Poetry*. Cambridge: Cambridge University Press, 2004.

Fowden, Garth. *The Egyptian Hermes: A Historical Approach to the Late Pagan Mind*. Cambridge: Cambridge University Press, 1986.

Freud, Sigmund. *Beyond the Pleasure Principle*. Translated by James Strachey. London: Hogarth Press, 1973. (German orig., 1920).

Gage, Jean. "Le Témoignage de Julius Proculus (sur l'Assomption de Romulus-Quirinus) et les Prodiges Fulguratoires dans l'Ancien 'Ritus Comitialis.'" *L'Antiquité Classique* 41 (1972): 49–75.

Goette, Hans-Rupprecht. *Studien zu römischen Togadarstellungen*. Mainz: Philipp von Zabern, 1989.

Hamilton, Neil Q. "Resurrection Tradition and the Composition of Mark." *Journal of Biblical Literature* 84 (1965): 415–21.

Hanson, Paul D. *The Dawn of Apocalyptic: The Historical and Sociological Roots of Jewish Apocalyptic Eschatology*. Philadelphia: Fortress Press, 1975.

Hegel, G. W. F. *Wissenschaft der Logik. Erster Band. Die objectiv Logik*. Nürnberg: Johann Leonhard Schrag, 1812.

Hershbell, Jackson P. "Philostratus's *Heroikos* and Early Christianity: Heroes, Saints, and Martyrs." Pages 169–80 in *Philostratus's Heroikos: Religion and Cultural Identity in the Third Century C.E.* Edited by Ellen Bradshaw Aitken and Jennifer K. Berenson MacLean. Leiden: Brill, 2004.

Johnston, Sarah Iles. *Restless Dead: Encounters between the Living and the Dead in Ancient Greece*. Berkeley: University of California Press, 1999.

Jong, Albert de. "Shadow and Resurrection." *Bulletin of the Asia Institute*. N.S. 9 (1995): 215–24.

———. *Traditions of the Magi: Zoroastrianism in Greek and Latin Literature*. Leiden: Brill, 1997.

Kittle, G., and G. Friedrich, eds. *Theological Dictionary of the New Testament*. 10 vols. Translated by G. W. Bromiley. Grand Rapids: Eerdmans, 1964–1976.

Lacan, Jacques. "Le Stade du miroir comme formateur de la fonction du Je, telle qu'elle nous est révélée dans l'expérience psychanalytique" (1949). Pages 93–100 in *Écrits*. Paris: Seuil, 1966.

———. "The Mirror Stage, as Formative of the Function of the I as Revealed in Psychoanalytic Experience." Pages 1–7 in *Écrits: A Selection*. Translated by Alan Sheridan. London: Tavistock, 1977.

Liebeschuetz, J.H.W.G. "Religion." Pages 984–1008 in *The High Empire, A.D. 70–192*. Edited by Alan K. Bowman, Peter Garnsey, and Dominic Rathbone. Vol. 11 of *The Cambridge Ancient History*. Cambridge: Cambridge University Press, 2000.

Litwa, M. David. *We Are Being Transformed: Deification in Paul's Soteriology*. Berlin: Walter de Gruyter GmbH & Co., 2012.

———. *IESUS DEUS: The Early Christian Depiction of Jesus as a Mediterranean God*. Minneapolis: Fortress Press, 2014.

Lohfink, Gerhard. *Die Himmelfahrt Jesu: Untersuchungen zu den Himmelfahrts- und Erhöhungstexten bei Lukas*. Studien zum Alten und Neuen Testaments 26. Munich: Kösel, 1971.

Luz, Ulrich. *Matthew 21–28: A Commentary*. Translated by James E. Crouch. Hermeneia. Minneapolis: Fortress, 2005.

MacDonald, Dennis R. *Two Shipwrecked Gospels: The Logoi of Jesus and Papias's Exposition of Logia about the Lord*. Society of Biblical Literature Early Christianity and Its Literature 8. Atlanta: Society of Biblical Literature, 2012.

Martin, Dale B. *The Corinthian Body*. New Haven: Yale University Press, 1995.

———. *Inventing Superstition: From the Hippocratics to the Christians*. Cambridge, MA: Harvard University Press, 2004.

Miller, Richard C. "Mark's Empty Tomb and Other Translation Fables in Classical Antiquity." *Journal of Biblical Literature* 129, no. 4 (2010): 759–76.

Most, Glenn W. *Doubting Thomas*. Cambridge, MA: Harvard University Press, 2005.

Nickelsburg, George W.E. *Resurrection, Immortality, and Eternal Life in Intertestamental Judaism*. Harvard Theological Studies 26. Cambridge, MA: Harvard University Press, 1972.

Ogden, Daniel. *Magic, Witchcraft, and Ghosts in the Greek and Roman Worlds*. Oxford: Oxford University Press, 2002.

Onions, Richard Broxton. *The Origins of European Thought about the Body, the Mind, the Soul, the World, Time, and Fate*. Cambridge: Cambridge University Press, 1951.

Pearson, Birger A. *Ancient Gnosticism: Traditions and Literature*. Minneapolis: Fortress Press, 2007.

Peppard, Michael. "The Eagle and the Dove: Roman Imperial Sonship and the Baptism of Jesus (Mark 1.9–11)." *New Testament Studies* 56 (2010): 431–51.

Pervo, Richard I. *Acts: A Commentary*. Hermeneia. Minneapolis: Fortress Press, 2009.

Puech, Henri Charles. In *Annuaire de l'École Practique des Hautes Études* (1966/67): 128–36.

Riley, Gregory J. *Resurrection Reconsidered: Thomas and John in Controversy*. Minneapolis: Fortress Press, 1995.

Rosenmeyer, Thomas G. "Ancient Literary Genres: A Mirage?" *Yearbook of General and Comparative Literature* 34 (1985): 74–84.

Rudolf, Kurt. *Gnosis: The Nature and History of Gnosticism*. Translated by Robert McLachlan Wilson. San Francisco: Harper & Row, 1983. (German orig., 1977).

Sagan, Carl. *The Demon-Haunted World: Science as a Candle in the Dark*. New York: Ballantine Books, 1996.

Sandmel, Samuel. "Parallelomania." *Journal of Biblical Literature* 81, no. 1 (1962): 1–13.

Setzer, Claudia. *Resurrection of the Body in Early Judaism and Early Christianity: Doctrine, Community, and Self-Definition*. Boston: Brill Academic, 2004.

Skinner, Christopher W. *John and Thomas: Gospels in Conflict?: Johnannine Characterization and the Thomas Question*. Princeton Theological Monograph Series 115. Eugene, OR: Wipf and Stock, 2009.

Smith, Daniel A. *The Post-Mortem Vindication of Jesus in the Sayings Gospel Q*. New York: T & T Clark, 2006.

———. *Revisiting the Empty Tomb: The Early History of Easter*. Minneapolis: Fortress Press, 2010.

Tabor, James D. and Michael O. Wise. "4Q521 'On Resurrection' and the Synoptic Tradition: A Preliminary Study." Pages 151–63 in *Qumran Questions*. Edited by James H. Charlesworth. Sheffield: Sheffield Academic Press, 1995.

Thomas, Richard F. "Genre through Intertextuality: Theocritus to Virgil and Propertius." Pages 73–92 in *Greek Literature*. Greek Literature in the Roman Period and in Late Antiquity 8. Edited by Gregory Nagy. New York: Routledge, 2001.

Todorov, Tzvetan. "Les Transformations narratives." Pages 117–32 in *Poétique de la prose*. Paris: Seuil, 1971.

Turner, Victor W. *Dramas, Fields, and Metaphors: Symbolic Action in Human Society*. Ithaca, NY: Cornell University Press, 1974.

Ustinova, Yulia. *Caves and the Ancient Greek Mind: Descending Underground in the Search for Truth*. Oxford: Oxford University Press, 2009.

Whitmarsh, Tim. *Greek Literature and the Roman Empire: The Politics of Imitation*. Oxford: Oxford University Press: 2001.

Wrede, William. *The Messianic Secret*. Translated by J.C.G. Grieg. Cambridge: J. Clarke, 1971. (German orig., 1901).

Wright, Nicholas Thomas. *The Resurrection of the Son of God*. Minneapolis: Fortress Press, 2003.

Zwiep, Arie. *The Ascension of the Messiah in Lukan Christology*. Leiden: Brill, 1997.

Index

Made in the USA
Monee, IL
11 December 2023

48845091R00122